KILLING TIME

Also by Donald Freed

Secret Honor (play and screenplay)
Circe & Bravo (play)
Executive Action (novel and screenplay with Mark Lane)
The Killing of RFK (novel)
The Secret Life of Ronald Reagan (history)
Agony in New Haven (history)
The Spymaster (novel)
Of Love and Shadows (screenplay)
Inquest (play)
The Glasshouse Tapes (history)
Death in Washington (history)
The White Crow: Eichmann in Jerusalem (play and screenplay)

KILLING TIME

The First
Full Investigation
Into the Unsolved Murders
of Nicole Brown Simpson
and Ronald Goldman

Donald Freed and
Raymond P. Briggs, Ph.D.

Macmillan ■ USA

MACMILLAN
A Simon & Schuster Macmillan Company
1633 Broadway
New York, NY 10019

Library of Congress Cataloging-in-Publication Data

Freed, Donald. 1932-
    Killing time : the first full investigation/by Donald Freed
and Raymond P. Briggs.
        p.   cm.
    Includes index.
    ISBN 0-02-861340-6 (alk. paper)
    1. Murder—California—Los Angeles.   2. Murder—
California—Los Angeles—Investigation.   3. Trials (Murder)
—California—Los Angeles.   4. Evidence (Law)—California
—Los Angeles.   5. Simpson, O. J., 1947-   —Trials,
litigation, etc.   6. Simpson, Nicole Brown, d. 1994.
7. Goldman, Ronald Lyle, d. 1994.   I. Briggs, Raymond P.,
1945-   .   II Title.
HV6534.L7F73   1996
364.1'523'0979494—dc20   96–17323
                                                    CIP

10   9   8   7   6   5   4   3   2

First Edition

Book design by Silver Editions

Printed in the United States of America

To
Mary Ann Lynch

Her conscience and her courage
made this book possible.

Contents

Acknowledgments

First, our thanks to the team that produced much of the material upon which this study depends. *Ian Bowater* led the research effort, conducting interviews, coordinating facts, and preparing the draft database for the book and future projects. *Robert Carl Cohen* provided photographic and forensic analyses. *Patricia Freed*, specializing in the study of "separation anxiety," was critical in the psychological analysis of the murders. She also discovered the key contradiction at the Simpson estate that led to the Bronco experiment in Chapter Two. *Alain Gansberg* excavated material for the Fuhrman Timeline. *Jack Lynch* kept the team current with the electronic dialogue, monitored Web sites, and researched trial documents. *Dr. David Berkowitz, Dr. Anthony Saidy, Dr. Stanton N. Smullens*, and *Dr. Ron Marasco* reviewed evidence and reports.

We are also indebted to several sources inside the Justice System, besides the major "Source" quoted throughout the narrative. William Pavelic, private investigator, was always available for consultation. We are grateful for the long, and necessarily anonymous, psychological meditation on the Simpson case by a close scientific observer.

Donald Freed would like to thank the following people who generously gave help, advice, or criticism—Joe Domanick and Alex Constantine, leading historians of Los Angeles law enforcement and organized crime, respectively; Patrick Fourmy, Andy Boehm, and *Prevailing Winds* magazine, Judy Osburn and the "Fully Informed Jury Association" (P.O. Box 59, Helmsville, Montana, 59843), Sherman Skolnick and the Citizens Commission, Dr. Samoan Barish, Professors Leon Katz and Barry Barish, Brenda and Tom Freiberg, Esq., Lynne Heidt, Ralph Schoenman, Michael Shephard, Jim Horwitz of Fairness and Accuracy in Media, Felice and Robert Harrison, Sally Allen and Carol Browning,

Farah Mansoor, Elia Katz, Fred Katz, Jim DiEugenio, Victor Moreno, Paul Ruiz, Robert Groden, and SaraKay Smullens.

A. J. Langguth, Linda Deutsch, Theo Wilson, and Sarah Jane Freymann— each helped to inspire this project by their own search for truth.

Raymond Briggs would like to thank simulator creator Jim Flack, for his guidance in figuring out how best to develop and stage scenarios and for helping to inspire the "Timeline" concept; Sven Linde, AIA, for days of stimulating discussion and analysis of all points of view; Dr. John Griffin, who often served as devil's advocate and articulated traditional views of the murders to clarify our thinking; economic analyst Derek Briggs for challenging our rationales and our logic for the book; Dr. David Yuan, for his ideas on computer staging; Isabel Peralta, for her many supporting activities; Attorney Ray Fountain, for his insight into how to simulate and stage a murder for trial; and former colleagues at California Peace Officers who allowed us to have direct on-the-street contact with law enforcement in California—including the LAPD.

Both authors wish to thank those at Macmillan who so enthusiastically supported and contributed to creating this book—in a remarkably short time:

First, our superb editor, Mary Ann Lynch, who never stopped believing in what this book could be and did everything possible to get us to that place.

Then, publisher Natalie Chapman, for her sound suggestions, Don Stevens and Dave Jagger for contractual and legal guidance, John Michel for his advocacy, and Olga Moya and Francisco Rios for dedicated service by fax, phone, and post; the artists and production staff who gave this book special care: Laurie Barnett, Michael Freeland, Michele Laseau, Cheryl Mamaril, Nancy Cochrane, Alberta Chalileh, Beth Jordan, Brian Phair, and Kathy Iwasaki; the marketing and publicity staff who beat the drum at just the right time: Claire Griffin, Jennifer Feldman, Margaret Durante, and Sharon Heede; those who met with the authors and gave valuable advice: Elliott Ehrlich, Abby Gillespie, Jeff Jacobs, Tom Heitzman, Rachele Schifter, Susan Skipper, and Kristin Sampson; and thanks to Ed Nothnagle, Kevin Howat, and Kevin Umeh at Macmillan Digital for their support of the first stage of a virtual reality version of *Killing Time*.

The Idea

I was at Dulles International Airport in August 1995, coming home from meetings having to do with a project involving the "Trial of the Century" of Adolf Eichmann in Jerusalem in 1960. The current Trial of the Century was playing on all the terminal television monitors: The "Fuhrman Tapes" were being argued in the O.J. Simpson case. As I watched, and listened to Fuhrman's racist statements about African-Americans, I muttered, "So they <u>did</u> frame the right man." A man standing next to me said, "We may never know because the lawyers are controlling the scientific evidence instead of the other way around." Four hours later we arrived in Los Angeles. Professor Raymond Briggs had taken the occasion to explain to me how it would be possible to get inside the real-time of the killings with the help of computer analysis, and to create a kind of virtual reality of the crime scene. Dr. Briggs spoke of "timelines" and "Einstein." I answered that this was all Greek to me, but I did, in parting, quote to him from Aeschylus concerning "The Long Foot of Time."

We exchanged cards . . .

Donald Freed
Los Angeles, July 1996

Prologue

You Are the Jury

Ladies and gentlemen of the jury:

Sometime between 10:00 PM and 12:00 midnight on the night of June 12, 1994, Nicole Brown Simpson and a friend, Ronald Lyle Goldman, were killed with a knife or knives at 875 South Bundy Drive in Brentwood, California. Ms. Simpson's former husband, the sports legend O.J. Simpson, was charged with the double murder. After a nine-month trial, Simpson was acquitted by a jury. And that is all we know for certain. We do not even know who the target was on that bloody night.

If a scientist had been invited to take charge of the Bundy murder scene, that scientist would have inevitably tried to reconstruct the series of events leading up to the murders, the murder events themselves, and the aftermath. Such an analysis would have produced a series of incomplete scenarios that could have guided the investigative process. With the gathering of evidence and further analysis, each of the scenarios would have faded away, or come closer to reflecting the actual events of the murder. As this occurred, one could eliminate, reduce, and clarify various possibilities until arriving at the most likely scenario.

The computer is invaluable for this kind of investigation. With the computer, we can sift through "mountains of evidence" to organize information in various ways. For *Killing Time*, information has been organized into a number of menus, or scenarios, each covering the period of time during which the murders occurred—the "killing time." We have also created timelines that track people, evidence, and events on the night of and day after the murders.

Our computer-inspired analysis, as the legendary detective Sherlock Holmes said, "eliminates the impossible, and what remains, however improbable, is the truth."

3

Ladies and gentlemen of the jury, in the autumn of 1995, the American people and their judicial system seemed to suddenly suffer a nervous breakdown. "The Simpson matter," in the words of the trial judge, worked like a powerful drug or poison on the body politic. This you know.

The trial that mesmerized this nation might or might not have been the "Trial of the Century"—but the Simpson matter, we believe, has become one of the greatest murder mysteries of all time, and a true American tragedy.

O.J. Simpson is a tragic figure in a particularly American sense. W. E. B. Du Bois, the African-American sociologist, wrote at the turn of the century about a kind of tragedy that he called Doubleness:

> . . . It is a peculiar sensation, this double-consciousness, this sense of always looking at one's self through the eyes of others, of measuring one's soul by the tape of a world that looks on in amused contempt and pity. One feels his two-ness—an American, a Negro; two souls, two thoughts, two unreconciled strivings; two warring ideals in one dark body, whose dogged strength alone keeps it from being torn asunder.

This Doubleness, you will find, seems to apply not only to race, but, in a much broader sense to almost everyone and everything connected to this crime. Our analysis cannot overcome the contradictory nature of the facts and the roles of principal players in this case, but it can isolate sequences of events and articulate an abstraction of time.

The computer, and technology as a whole, are now functions of time and tragedy as well as history. Take four American examples:

- **The Zapruder Film:** Abraham Zapruder took a home movie in Dallas just as President Kennedy was assassinated. The film was embargoed and kept from the public for ten years. However, when independent researchers, including one of the authors, bootlegged and broadcast the less-than-thirty-second film of Kennedy's assassination, the official Government investigation and record of the crime began to fall under its own weight.

- **The Pentagon Papers:** Daniel Ellsberg and Anthony Russo used a Xerox machine to copy the Pentagon's secret history of the war in Vietnam, and printed in the nation's great newspapers the searing truth of an illegal war. The Xerox machine, like the motion picture camera, had "disenthralled" the nation, to use Abraham Lincoln's word.

- **The Watergate Tapes:** A tape-recording system caught enough fragments of both truth and lies in Richard Nixon's Oval Office to bring down a dangerously out-of-control government.

- **The Rodney King Videotape:** A neighbor with a video camera produced a tape of the Los Angeles Police beating a black man, which stuck to the conscience of the world and sparked riots that nearly razed a city.

The technology that assists us in this double-murder case is the computer. First, the computerized telephone records from June 12 offer us time-locked information. Nicole and O.J. Simpson, Kato Kaelin, and the limousine driver, Allan Park, each made telephone calls that anchor them in time. And second, our timelines tell and retell the crime story from contrasting points of view.

This approach to presenting an incident from multiple perspectives was brilliantly used in *Rashomon,* a film by Akira Kurosawa based on a Japanese epic. *Rashomon* presents the "facts" of a rape and murder from four viewpoints: that of a nobleman, his wife, a charismatic bandit, and a hidden peasant observer. We use this classic device, with competing storylines, or scenarios, as our text. Our various scenarios are then positioned on timelines.

Albert Einstein concluded that, "Anything that measures the passage of time is a clock." This study will focus on the many clocks of June 12, 1994, from the telephone time logs to the burning candles at Bundy, to the barking dogs: These are all clocks, as are the witnesses and their respective dogs who heard or saw "something" or "nothing" between 10:00 and 10:55 PM on that night.

Then, there is the LAPD's clock, which starts to tick with the discovery of the murder victims and reaches high noon with the finding of the bloody glove at the Simpson estate by Detective Mark Fuhrman. This glove is the clock that links the police timeline to the killer's or killers' timeline.

As independent jurors we have to follow the "Long Foot of Time" wherever it leads. The juror, at the end of this search for truth, will have earned his or her opinion, because while the book cannot come to a final verdict, the reader may. There are truths about this awful event that may never be described or known. Indeed, you may or may not like your final conclusion—but once you have reached it, no one will be able to accuse you of ignorance or blind bias. Your "truth" may not be ours (and we have differences within our own team) but at the very least, you, too, will have come to your own firm conclusion as to whether this case is open or closed.

Your instructions come from Thomas Jefferson:

> *I consider trial by jury as the only anchor yet imagined by man, by which a government can be held to the principles of the Constitution.*

The revolutionary fundament of our system is that the jury bases its verdict on its own intelligence and conscience. If jurors were meant to judge "only the facts," their task could be executed by a computer. Jurors have feelings, opinions, experience, and conscience. Computers, and the analytical tools of this book, do not. Our analysis is your servant, not your master.

You are the soul and spirit of the inquiry that lies before you. You, the juror, are the final check and balance of our system. That is your one and only charge: Use your critical powers, your mind and your heart, to do justice.

The People vs. Orenthal James Simpson
June 1994—October 1995

1994   JUNE

13   The bodies of Nicole Brown Simpson, 35, and Ronald Lyle Goldman, 25, are found shortly after midnight outside Nicole's Brentwood townhouse on South Bundy Drive. Police find the Simpsons' two children, Sydney and Justin, asleep inside. LAPD detectives go to Simpson's Rockingham estate. When blood is found on the Bronco, Detective Mark Fuhrman scales the wall. Simpson in Chicago is notified of his ex-wife's death and returns. Robert Shapiro becomes Simpson's defense counsel.

16   Simpson joins his children and the Brown family at a service for Nicole.

17   Simpson fails to surrender and flees with Al (A.C.) Cowlings in Cowlings's white Bronco. Simpson has left behind a farewell note that is read to the media. Cowlings and Simpson lead police on an internationally televised "slow-speed chase." It ends at Rockingham, where Simpson is arrested and charged with two counts of murder.

20   Simpson enters a plea of not guilty at arraignment. He offers a $500,000 reward for tips leading to the killers.

22   Nicole Simpson's 1993 call to 911 is released to the media by authorities.

24   Responding to the Defense's charges that publicity has tainted the panel's ability to deliberate fairly, the Grand Jury is dismissed.

30   The preliminary hearing begins with Judge Kathleen Kennedy-Powell presiding. The hearing is televised.

JULY

8   Judge Kennedy-Powell rules there is ample evidence for Simpson to stand trial.

22   Superior Court Judge Lance A. Ito is assigned to the case. Ordered held without bail, Simpson pleads "absolutely 100 percent not guilty." Attorney Johnnie L. Cochran, Jr., joins the Defense.

27   Goldman's mother files wrongful death lawsuit against Simpson.

AUGUST

18   The Defense files motion seeking Fuhrman's military and personnel files. Motion will be denied.

SEPTEMBER

9 The District Attorney announces that the People will not seek the death penalty and instead will ask for life in prison without parole.

19 Judge Ito upholds the legality of the search of Simpson's home, but states that in the matter of the warrant there was "reckless disregard."

26 Jury selection begins.

OCTOBER

18 Judge Ito suspends jury selection to evaluate the impact of Faye Resnick's "tell-all" book about Nicole, *Nicole Brown Simpson: Private Diary of a Life Interrupted.*

NOVEMBER

3 Jury of eight women and four men sworn in: one Caucasian, one Hispanic, eight African-American, and two of mixed race.

DECEMBER

7 Judge Ito announces the trial will be televised.

8 Nine woman and three men selected as alternates: seven African-American, four Caucasian, and one Hispanic.

1995 JANUARY

11 Jurors begin their sequestration.

18 Cochran takes the lead in the Defense, following much publicized disagreements between Defense attorneys Robert Shapiro and F. Lee Bailey.

Juror Roland Cooper is dismissed because he allegedly met Simpson at a Hertz function. Before the end of the trial, a total of 10 jurors will be dismissed.

24 Prosecutors Marcia Clark and Christopher Darden deliver opening statements.

25 Cochran begins opening statements for the Defense.

27 Simpson's book *I Want to Tell You* goes on sale.

30 Cochran completes the Defense's opening statements.

31 The first Prosecution witness Sharon Gilbert, the 911 operator who took Nicole's call in 1993, is called as the first of nearly a dozen domestic violence witnesses.

FEBRUARY

3 Denise Brown testifies that she witnessed O.J. abuse her sister Nicole both verbally and physically.

9 Sergeant Robert Riske, the first LAPD officer at the crime scene, describes the bodies and the efforts made to keep evidence from being contaminated.

12 Judge Ito, jurors, attorneys, and Simpson take daytime tour of Simpson's Rockingham estate, the crime scene, and other key Brentwood sites.

MARCH

13 Bailey unveils for the jury a crucial Defense argument that Fuhrman, a key Prosecution witness, is a racist who may have planted evidence. Fuhrman denies all allegations.

15 Bailey cross-examines Fuhrman, who denies using the word "nigger" anytime in the previous ten years.

21 Kato Kaelin bolsters the Prosecution's murder timeline by confirming that he can't account for Simpson's whereabouts during the crucial hour.

APRIL

3 Over nine days of testimony, Dennis Fung, an LAPD criminalist, describes the process of analyzing blood evidence. Under cross-examination by Defense Attorney Barry Scheck, he admits errors at the crime scene.

11 Fung testifies that he did not initially see blood on the Bundy back gate or on the socks found in Simpson's bedroom, although he did weeks later.

MAY

1 Tracy Hampton, stating she "can't take it anymore," is the seventh juror to be dismissed.

4 Ronald Goldman's father and sister file wrongful death suit against Simpson.

8 Testimony about DNA blood analysis begins. Cellmark Laboratory director Robin Cotton links Simpson to the murders when she testifies that lab test results indicate that a blood spot on Simpson's sock matches Ms. Simpson's DNA.

JUNE

2 Coroner Lakshmanan Sathyavagiswaran testifies that a lone assassin could have committed both murders.

5 Two more jurors are dismissed. The final jury is composed of ten women and two men: nine African-American, one Hispanic, and two Caucasians.

12 The estate of Nicole Brown Simpson files wrongful death suit against Simpson.

15 Simpson struggles to put on the bloody leather gloves allegedly worn by the killer. The failed demonstration causes friction between Prosecution attorneys Darden and Clark.

JULY

6 The Prosecution rests.

10 The Defense begins its case by calling Simpson's adult daughter Arnelle, who lives at Rockingham.

25 Several of the Defense's expert witnesses describe contamination in the LAPD lab. The Defense suggests the possibility that evidence was planted.

AUGUST

29 Sixty-one excerpts from the "Fuhrman tapes" are played for the first time in open court without the jury present. Ito later rules that the Defense can only present two excerpts of Fuhrman's racism to the jury.

SEPTEMBER

5 Jury hears taped excerpts of Fuhrman using the word "nigger."

6 Fuhrman refuses to answer the Defense's questions, invoking his Fifth Amendment privilege.

12 Judge Ito orders the Prosecution to begin its rebuttal case even though the Defense has not yet rested.

19 The Defense calls mob informants to impeach Detective Philip Vannatter's testimony that Simpson was not a suspect when the police first went to Rockingham. Judge Ito does not allow this to be televised.

21 The Defense rests.

22 The Prosecution rests.

Simpson tells Judge Ito "I did not, could not, and would not commit this crime."

Judge Ito reads 55 instructions to the jury, allowing them to find Simpson guilty of second-degree murder if they can't agree to convict him of first-degree charges.

26–7 Clark and Darden deliver the Prosecution's closing argument.

27–8 Cochran and Scheck deliver the closing argument for the Defense.

29 Clark completes the Prosecution's rebuttal with Nicole's 911 tape and a montage of autopsy photographs.

Judge Ito delivers final jury instructions. A forewoman is selected in four minutes.

OCTOBER

2 Jury reaches verdict in less than four hours. The only testimony the jurors request is that of limousine driver Allan Park. Judge Ito decides the verdict will be announced the next day.

3 Verdict read. Simpson is acquitted of all charges and returns home to his Rockingham estate.

One

The Prosecution

The [D.A.'s] office leaked out two different so-called timelines and they got caught and they never were able to straighten it out, that's why in the final summation they had to try to add ten minutes and have Kato hear the thumps at 10:50. But the jury didn't buy it.

This is the "Source," a person who works or did work for the criminal justice system. This courageous and frustrated individual would also say, shrewdly, that the District Attorney's office was utterly sincere, "too sincere": They believed, as an article of faith, that Orenthal James Simpson murdered Nicole Brown Simpson and Ronald Lyle Goldman. And, the Source continued, "until the Thursday they thought they were going to find the knife—they had the blood and the gloves—but they never did, and that's when the trouble started." This "trouble" will occupy us in this study and possibly for years to come.

Please bear in mind, Ladies and Gentlemen, that it is the Prosecution's case, theory, and storyline that define our first reality of the crime and case. It is the Prosecution's duty to present their best evidence, theories, and witnesses to the jury with the hopes of convincing them "beyond a reasonable doubt" of their view of the crime. The Defense, however, only has to present the jury with that "reasonable doubt." The Defense does not create a counter-universe or theory of the crime except by cross-examination and implication. Theirs is not the responsibility of proving anything—their client is "innocent" by definition.

The Prosecution Scenario

By week two of June 1994, the District Attorney had pieced together a storyline of the crime that was well summarized by the *Los Angeles Times*:

> O.J. glared at Nicole during their daughter's dance recital the afternoon of June 12, 1994. Nicole had recently dumped him for good. He had always tried to control her, even beat her, and could not stand the thought of her waltzing off without him. And so he plotted his revenge. At about 10 PM that evening, in the dim light of a crescent moon, O.J. grabbed a knife, leather gloves, and a dark knit cap, jumped into his white Ford Bronco and sped to Nicole's condominium.
>
> As he drove, O.J. twice tried to call his new girlfriend, Paula Barbieri. He could not reach her. Spurned by Paula, rejected by Nicole, O.J. fumed. He leaped out of the car at Nicole's back gate and sneaked up the dark alleyway. Perhaps hearing a noise, Nicole opened her front door and stepped down the tiled walk. O.J. struck, cutting her and knocking her unconscious. Then a man appeared on the walk. Panicked, O.J. lashed out again. Ron Goldman struggled and tried to flee. But O.J. jabbed the knife deep into his neck. Turning to Nicole's limp form, O.J. yanked back her hair and delivered a vicious, final swipe across her neck.
>
> Then he fled, dripping blood from a cut on his left finger and leaving footprints from his size 12 Bruno Magli shoes. In his haste, he had dropped one glove and the hat.
>
> Back home, O.J. hurried down the narrow, overgrown path behind his guesthouse—and slammed into the air conditioner sticking out of the wall. The collision shook Kato Kaelin's guesthouse and made O.J. drop the other glove. He dashed across the yard, raced up to his bedroom, peeled off his bloody socks, showered, changed, and zipped outside to a limousine that had waited for its missing passenger for 35 minutes. As he sweated and fussed with his bag in the back seat, the limo whisked him off to the airport.[1]

The Prosecution's overarching theme and thesis of the crime is homicidal jealousy—beginning with the smoldering rage of the defendant at young Sydney Simpson's dance recital. This scenario includes many of the critical items that would be discussed during the trial: a knife, leather gloves, a dark knit hat, a white Ford Bronco, Bruno Magli shoes, bloody socks, an air conditioner, and a waiting limousine and driver. However, you will note as we proceed that virtually every phrase in this first draft of the Prosecution's case would be amended and, in some cases, deleted.

In fact, in nearly every assertion of the Prosecution—from blood chemistry, to the psychology of obsessive jealousy, to the philosophy of gender conflict, to the farewell note and "slow-speed chase"—there would be a profound ambivalence, contradiction, overdetermination, and confusion of conflicting elements: "Doubleness"—some pointing to guilt, some to innocence, and, as we shall see, some to both.

The two major bases for the Prosecution's case—the jealousy/abuse motive, and the trail of blood from the Bundy to the Rockingham residence—require separate, in-depth, discussion and the place for that is Chapter Two. At this point in time, it is the Prosecution's story line that must be accepted by the jury in order to find the defendant guilty. We must be convinced beyond a reasonable doubt that O.J. Simpson is guilty of the double murder.

The Timeline Approach

In the sections to come, you, the jury, will follow the evolution of the Prosecution's killing time scenario. First, we broadly sketch the overall timeline. Then, we follow the story minute by minute in both narrative and graphic timelines. As we revisit the timelines, we add, alter, or discuss certain elements. We point out changes in the scenario; the Defense's responses; and other information pertinent to the killing time. As we proceed, we will also evaluate the credibility of the Prosecution's scenario as measured against events known to have occurred at fixed points in time on June 12, 1994. Before we proceed to the Prosecution master timeline, we will review some of its components.

Prosecution Clocks

The Prosecution was constantly ridiculed for using a bark-ing dog as a clock. But it was a valid and resourceful strat-egy to create a murder timeline employing a series of clocks—dogs, people, telephone logs.

The unofficial clocks of the events of June 12 include everything from burning scented candles, to wailing and barking dogs, to witnesses passing the crime scene between 10:00 PM and 12:00 midnight. That dark night was full of dogs and people—neighbors, visiting lovers, innocent by-standers, and tragic homicides—all under nature's clock, a crescent moon.

Telephone calls are the uncontested fixed points bur-ied in the timelines; they are the official clocks of the mea-surement of the killing time, times that both the Prosecu-tion and the Defense accepted as accurate. The basic times of the following computer–clocked calls are taken from tele-phone company records. All of these telephone calls were logged between 9:30 PM and 10:55 PM on June 12, 1994. They will be critical parts of all scenarios to come.

Telephone Calls—June 12, 1994
• O.J. Simpson to Sydney Simpson
• Juditha Brown to the Mezzaluna Restaurant
• Juditha Brown to her daughter Nicole
• Nicole to Mezzaluna, where Ron Goldman worked
• Faye Resnick to Nicole Simpson
• O.J. Simpson to Paula Barbieri (2 calls)
• Limousine driver Allan Park to his employer (4 calls); Park to his mother
• Kato Kaelin to his friend (3 calls)
• Denise Pilnack to her mother

Witnesses

It is time now to meet some of the human clocks, the timeline witnesses, whose fate positioned them to become important components in the mystery of the Bundy killings that Sunday night. Three separate legal hearings at which witnesses appeared were held in the Simpson matter:

Grand jury: Conducted in secret, to determine if there was sufficient cause to try Simpson for murder. Dismissed June 24, after the Defense charged and the judge found that the massive media coverage and release of Nicole's 911 tape had tainted the panel.

Preliminary hearing: Open to the public, held June 30 to July 8 before Municipal Court Judge Kathleen Kennedy-Powell. This was, in a way, a mini-trial, with the Prosecution calling 21 witnesses; the Defense is not allowed to call witnesses at a preliminary hearing. Both the Defense and Prosecution delivered final arguments. On July 8, the judge ordered Simpson to stand trial.

Trial: On July 22, Superior Court Judge Lance A. Ito was assigned to preside over the Simpson trial.

The witnesses listed here offered information relating to either Ron Goldman's timeline (Mezzaluna witnesses) or events at Bundy immediately around the time of the murders. They are grouped according to their testimony. Although many other witnesses testified, those listed below were critical in establishing the killing time. (See Appendix for master list of all witnesses at trial.)

Witnesses Testifying about Mezzaluna

Karen Lee Crawford: *Grand Jury, preliminary, and trial.* Took Juditha Brown's telephone call. Testified that Ron Goldman left at 9:50 or 9:55 PM the night of the murders.

Stewart Tanner: *Grand Jury, preliminary, and trial.* Also testified that Ron left at about 9:50 PM, arranging to meet Tanner later at a Mexican restaurant in Marina Del Rey.

John Debello: *Grand Jury.* Confirmed the above.

Prosecution Witnesses about Events at Bundy

Pablo Fenjves: *Preliminary and trial.* Testimony changed slightly between two hearings. First reported hearing a dog barking at 10:20. Then, at trial, described the barking as a plaintive wail that began at 10:15 PM.

Mark Storfer: *Trial.* Heard a dog at 10:28 PM.

Eva Stein: *Trial.* Awakened by a dog between 10:15 and 10:45 PM.

Louis Karpe: *Trial.* Alarmed by a dog while picking up mail at 11:00 PM.

Elsie Tistaert: *Trial.* Heard a dog barking for about thirty minutes in late evening. No time given.

Steven Schwab: *Trial.* Found Nicole's dog roaming the neighborhood. Estimated time 10:55 PM. Originally told detectives it was after 11:00 PM. Returned home and later gave the dog to his neighbor Sukru Boztepe.

Sukru Boztepe: *Grand Jury, preliminary, and trial.* With his wife, Bettina Rasmussen, took the dog out a little after midnight and discovered the crime scene at Bundy.

Bettina Rasmussen: *Grand Jury, preliminary, and trial.* She saw bodies briefly at the crime scene and then called 911.

Jill Shiveley: *Grand Jury and preliminary.* Saw Simpson speeding in his Bronco on streets near 875 South Bundy and running a red light at 10:50 PM. The Prosecution did not call her to testify at trial once they learned she had taken money from a tabloid and *Hard Copy.* The Defense will insist that she was not called because she swore that she saw a white Bronco at 10:50 PM, a time that conflicted with the Prosecution murder timeline, which had Simpson at Rockingham at 10:45 PM, crashing into the air conditioner.

Defense Witnesses about Events at Bundy

Ellen Aaronson: She passed the Bundy crime scene around 10:28 PM. She was walking with Danny Mandel.

Danny Mandel: Remembered them passing the front gate of Bundy about 10:30 PM. They saw nothing—no blood, no dog. They heard no barking or wailing.

Francesca Harmon: Drove past 875 South Bundy about 10:25 PM, saw and heard nothing unusual.

Judy Telender: Drove past 875 South Bundy at 10:24 PM, saw and heard nothing unusual.

Denise Pilnak: A neighbor of Nicole's, she came out when her friend Judy Telender left at 10:21 PM. Testified that she saw and heard nothing unusual. At 10:35 PM, she heard a dog barking.

Robert Heidstra: Was in the alley across from the Bundy crime scene at 10:35 PM. Heard a dog barking, the sound of men talking, and a man's voice yelling, "Hey, hey, hey!"

Did Not Testify

Mary Anne Gerchas: Reported that she saw four men fleeing the crime scene. Two Caucasian, two Hispanic. None was O.J. Simpson. The Prosecution claimed she was not even in the area that night. She pleaded guilty for fraud unrelated to the Simpson matter.

Lief Tilden: Stated that he saw four men at Bundy.

Frank Chiuchiolo: Claimed to be near the crime scene, casing a house for burglary. Saw Caucasian and Latino men at the crime scene about the time of the murders. The Defense decided not to call the convicted felon to testify.

The Prosecution Master Timeline

The events preceding, during, and following the murders of Nicole and Ron are presented here with times assigned as in the Prosecution's scenario. The descriptions of events are from the point of view taken by the Prosecution unless otherwise noted. This master timeline stretches from Sydney Simpson's afternoon recital to the murder of Ron and her mother and on to the arrest of her father, O.J., for the murders.

The Prosecution Master Timeline June 12–17, 1994	
PM	**JUNE 12**
5:00	Nicole attends her daughter's dance recital. O.J. arrives late. He glares at Nicole.
6:30	Nicole and the Brown family go to dinner at the Mezzaluna Restaurant. They do not invite Simpson. He leaves the recital angry and upset.
6:30	Simpson returns to his Brentwood estate on Rockingham Avenue. He tells his house guest Kato Kaelin that his relationship with Nicole is over.
8:30	Nicole, Justin, Sydney, and Sydney's friend leave the restaurant and go to a Ben & Jerry's ice cream shop.
8:30	Simpson and Kaelin drive to a McDonald's restaurant for hamburgers.
9:00	Nicole and three children arrive home at 875 South Bundy Drive.
9:35	Simpson and Kaelin return from McDonald's. Kaelin retires to his guesthouse.
9:37	Kaelin telephones a friend in San Diego.
9:37	Nicole's mother, Juditha, calls Mezzaluna to see if anyone has found her eyeglasses. The manager finds the glasses in the street outside.
9:40	Juditha Brown calls Nicole to tell her that she left her glasses at Mezzaluna.
9:42	Nicole calls Mezzaluna and speaks to her friend Ronald Goldman, who offers to drop off the glasses at Nicole's residence after his shift.

9:50	Ron leaves the restaurant for his apartment nearby. He changes and then heads to 875 South Bundy.
10:15	O.J. Simpson murders his ex-wife Nicole and her friend Ron Goldman. Neighbor Pablo Fenjves hears Nicole's Akita announce her death with its "plaintive wail."
10:20–25	Allan Park, a limousine driver, arrives at the Simpson estate to drive Simpson to the airport for his flight to Chicago.
10:30–40	Park moves back and forth between the Rockingham and the Ashford Street gates.
10:40	Park rings the buzzer. Nobody answers. It appears that one light is on upstairs and the downstairs is dark.
10:40–45	Kaelin, still on the phone, hears three loud "thumps" on his guesthouse wall.
10:49	Kaelin goes out to check the grounds after hearing the thumps.
10:49	Park again rings the buzzer at the gate, still no answer.
10:55–57	Park sees a tall person in dark clothing walk across the driveway and enter the mansion. The downstairs lights go on. The driver rings the buzzer again, and Simpson answers immediately. He explains that he had over-slept.
10:55	Neighbor Steven Schwab, walking his dog, discovers Nicole's barking Akita. The dog has no tags and its legs and paws are bloody. Schwab takes the dog to his nearby residence.
11:00	Kaelin sees Simpson for the first time since returning from McDonald's restaurant.
	Kaelin helps Simpson load his luggage into the limousine. He informs Simpson of the mysterious thumps.
11:06–15	The limousine, with Simpson, leaves for the airport and a flight to Chicago.
11:20	Simpson calls Kaelin from the limousine and asks him to set the alarm in his mansion.
11:45	The Akita is so restless that Schwab's neighbors Sukru Boztepe and Bettina Rasmussen, who have received the dog from Schwab, take it for a walk to try to find the owner.
11:50	The dog leads them to Nicole's townhouse. Nicole's body is discovered and the police are summoned.

AM   **JUNE 13**

12:17 The LAPD arrive at the Bundy crime scene. Sergeant Riske discovers Ron Goldman's body. Soon many more LAPD officers are at the scene.

Sydney and Justin are discovered asleep and unharmed inside. They are taken to the police station.

2:10 Detectives Mark Fuhrman and Ron Phillips arrive at Bundy.

2:50 Fuhrman and Phillips are told that detectives from Robbery/Homicide are being called in to take charge of the investigation. Fuhrman later testifies that from 2:50 AM to 4:05 AM, when Detectives Lange and Vannatter arrived, no "detecting" was done.

5:00 Detectives Tom Lange, Philip Vannatter, Ron Phillips, and Mark Fuhrman drive to Simpson's Rockingham estate to notify him about his ex-wife's death and to make arrangements for his two children. They are unable to rouse anyone inside the estate.

Fuhrman sees blood near the door handle of Simpson's white Bronco. Suspecting "more crime victims," the detectives decide they must enter the estate. Fuhrman climbs over the fence and lets the others in. When no one answers at the front door, the four proceed to the nearby guesthouse, where they awaken Kato Kaelin. He directs them to Arnelle Simpson's quarters.

Fuhrman remains to talk with Kaelin, who describes the three thumps that he heard on the wall.

Fuhrman searches the grounds and finds a right-hand bloody glove on the ground in back of the guesthouse.

6:00 Detectives note blood drops leading from the Bronco on Rockingham Avenue up to the mansion.

6:05 Arnelle helps police locate her father. Phillips notifies Simpson in Chicago of his ex-wife's death.

7:41 (9:41 Central time) Simpson's flight back to L.A. leaves Chicago.

9:30 (11:30 Central time) Chicago police search Simpson's hotel room, find blood on the sink, a broken glass, and a bloody washcloth.

12 noon Simpson, back at Rockingham, is handcuffed briefly.

PM   **JUNE 13**

12:20 The bodies of Nicole Brown Simpson and Ronald Goldman arrive at the coroner's office for autopsy.

1:35	Simpson, after sending his attorney away, talks with Lange and Vannatter at police headquarters. A photograph is taken of a cut on his left hand, he volunteers a blood sample, and he is released. (See Appendix for Simpson's statement.)
AM	**JUNE 17**
9:00	A warrant is issued for the arrest of Orenthal James Simpson for two counts of first-degree murder. Simpson agrees to turn himself in at 11:00 AM.
PM	**JUNE 17**
3:00	L.A. County District Attorney Gil Garcetti announces that Simpson is a fugitive.
6:30	Simpson and his friend A.C. Cowlings lead police on a "slow-speed" freeway chase to Simpson's home where Simpson is handcuffed and arrested at 8:50 PM.

O.J. Simpson During the Killing Time

The Prosecution was concerned that their circumstantial clock or clocks validate their charge that O.J. Simpson did have time on the evening of June 12, 1994, to murder his former wife and her friend and then—and this is crucial—have time to dispose of incriminating evidence and a weapon before leaving on a planned business trip to Chicago.

The killing time had to be sometime after 9:42 PM that evening. This we know because Nicole was still alive at that time, phoning Mezzaluna. The first clock the Prosecution found anchoring Simpson to the critical time frame was a telephone call at 10:02 PM that was recorded on his cellular telephone bill. The other clock was at about 10:56 PM, when the defendant was seen by the limousine driver entering his mansion. Less than one hour. The Prosecution needed to plug the gaps in that rudimentary timeline to account for the murders. They tried.

They looked closely at the reports of dog activity in the Bundy area the night of the murders, focussing on one particular report of a dog with a plaintive wail.

The Wailing Dog Timeline
June 12–13, 1994

PM

10:15   Pablo Fenjves lived behind Nicole Brown Simpson. He told police that he had heard Kato, Nicole's Akita, "wailing plaintively" at 10:15 PM, meaning, the Prosecution argued, that the murders were in progress.

10:25   Four witnesses testified they heard a dog that night, but only one of them, Fenjves, heard the dog wailing as early as 10:20 PM. Francesca Harmon, who testified that she drove past Bundy around 10:25 PM, said she heard no dog.

Prosecution witness Fenjves testified that he first heard the dog wailing during the news, at about 10:20 PM; then, on the stand, he changed the time to 10:15. Fenjves also stated that he continued to hear the same dog between 11:00 and 11:40 PM. Any dog he heard at that time could not have been Nicole's Akita because the Akita had been found around 10:55 PM by another neighbor, Steven Schwab.

10:50-55   Schwab encountered Nicole's dog barking furiously, roaming loose, and spotted with blood. Schwab was certain of the time of this canine encounter because he had his own clock: He left his residence at the end of *The Dick Van Dyke Show*, at 10:30 PM, and returned before the beginning of *The Mary Tyler Moore Show*, at 11:00 PM.

Schwab found the Akita around 10:55 PM and left the immediate neighborhood with him.

11:50   Near midnight, Sukru Boztepe and Bettina Rasmussen took the Akita from Schwab and walked with it, trying to find an owner. The dog led the young couple to 875 South Bundy. The dog stared into the dark walkway, thick with lavender, white lilies of the Nile, Austrian ferns, two palm trees, pink and white ground cover. The Boztepes looked, too, and then they saw, in the moonlight, blood trickling down the Spanish tile walkway on the street side of the gate; then they made out a woman's body crumpled in the gateway.

Members of the jury, we must draw your attention to the Prosecution's murder clock, on which all the rest of their case depends. Their clock stopped here at 10:15 PM, the time Fenjves heard the dog wail, the time they said meant that the murders were in progress.

Of the nine time witnesses called by Prosecution and Defense, only Fenjves offered testimony that supported the Prosecution's 10:15 PM timeline. Christopher Darden in his book *In Contempt* comments on the Prosecution's early time frame for the murders:

> *We had staked much of our case on the idea that the murders occurred at 10:15 PM, yet I didn't think we should have allowed ourselves to be pinned down by that. To me, the murders could have occurred as late as 10:40 PM, and Simpson would still have had time to drive five minutes back to his estate.* [2]

Is that possible? We will see later. The official Prosecution timeline set the murders around 10:15 PM, and it is that timeline we will now begin to analyze.

Below are the key elements, or clocks, of the Prosecution's scenario of the murders, positioned on a timeline.

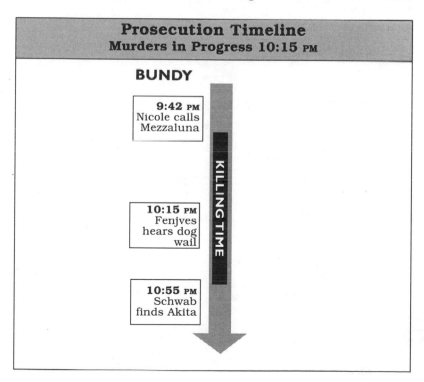

Prosecution Timeline
Murders in Progress 10:15 PM

BUNDY

9:42 PM
Nicole calls
Mezzaluna

10:15 PM
Fenjves
hears dog
wail

10:55 PM
Schwab
finds Akita

KILLING TIME

Note that there is an important time that is not noted in this scenario—a point that was established once the Prosecution decided that it was Simpson who made the thumps Kaelin heard about 10:40–10:42 PM. The crime scene at Bundy is about five minutes' drive from Simpson's Rockingham estate. Therefore, Simpson had to have left the crime scene by 10:35 PM or so in order to make the "thumps" at the reported time (a time that was "fixed" by the time Kato hung up from a phone call to check on the noise). Therefore, the public and the jury were encouraged by the Prosecution and much of the media to visualize a timeline of criminal opportunity of 62 minutes, from roughly 9:35 PM—when Simpson returned to his home from a McDonald's restaurant—to 10:37 PM. This would have been the latest possible moment Simpson could have fled the South Bundy killing area and sped home to Rockingham in the five minutes–plus required to cover the winding two miles, then entered the grounds, raced around the mansion, crashed into Kaelin's wall between 10:40 and 10:42 PM, and dropped his second bloody glove.

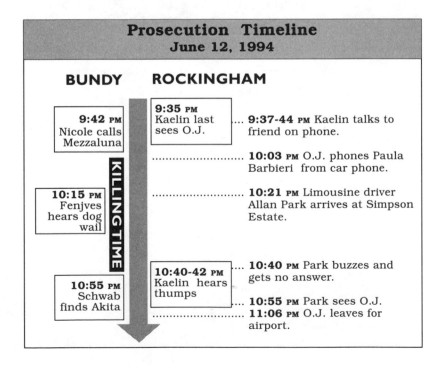

Prosecution Timeline
June 12, 1994

BUNDY   **ROCKINGHAM**

9:42 PM
Nicole calls
Mezzaluna

9:35 PM
Kaelin last
sees O.J.

.... **9:37-44 PM** Kaelin talks to
friend on phone.

.... **10:03 PM** O.J. phones Paula
Barbieri from car phone.

10:15 PM
Fenjves
hears dog
wail

.... **10:21 PM** Limousine driver
Allan Park arrives at Simpson
Estate.

KILLING TIME

10:40-42 PM
Kaelin hears
thumps

.... **10:40 PM** Park buzzes and
gets no answer.

10:55 PM
Schwab
finds Akita

.... **10:55 PM** Park sees O.J.
.... **11:06 PM** O.J. leaves for
airport.

Having fixed the killing time, the Prosecution's next task was to track Simpson movements moment to moment. The following scenario integrates various assertions made by the Prosecution, some of which would later be changed.

	Prosecution Timeline O.J. Simpson Acting Alone
PM	
10:03	Simpson, at his mansion, is unable to reach Paula Barbieri on his cellular telephone. He erupts with rage; gathers up a knife, leather gloves, mask, stocking cap, a plastic bag, and shovel in preparation for murder.
10:10	Simpson, in white Bronco, pulls up in front of Nicole's condominium, headlights on.
10:12	Simpson drives behind the residence into the alley, parks, and, using stolen keys, enters through the back gate.
10:13	Simpson "lies in wait" in the very small front courtyard of 875 South Bundy.
10:14	Nicole exits her residence. Simpson stabs her. She collapses at her front gate, still alive.
10:15–16	Ronald Goldman enters through the front gate. Simpson stabs and kills Goldman, then completes murder of Nicole by slashing her throat "through and through." Nicole's Akita, Kato, begins to wail piercingly.
10:17	Simpson walks slowly to the back gate (dripping blood from a cut on his left hand). Then he returns to the murder scene to search for his missing left glove and stocking cap—but fails to locate them.
10:19	Simpson speeds away toward his Rockingham estate.
10:20-40	Simpson disposes of the murder weapon and bloody clothes, including shoes, and drives back to Rockingham estate.
10:21	Limousine driver Allan Park arrives early at Rockingham to chauffeur Simpson to the airport. He parks near the Ashford Street entrance to the estate for his 10:45 PM appointment.
10:40	Park begins to ring the gate buzzer. No answer.
10:41	Simpson speeds up to the Rockingham Avenue entrance, parks at an angle. He runs along the driveway

to the path curving in back of house, smashes into the air conditioning unit on Kato Kaelin's guesthouse outer wall, and drops his remaining right-hand glove.

10:48 Kaelin hangs up from his phone call to search the grounds for the source of the noise he heard while on the phone.

10:52 Kaelin meets driver Park at Ashford gate, then continues search.

10:56-57 Park notes a large African-American entering the mansion.

10:58 Park buzzes again and this time Simpson answers and states that he has overslept.

11:02 Simpson exits the mansion with his suitcases.

11:03–06 Simpson insists on putting certain bags in the limousine, talks with Kaelin concerning the thumps, enters and exits the mansion, then leaves for his pre-planned business flight to Chicago. Park did not, then, note the presence of the white Bronco, as he had not earlier noted it when he arrived at 10:21 PM.

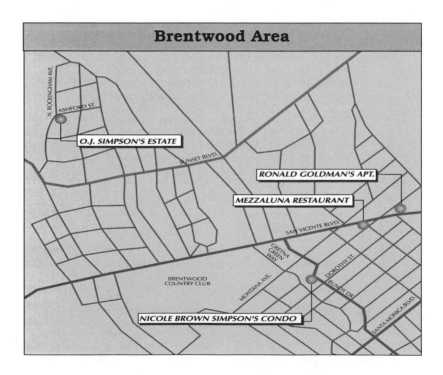

Brentwood Area

Prosecution Timeline
O.J. Simpson Acting Alone

BUNDY

ROCKINGHAM

9:42 PM Nicole calls Mezzaluna

KILLING TIME

10:15 PM Fenjves hears dog wail

10:55 PM Akita found loose

.... **9:35 PM** Simpson returns home from McDonald's and is last seen by Kaelin.

.... **10:03 PM** Simpson makes decision to murder Nicole Brown Simpson.

.... **10:14–17 PM** Simpson murders his ex-wife and Ronald Lyle Goldman.

.... **10:20–40 PM** Simpson unaccounted for.

.... **10:21 PM** Limousine driver Allan Park arrives at Simpson estate.

.... **10:40–42 PM** Kaelin hears three loud thumps on his outside wall.

.... **11:02 PM** Simpson exits mansion.

.... **11:06 PM** Limousine with Simpson leaves for airport.

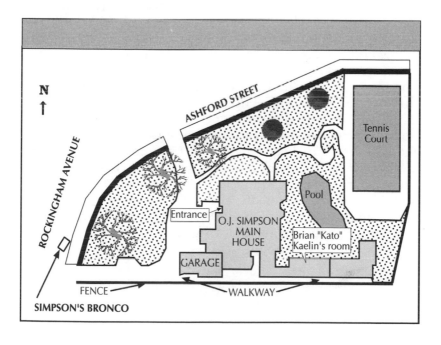

The Prosecution's History
of Abuse Within
the Simpson Household

In order to fully understand the Prosecution's theory of events, it is necessary to discuss their emphasis on the history of spousal abuse in the Simpson household. The element of motive is not required by law but the Prosecution seemed to feel compelled to find the nexus of spousal abuse and murder.

The Prosecution begins its timeline at 10:03 PM, with Simpson's second call of the evening to Barbieri. In July of 1994, a month after the murders, the District Attorney's office had leaked information that Simpson called his companion knowing that she would not answer, and that he left a message for her to call him as part of an elaborate alibi. But a year later, according to Darden's summation, the killer—described as a "burning fuse" of rage and frustration—was triggered into lethal action when unable to reach Barbieri. Over and over again, the Prosecution swung from one extreme to another ("cold-blooded" to "burning fuse") in their attempt to prove motive for the crime. In either case, what did remain constant was the Prosecution's view that Simpson's prior history of abusing Nicole revealed him as capable of murdering her—whether in a cold-blooded, calculating state, or in an eruption of blind fury.

There is indeed a nexus of abuse and murder, and it cannot be repeated or revealed too many times to a male-chauvinist culture based on denial. The question for the jury is whether or not there is a connection in this case. Here follow short excerpts from the 911 tape leaked by the District Attorney to the media and public during the preliminary trial. It is the emotional blueprint of the Prosecution's case, and it would be used during their closing argument.

Nicole Brown Simpson Call to 911
October 25, 1993

Nicole: My ex-husband has just broken into my house and he's ranting and raving outside in the front yard.
Dispatcher: Has he been drinking or anything?
Nicole: No. But he's crazy.
Dispatcher: Did he hit you?
Nicole: No.
Dispatcher: Do you have a restraining order against him?
Nicole: No.
Dispatcher: What is your name?
Nicole: Nicole Simpson.

. . . .

Nicole: Could you get somebody over here now, to... Gretna Green. He's back. Please.
Dispatcher: What does he look like?
Nicole: He's O.J. Simpson. I think you know his record. Could you just send somebody over here?
Dispatcher: What is he doing there?

. . . .

Nicole: Screaming at my roommate [Kato Kaelin] about me and at me.
Dispatcher: OK. What is he saying?
Nicole: Oh, something about some guy I know and hookers and keys and I started this s--- before and...
Dispatcher: Um-hum.
Nicole: And it's all my fault and now what am I going to do, "Get the police in this" and the whole thing. It's all my fault, I started this before. (Sigh) Brother. (Inaudible) kids (inaudible).
Dispatcher: OK, has he hit you today or...
Nicole: No.
Dispatcher: OK, you don't need any paramedics or anything.
Nicole: Uh-uh.
Dispatcher: OK, you just want him to leave?
Nicole: My door. He broke the whole back door in.
Dispatcher: And then he left and he came back?
Nicole: He came and he practically knocked my upstairs door down but he pounded it and he screamed

and hollered and I tried to get him out of the bedroom because the kids are sleeping in there.
Dispatcher: Um-hum. OK.
Nicole: He wanted somebody's phone number and I
gave him my phone book or I put my phone book down
to write down, the phone number that he wanted and
he took my phone book with all my stuff in it.
Dispatcher: OK. So basically you guys have just
been arguing? * (Simpson continues yelling unintel-
ligibly.)

. . . .

O.J.:   ... I don't give a s--- anymore ...
Nicole: Would you just leave, O.J., O.J., O.J.,
O.J., could you please (inaudible) Please leave.
O.J.:   ... I'm not leaving...
Nicole: Please leave. O.J. Please, the kids,
the kids are sleeping, please.
Dispatcher: Is he leaving?
Nicole: No.
Dispatcher: Does he know you're on the phone with
police?
Nicole: No.

. . . .

Dispatcher: What is he saying now? Nicole, you
still on the line?
Nicole: Yeah.
Dispatcher: Do you still think he's going to hit
you?
Nicole: I don't know. He's going to leave. He
just said that. He just said he needs to leave.
O.J.:   ... Hey! I can read this b---s--- all
week in the *National Enquirer*. Her words exactly.
What, who got that, who?

. . . .

Dispatcher: Has this happened before or no?
Nicole: Many times.
Dispatcher: OK. The police should be on the way. It
just seems like a long time because it's kind of
busy in that division right now.
(Yelling continues.)

When this dramatic cry for help was broadcast, one part
of the public jury instantly voted guilty in their hearts. Leaks
like this about the case were a regular occurrence in the early

days, particularly in the period between the preliminary hearing and jury selection. This most notorious 911 leak was, in fact, officially sanctioned. Its release was rationalized as "in response to requests from the news media."

Selections from this tape, with Nicole pleading for help just seven and a half months before her death, would be one of the last things the jury heard at the end of trial, played as a sound track to a grisly murder photo of the former homecoming queen. This montage wrung groans of pain and sobs from the courtroom audience of victims' family and friends. Some of the jurors, however, saw this as an attempt to manipulate them to convict in a case that had not been proven to their satisfaction.

At this point, we must also call the jury's attention to something else in the tape: What O.J. is saying. Note his references to "keys," "hookers," "sex," and the *National Enquirer:* there is a subtext here not necessarily connected to domestic jealous violence but to another dangerous borderline subculture. Bear this in mind for scenarios to come in later chapters.

Nicole's desperate voice on the 911 tape was powerful evidence. The Prosecution had promised to call many witnesses, including experts, to testify to the links between Simpson's attacks on his wife and her murder on June 12, 1994. They called only Nicole's sister Denise Brown, who cited other instances of Simpson mistreating Nicole. They called no expert witnesses.

Certainly, no juror could honestly rule out the relevance of such abuse leading to homicide—that is, if the Prosecution could "hook it up." There is a powerful historical predicate for the murder of Nicole: Four women a day are murdered as a result of domestic disputes. According to the FBI, 33 percent of women murdered in the United States are killed by a husband or boyfriend. The American Medical Association reported in 1990 that 50 percent of all female homicide victims are killed by a husband or boyfriend.

Further, the Prosecution would argue, 74 percent of all murders of women from domestic violence occur after the woman has left the relationship, filed for divorce, received a divorce, or filed an order of protection against the abuser. When women leave the abusive relationship, the violence against them often escalates.

Nicole Brown Simpson's history as a battered wife extended back to 1985, as far as police and public records are concerned. The Prosecution presented this history in full.

Police Records of Nicole's Battery by O.J.

- In 1985, there was an alleged incident at the Rockingham residence to which police were called. Mark Fuhrman, then a patrolman, and his partner responded to a 415, or family dispute call. No report was filed at that time, but in 1989, after an incident of abuse at Rockingham, the City Attorney's Office asked for information from any officers who knew of previous trouble there. Fuhrman then prepared a report of the 1985 incident.

  Fuhrman stated that when he arrived, O.J. Simpson was standing on the driveway and a sobbing blonde Caucasian woman was leaning on the side of a Mercedes nearby. The window of the Mercedes was shattered and a baseball bat was leaning against the wall. During the 1995 trial Fuhrman testified about this 1985 incident. He stated that Simpson had been "agitated" but "not out of control," and that he had said, "She's my wife. She's okay. I broke the windshield. It's mine. There's no trouble here." Nicole did not wish to report the episode or file charges, so no report was filed.

- On New Year's Day 1989, there was an incident in which Simpson beat Nicole and threw her out of the house. Police responding to her call reported that she ran to them from the bushes, sobbing, "He's going to kill me." She said that O.J. had said, "I'm going to kill you," and that he had slapped her with both open and closed fists, kicked her, and pulled her hair. Simpson came out and said that he had not beaten Nicole, argued that the LAPD had come to the house eight other times and that now these officers were making a "big deal" out of "a family matter." When Officer Edwards told Simpson that Nicole wanted him arrested for beating her up, Simpson eluded arrest by leaving in his Bentley. Nicole was taken to the West L.A. Police Station where photographs were taken of her badly beaten face and muddied clothes. Simpson pleaded "no contest" to a misdemeanor spousal battery charge. The photographs were introduced as Prosecution evidence in the murder trial.

- In October 1993, Nicole made the 911 call to which police responded. Sergeant Lerner testified that Nicole appeared frightened, and that he was able to calm down Simpson, who was "agitated." Authorities took no action because Nicole declined to press charges.

The above are the only incidents on the police record, but friends and relatives also offered testimony of Simpson's physical and verbal abuse of Nicole. Her sister Denise testified that on one occasion in 1986, Simpson called Nicole a "fat pig" and made fun of her when she was pregnant. She also testified that on another occasion in the late 1980s, Simpson became enraged—when Denise told him he took Nicole for granted—and threw Denise, her date, and Nicole out of the house. "He picked her up and threw her against a wall," sobbed Brown. The Prosecution abuse timeline also included a 1992 incident in which Simpson was said to have stalked Nicole and spied on her being intimate in her home with Keith Zlomsowitch, a Mezzaluna manager.

The Prosecution contended that these, and other incidents of abuse during the Simpsons' 17-year relationship led to Simpson's murdering Nicole. The question is: Did these events form a pattern leading to murder? The Prosecution did not call any domestic violence experts to bolster their argument that O.J. Simpson fit the pattern of abuser-turned-murderer.

According to the Source:

> They [D.A.] were afraid of Scheck and Neufeld and especially Dershowitz on the abuse question. You know, "Men who kill are often abusers, but men who abuse almost never kill." And they only had the 1989 fight—all the rest was Faye Resnick's hype...

Had Simpson testified we now know what he might have said, based on statements given in his post-trial video:

> ... no excuse for 1989. I went into therapy, I still go

to this day. I accepted punishment. It was mutual, but it was my responsibility . . . The 911 call—I don't apologize at all! First, I didn't break down the door, it was already broke. Now, they played the tape, but what you didn't know was that Nicole had called me and insisted that I come over to talk this problem out . . . She went upstairs and I thought she was talking to her mother! Or I wouldn't have yelled like that . . . No, she wasn't scared of me, she came down and talked on the phone right in front of me. Then when the cops came they made another tape, secretly, where Nicole didn't make any charges. And she called me the next day to apologize for calling the police! [3]

To hear Simpson's fuller version of events—albeit a version presented outside of the courtroom and one not subject to Prosecution's cross-examination—the jury may choose to view the tape. But now, let us move on to how the Defense answered the Prosecution's view that Simpson's abusive treatment of Nicole was the prelude to murder.

Defense Perspective of Abuse Within the Simpson Household, 1985–94

Point by point, the Defense offered contrasting views to the Prosecution's theories.

1985: Simpson claimed that he never attacked Nicole's Mercedes with a baseball bat during a domestic dispute. The police report was not written until four years after the incident.

January 1989: Simpson pleaded "no contest" to a misdemeanor spousal battery charge. After the case, he signed an agreement that if he ever laid a hand on Nicole again, their prenuptial agreement would be null and void. During their 1992 divorce proceedings, Nicole testified that since the 1989 beating, Simpson had not touched her in anger. This indicated that he was reformed and the abuse had stopped.

April 1992: Simpson never "spied on" Nicole having oral sex with Keith Zlomsowitch. He only happened to drop by after visiting a nightclub. He mentioned the incident the next day when he again went to her home, because he was concerned that their children might have seen their mother having sex.

October 1993: Simpson did not kick in Nicole's back door at her house on Gretna Green. The door was already broken. Simpson was upset because of sexual and other activity in the home where his children resided, and a photograph of Nicole's restaurateur-lover holding Justin Simpson on his lap.

May 1994: Nicole was as much a party to their reconciliation as Simpson. She still loved him when she was murdered in June. During May, she had pneumonia. Simpson went to Bundy to care for her. Three weeks before the murder, Nicole had a pizza party at Rockingham.

June 12, 1994: Simpson did not glare at Nicole during the dance recital at which Sydney was performing. The Brown family invited him to dinner. He declined. The Defense introduced a video showing Simpson smiling and laughing as he was leaving the event, hugging his ex-wife's family.

June 12, 1994: Simpson did not make a last-minute flight to Chicago. The business trip had been scheduled for some time by the Hertz Corporation. He had flown in from New York on June 10, specifically to attend his daughter Sydney's dance recital.

Defense attorneys Barry Scheck and Peter Neufeld specialize in cases of gender abuse as well as DNA, major themes of the trial. Scheck suggested a reason why the Prosecution never put on one expert to argue that Simpson's marital troubles and incidents of physical abuse were part of a pattern that led inexorably to the murders. According to Scheck:

> *We specialize in spousal abuse—defending women who have to strike out against their abusers in order to defend themselves. Abuse can lead to murder but there is always a pattern and a momentum—but not in this*

case. It didn't fit. He didn't fit the pattern! They couldn't get an important authority in the field to endorse their leap in logic. . . .[4]

The Defense also had Nicole Simpson's own deposition—given at the height of her bitter divorce action against Simpson—in which she stated that the 1989 incident was the one and only time Simpson had hit her.

Whatever the jury concludes about the nexus of abuse and murder as it pertains to this case, at this point, it is only required that the jury accept that abuse is an important aspect—if not the very libido—of the Prosecution's case.

Analysis of the Prosecution Timeline

We return now to the Prosecution timeline, with a critical analysis of each of the components as the Prosecution continued to develop their killing time scenarios.

10:03: *360 North Rockingham Avenue.* Simpson makes his fateful decision to murder Nicole. He changes his shoes and socks and gathers up his knife, cap, gloves, ski mask, plastic bag, and shovel, and speeds toward Nicole's.

Over the year and some months of hearings and trial, only the knife, gloves, and stocking cap will remain in the Prosecution's inventory of Simpson's props at the crime scene, with the argument over shoes still unresolved. Lead detective Tom Lange took from Rockingham a pair of Simpson's athletic shoes that Simpson said he had worn June 12. These were never introduced against the defendant. The Defense reminded the jury that the Prosecution had been unable to prove that Simpson ever owned a pair of Bruno Magli shoes, though admitting that the defendant did wear a size 12, the size of footprints found at the scene.

The gloves, plastic bag, and shovel were connected to evidence found by Mark Fuhrman and will be examined in our scrutiny of his scenario. The ski mask was a figment leaked to the media, which the Prosecution was forced to retract during the preliminary hearing. The Prosecution believed that the knife used in the murders could be traced to a purchase Simpson had made at a Ross Cutlery store.

Shortly before the murders, Simpson had been filming in Los Angeles on a street adjacent to Ross Cutlery, a store where he had, indeed, purchased a large knife. The owner and an employee of the store were the first witnesses called during the preliminary hearing. They testified to Simpson's purchase while, as was his habit, he signed autographs for people in the store. The nation watched on television as similar knives were displayed for the hearing officer, Judge Kennedy-Powell, the media, and the public.

The next week, the defendant's attorney, Robert Shapiro, walked into court with a sealed brown manila envelope, obviously containing a knife, and turned it over to the judge. The Prosecution never again referred to either "a 15-inch stiletto" or the knife from Ross Cutlery, and although Judge Ito refused to allow the Defense to introduce the innocent instrument (that was in the manila envelope) into the trial, or to inform the jury of the Prosecution's jump to a false conclusion, it was clear to many that this had been a Prosecution blunder, based on its profound belief in the defendant's guilt.

According to our law enforcement Source, when the LAPD searched Simpson's home on June 13–15, they did find the unused Ross Cutlery knife, but because it was obviously unused, and not the murder weapon, they did not collect it as evidence.

No knife used in the murders was ever found, nor any bloody clothes, except for a pair of black dress socks discovered on a rug in Simpson's bedroom. These socks would lead to a new set of problems for the Prosecution, when Defense expert witnesses argued that the blood found on the socks was consistent with evidence-tampering. We will discuss this in greater detail in Chapter Two.

10:10 PM: Simpson, in his white Bronco, pulls up in front of Nicole's condominium, headlights on.

The Prosecution later eliminated this appearance of the Bronco in front of Bundy and argued that Simpson parked immediately in the alley behind Nicole's residence.

10:12 PM: Then, using a stolen key, he enters through the back gate.

The stolen keys that the defendant supposedly used to enter the premises were never produced at trial.

10:13 PM: Simpson "lies in wait" in the very small front courtyard.

The defendant now lies in wait, the Prosecution insists. Where, and for how long, and to what end? The area in front of the residence is very small, indeed—ten feet by ten feet— with no natural hiding place for a six-foot-two marauder (who must have been on a tight timeline of his own and therefore would have had to lure his victim to open the door).

10:14 PM: Nicole exits her residence. Simpson stabs her. She collapses at her front gate, still alive.

Note that the reason Nicole comes out is not clear. (The Prosecution will point to a photograph of a large knife in- side the residence resting alone on a clean kitchen surface that, according to Clark's assertion to Judge Ito, lay ready for Nicole to defend herself because she was in mortal fear of her ex-husband.) Nevertheless, Nicole went outside with- out the knife. Was it to talk to Simpson? Or for some other unexplained reason? The disputed facts of this encounter between Nicole, Ron Goldman, and their slayer or slayers will come back to haunt us in every scenario of the crime.

If Nicole had a knife in readiness, why did she come out without it? If she came out to admit Goldman when he arrived with her mother's glasses, and if that is when she was stabbed, then the killer "lying in wait by the front gate" had to be aware of a man buzzing for entrance and identify- ing himself over the speaker. Thus, the murderer would have to take the improbable actions of (1) waiting for Nicole to buzz Goldman in, (2) watching her coming out to greet him, and then (3) leaping from his hiding place to murder two people at once, one of them as big and strong as he and much younger. But, again, the murderer does not know Goldman is coming, so why would he be "lying in wait" by the front gate at all, for events to then unfold in this way?

The Prosecution, for good reason, never dealt with these possible contradictions, which we will examine in later scenarios. They merely suggested that the gate might not have functioned in its security mode so that Goldman did not have to buzz for entry. Then if the gate was known to be not secure, and Simpson had stolen Nicole's keys, but the knife remained in the kitchen—was she or was she not in mortal fear of her ex-husband? Here, as everywhere, there is a potent mixture of fact and fiction, put forth by both the Prosecution and Defense, that requires analysis.

Nicole steps out, and, Defense and Prosecution experts will agree, she was hit on the head and then, perhaps, fell near or on the steps leading to the gate only a few feet away. The Prosecution argues that she fought off her attacker for a minute or two, in the process sustaining stab wounds to her body and knife cuts on her hands. Questions remain: Blood above the body could suggest that she was moved after her death; compared to Goldman, Nicole was not nearly so lacerated as the Prosecution kept insisting as part of its "insanely jealous" Simpson torture theme.

Many hours later, criminalists and coroners at the scene will disregard blood found under one of Nicole's fingernails that did not match Simpson's, and blood on her back, arguably, from an unidentifiable person. This oversight, together with the disposal of Nicole's stomach contents, and the failure to take a vaginal swab to test for sexual intercourse, will begin to arouse the concern of the scientific community.

10:15 PM: Goldman enters through the front gate. Simpson stabs and kills him, then completes the murder of Nicole by slashing her throat "through and through." Nicole's Akita begins to wail.

Goldman, somehow, enters the premises with an envelope containing Juditha Brown's glasses—left behind earlier at Mezzaluna, where the Brown family dined and Goldman worked as a waiter—and falls victim to Simpson within a minute. How did Goldman enter the locked front gate, or, was it left unlocked?

The murder of Ron Goldman requires a close study, because the Prosecution advanced various and contradictory theories. During the week of June 12, 1994, the LAPD and the D.A.'s office featured, in their steady stream of leaks to the media, the fact that the 25-year-old Goldman at near six feet and heavily muscled—as large, though not as heavy, as the 46-year-old Simpson—and in superb physical condition, put up a "ferocious struggle" and a "fierce battle" with his attacker. All this talk of self-defense soon changed, however, when photographs of Simpson taken the same week as the murders revealed his body to be unmarked. Now, according to the Prosecution, the lithe and powerful Goldman could neither flee nor fight effectively, but, instead, was cornered by the assailant and brutally killed.

The Prosecution at summation returned again to the theme of struggle, when Clark appealed to the jury to recognize that Goldman's heroic efforts caused Simpson to drop his left glove, cut his left hand, lose his stocking cap, and then flee the scene, leaving behind this damning evidence and dripping drops of his own blood.

We may also wonder how the killer could drop the glove, unless the glove was much too large. This is a possibility to be examined in another timeline, with another killer.

There was no attempt to reconcile a two-minute killing with an heroic battle, but the Prosecution had no choice but to limit the struggle to this time period because it was now 10:15, plus seconds, and the Akita had to begin the "plaintive wailing" that Fenjves heard, and that the Prosecution had identified as the clock marking the killing time.

10:16 PM: The Prosecution alleges that Simpson turns away from Goldman, moves back to the prone and bleeding Nicole and, from behind, slits her throat almost to the spine.

Later, the Defense's criminalist, Dr. Michael Baden, would question the Prosecution's assertion that both victims were cut fatally from behind.

10:17 PM: In June 1994, the local press will report that Simpson fled from the scene bleeding from a cut on his ungloved left hand.

This assertion will change dramatically during trial when it becomes apparent that (a) someone—presumably the killer—walked out the back stairway and walkway slowly; (b) returned (to look for his lost glove and cap, according to the Prosecution) but, did not retrieve the glove and cap; and (c) walked slowly away again—thus explaining the several sets of size-12 shoe prints going in opposite directions.

10:19 PM: Simpson speeds away to Rockingham estate.

The Prosecution timeline at the crime scene concludes with a witness asserting that he saw a white vehicle leaving Bundy Drive. This assertion is based on the testimony of one of the trial's most fascinating witnesses, Robert Heidstra, a luxury automobile caretaker, or detailer. The problem was that Heidstra insisted that he saw the white vehicle not at 10:19 PM the night of the murder, as the Prosecution argued, but, rather, close to 10:40 PM. And no matter what the Prosecution did, Heidstra stuck to his own timeline, because he had two clocks: one dog fourteen years old and one twelve. He slowly walked his dogs each night at the same time.

10:20–40 PM: Simpson disposes of the murder weapon and bloody clothes, including shoes.

The police and Prosecutors began their search for the murder weapon and bloody clothes in the early morning hours of June 13, 1994, and they continue to this day, so far in vain, to hunt the evidence of guilt. Though the evidence was never located, the Prosecution did not at any time broaden their search for other suspects.

In the early hours and days of the investigation, authorities had no doubt that the evidence would turn up. Police, and hundreds of Boy Scouts and volunteers searched the area between Bundy and Rockingham—bushes, dumpsters, yards, drains, lots—while in Chicago, the police scoured the environs of the hotel where Simpson was staying, before being called back to Los Angeles. Nothing. The airports, LAX and O'Hare: A massive search, including all disposal units and sanitation and refuse carriers and dump sites.

According to the Source:

> *There's never been anything like it. They tore those airports apart. They couldn't believe they hadn't found it. That's why they waited until Thursday, because they*

wanted the arrest to come after they found the knife and the clothes. That's when they started to panic because they had already taken the line that O.J. got rid of the stuff between 10:20 and 10:40, but then, again, they had the limo driver saying he saw someone in dark sweats going into the house around 11:00. But there weren't any sweats in the house. And there was nothing in Chicago, and they were freaking, and his golf bag had another little ball bag in it, but if he had used that then the problem still came up the same–where in the hell was it?. . .

Later the Prosecution would hint broadly that the bloody evidence had been carried to Chicago and back in Simpson's Louis Vuitton suitcase, then taken away and disposed of by longtime Simpson friend and consultant Robert Kardashian. Yet, the police did not request the bag when they searched Kardashian's home on June 17, made minimal legal motions but did not question or call Kardashian during trial, and at summation merely held up the empty case for the jury to see and speculate on.

This Prosecution theory on carrying bloody evidence to Chicago raises another issue: In this scenario of evidence disposal, there was no need to posit a twenty-minute window of time for the killer to cover his tracks. No need to insist that the murders were completed by 10:15 PM, no reason to deny the contradictory testimony of other neighbors, because Simpson could have left the crime scene much later and still vaulted over the Rockingham back fence (first Prosecution version), or raced through the front gate and around the mansion (second version) and bumped into the wall and dropped the glove. Then why didn't the Prosecution seize this logical timeline and feature Heidstra's testimony (of voices and a dog barking around 10:40 PM) as the second hand of their crime clock?

They were on the horns of a dilemma: (a) Simpson disposed of the evidence between 10:20 and 10:40 PM (except for the glove?). Period. So, no need to search in Chicago or at LAX. This scenario works as long as the murders are done by 10:15 PM. Or (b) Simpson commits double murder by 10:35 PM, speeds home and drops his glove and takes the rest of the evidence with him to Chicago. Period.

According to the Source:

. . . So they said, we'll make a commitment depending on where we find the knife. And you had two factions in the office—one said L.A., the other said Chicago, and they were both giving the media their versions. So they got caught, got stuck with both versions, when they never found the evidence. And that's when . . . that's when there was a third group . . . But they believed . . . something else . . .

In those elliptical pauses, in the silence, the Source was pointing us toward another hypothesis—to be analyzed later—that might have resolved the Prosecution's dilemma.

Defense Forensic Challenges

At trial on June 15, the Prosecution brought on not the coroner who had performed the autopsy, Dr. Irwin Golden, but the Chief of the Los Angeles County Coroner's Office, Dr. Lakshmanan Sathyavagiswaran. According to the chief coroner and expert observers, it was unheard of not to question the actual coroner who had presided over the victims. However, during the preliminary hearing the officiating coroner, Dr. Golden, had been called, and he had stated his opinion that two knives could have been used at the scene. Two knives could have pointed to two killers, but the Prosecution had only one in their scenario.

At the trial their scenario prevailed. Golden's superior, Dr. Lakshmanan, supported the Prosecution's hypothesis that a single, powerfully built killer had surprised both victims, rapidly overpowered them, and knifed them to death in as few as two minutes.

Under cross-examination, Dr. Lakshmanan was forced to admit that he could not with "medical certainty" answer how many assailants were involved in the attack or accurately reconstruct what took place.

On August 10, lawyers for Simpson brought former New York medical examiner Dr. Michael Baden to the stand to testify about the injury to Nicole Simpson's head. On cross-examination, Dr. Baden refuted the Prosecution's death scenario as just one of many possible ones: "It's possible that it happened by a bushy-haired stranger from behind, yes, but it's also equally consistent with a bald-headed midget from the front who is left-handed."

Dr. Baden held the jury's attention when he explained that he had been called upon to deliver autopsy opinions in the cases of President Kennedy, Dr. Martin Luther King, civil rights leader Medgar Evers, and football star Ron Settles, who had died mysteriously while in police custody. Then, as jurors scribbled notes furiously, the Defense continued with their witness:

> **Defense:** *If Ronald Goldman began a struggle with the assailants at 10:40 PM, within a reasonable degree of medical certainty, can you tell us when the [fatal] stab wound to the chest would have occurred?*
> **Baden:** *My opinion would be at least five minutes, more likely around ten minutes after the neck started to bleed.*
> **Defense:** *So, what is the earliest time he would have been cut in the chest, in your opinion?*
> **Baden:** *In my opinion, 10:45.*

Here we have the Defense suggesting a later time for the murders than that of the Prosecution—and an expert supporting a struggle of five to ten minutes' duration. These theories require a different scenario, which we will present in the next chapter.

Clocks Left Unexamined

At the time of the crime, inside Nicole's residence, there were at least four unexamined clocks: (1) candles burning; (2) bubble bath water cooling; (3) a CD playing; (4) ice cream melting in a cup. Each and every one of these clocks was capable of measuring time on that night if they had been tested or evaluated forensically—but, they were not.

The coroner, whose task it is to estimate the time of death, was not called onto the crime scene until ten hours after discovery of the bodies, according to the court record. This left the coroner's office unable to do more than estimate the clock of death as between 9:00 PM and midnight.

The question of how and why the coroner was deliberately delayed, and by whom, also figures in a later scenario. The LAPD Special Order of November 17, 1993, spells out the police responsibility to contact the coroner immediately.

> *The investigating officer at the scene of a death . . . shall make notification immediately upon determining that the death falls within the purview of the coroner's office. If the coroner is not immediately needed at the scene, the investigating officer shall advise the coroner of an approximate time when the coroner's deputy can respond.*

Because law enforcement intervened before anyone could analyze the crime scene, we can never know what the coroner might have discovered, and we can only guess why he was kept away so long. For now, let us take a look at what the police did discover as they investigated the murders.

LAPD Investigation Timeline
June 13–September 4, 1994

AM	June 13
12:00	Rosa Lopez, the maid next door to Simpson's home, hears voices coming from his property between midnight and 4:00 AM and has trouble sleeping (later disputed and denied by the Prosecution).
12:17	Uniformed police officers arrive at Bundy and discover Goldman's body. Sergeant Robert Riske testifies at the trial that he established the crime scene parameters, and that he took note of a single glove, a cap, bloody footprints and other evidence outside, and the bath, candles, music playing and a cup of melting ice cream inside. He found the two sleeping children and called for backup.
2:10	LAPD detectives Mark Fuhrman and Ron Phillips of the West L.A. station arrive at the murder scene.
4:05–25	Detectives Philip Vannatter and Tom Lange from Robbery/Homicide arrive to take over the investigation. Fuhrman is officially off the case, though he and Phillips will continue to assist Vannatter and Lange.

5:00   Vannatter, Lange, Fuhrman, and Phillips leave for Simpson's home at Rockingham to make personal notification. They ring the buzzer at his gate on Ashford but nobody answers. After seeing a dot of blood on Simpson's Bronco, Fuhrman is authorized by Vannatter to climb the fence and enter the property without a search warrant. The Defense will emphasize that the blood spot is much smaller than a dime, and that it is Fuhrman alone who spots the blood drop and then calls it to the others' attention.

5:35   Fuhrman talks with Kato Kaelin in the guesthouse, where he has been roused from sleep. Kaelin mentions he heard three thumps on his wall the night before. Fuhrman, by himself, walks around to the back and allegedly finds a bloody right-hand glove near the wall of the guesthouse.

6:05   Phillips calls Simpson, who has checked into his Chicago hotel room, to notify him of his ex-wife's death. When Simpson calls back for more information, Lange takes the call.

PM

12:30   Simpson arrives at Rockingham and is briefly handcuffed.

1:30   Simpson goes to LAPD headquarters voluntarily and is questioned about the murders outside the presence of his lawyer. (See Appendix for Simpson's Statement) After the interview is over, he agrees to give a blood sample. Vannatter takes the vial of blood and instead of checking it in, he puts it in his pocket.

5:30   Vannatter returns to Rockingham to continue his investigation. Several hours later, he turns over the sample of Simpson's blood to Dennis Fung, police department criminalist. According to the Defense, Vannatter had ample time and opportunity to create the "trail of blood" leading to the house. Vannatter states after the trial that he carried the blood with him to protect the chain of evidence.

Lange removes a pair of running shoes from the residence (the shoes Simpson said he wore the previous night) and takes them home before booking them into evidence the next day.

According to a source, the LAPD went through Simpson's home inch by inch, using their warrant as "a roadmap." This warrant contained so many misstatements that Judge Ito called it "at least reckless."

JUNE 15

The LAPD impounds Simpson's Ford Bronco at a storage lot. Some days later, the Bronco is broken into and items are removed.

JUNE 17

A warrant is issued for Simpson's arrest. To the astonishment of everyone assembled at Robert Kardashian's home, where the police are to pick up Simpson, Simpson and his friend A.C. Cowlings slip out of the residence. The police declare Simpson a fugitive. At a news conference, Kardashian reads a letter from Simpson that will be termed by the media "a suicide note."

Toward evening, Simpson and Cowlings are spotted in the Bronco on the 405 freeway. Video cameras capture Simpson lying in the back seat with a gun to his head as he talks to Detective Tom Lange, who has obtained the number of Simpson's cellular phone. Lange will later state, "My one intent was to get him to throw the gun out the window." The chase ends at Simpson's home, where he is detained in accordance with the warrant.

JULY

Approximately three weeks after the murders, blood is found on the back gate of 875 South Bundy. Blood was seen there, but not inventoried during the original search, according to the LAPD.

AUGUST 26–SEPTEMBER 4

LAPD investigators conduct additional searches inside Simpson's Bronco, looking for biological and trace evidence, even though the vehicle had been broken into at the storage lot and a number of employees and sightseers had climbed in and out of the vehicle.

Clocks: Slow and Fast

There were other neighbors of Nicole Brown Simpson who came forward, who had walked past 875 South Bundy, and who were ready to testify as to what they heard and saw on that June evening. But the Prosecution rejected them without exception because these human clocks were out of synch with their chosen timeline—they placed the dog's wails or barking later than 10:15 PM.

Clocks: Slow and Fast
June 12, 1994

PM

10:15–30 Rosa Lopez testified that she had seen the defendant's white Bronco parked at his Rockingham Avenue gate between 10:15 and 10:30 PM, when she walked her family dog. Like Heidstra, who serviced homeowners' expensive cars, Lopez was not a property owner in wealthy Brentwood but a worker who served a homeowner.

10:21 Denise Pilnak and her friend Judy Telender left Pilnak's house at 10:21 PM. The neighborhood was quiet until the dog's intense barking (not wailing, not yet) was heard at 10:35 PM, continuing for about 45 minutes.

10:25 Francesca Harmon, a hotel executive, drove slowly past 875 South Bundy at 10:25 PM. She saw and heard nothing.

10:30 Ellen Aaronson and Danny Mandel passed very close to 875 South Bundy on their way home from Mezzaluna Restaurant. They saw no blood or bodies, heard no dog.

10:35–45 Robert Heidstra might well have been the Prosecution's key witness because he, and he alone, had heard voices at the murder scene and then seen a white sports car that "could have been a Bronco" speeding away (south, not north). But, instead, the Prosecution tried to humiliate Heidstra. Why? Could it have been because he heard what he heard at "about 10:40 PM," a time that was much too late for the Prosecution's timeline?

Both Heidstra and Lopez were pummelled with questions as to whether or not they were hoping to gain money from various tabloid papers or programs. Over and over again, they denied that they were being paid by anyone.

Lopez on the stand was clearly uncomfortable. Like Heidstra, she had been intimidated with accusations of being an illegal alien, and her employers and former employers who were present in the courtroom also seemed to intimidate her. Prosecution Attorney Christopher Darden believed that Lopez had been coached and that as a witness she was unreliable at best—he cites her as saying, "No me recuerdo" ("I don't remember") more than ninety-five times.

The Trail of Blood

The trail of blood

Genetic fingerprints of O.J. Simpson, Nicole Brown Simpson and Ronald Goldman match blood stains collected at the scene of the murders and at O.J. Simpson's home. Where matches were found:

At the crime scene

1. **REAR GATE** *Simpson*
2. **SHOEPRINT** *Ms. Simpson*
3. **GOLDMAN'S SHOE** *Ms. Simpson*
4. **MS. SIMPSON'S FINGERNAILS** *Ms. Simpson*
5. **WALK** *Simpson*

At O.J. Simpson's mansion

6. **SIMPSON'S SOCKS** *Simpson, Ms. Simpson*
7. **GLOVE** *Simpson, Ms. Simpson, Goldman*
8. **FOYER** *Simpson*
9. **DRIVEWAY** *Simpson*

BRONCO

10. **Instrument panel** *Simpson*
11. **Inside door** *Simpson*
12. **Steering wheel** *Simpson, Ms. Simpson*
13. **Carpet** *Ms. Simpson*
14. **Console** *Simpson, Ms. Simpson, Goldman (alone or in combination)*

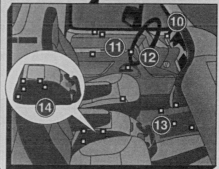

Source: Los Angeles Police Department, courtroom testimony

AP/Karl Gude, Eileen Glanton, Wm. Schroeder

Reprinted by permission.[5]

But he also admits, "I took no joy in watching Rosa Lopez limp off the stand." [6]

To many observers, the brutal handling of these vulnerable servants to the rich was apparent, especially in view of the fact that both of their statements disputed the Prosecution's timeline. This was certainly apparent to the Defense, who demanded to know why the Prosecution had called on only those two neighbors who partly verified the Prosecution's theory of the crime and ignored the far greater number who contradicted it.

Heidstra and his dogs could have been the turning point in the Simpson case for the Defense—had his testimony been accepted by the Prosecution. Heidstra calculated the time by when he left his home and by how fast his dogs could walk. The labored and arthritic pace of his 14 and 12-year-old canine companions on their nightly walk gave Heidstra his clock for when he heard voices at 875 South Bundy, since he did not begin his nightly walk until after 10:10 PM and did not reach 875 South Bundy until twenty minutes later. Heidstra was on Bundy only about twenty-five yards from the murder scene when the barking erupted in the silence. To protect his elderly dogs, Heidstra retreated into the alley east of Bundy, and it was there that he heard a man call out "Hey, hey, hey!" and fierce further barking (the Akita, though a gentle companion, is bred to hunt bear). As Heidstra headed back home, leaving the alley at 10:45 PM, he saw the "white sports vehicle" speed south. 10:45 PM—the very latest time that Kato Kaelin could have heard the thumps. The Prosecution timeline ends at 10:45 PM with those three thumps made by the returning killer.

Ironically, Heidstra, like the other earwitnesses, felt certain that Simpson was the single killer—yet it was precisely their timeline that calls into question the entire Prosecution case. Heidstra reflected after the trial:

> *My dogs saved my life. This is how close I was. Here is where I turned back and went into the alley. Right here is where I heard "Hey-hey-hey!" I came out here and right at this tree is where I saw the white vehicle. They tried to get me to say that I saw it come out of the alley, that it was a Bronco, that it was heading north. But it wasn't.*[7]

Mr. Heidstra today enjoys the respect of his neighbors. He feels that he has maintained his honor. He has never sold his story. If one accepts his recollection of time and events as accurate, his account destroys the Prosecution's timeline.

Finally, the Defense joked that Simpson had to have returned home naked except for one glove and dress socks, according to the Prosecution's theory. After the verdict, Simpson told anyone who was interested in viewing his videotape that, yes, the large figure seen entering the front door at 10:57 PM was him, and that he was already showered and immaculately dressed for his trip, that he had only to reenter the foyer to finish bringing out his bags and cases for Chicago—because he had:

- chipped golf balls in the yard from 9:40 to 10:02 PM.

- tried to return Barbieri's call from the cellular phone in the parked car at 10:02 and 10:03 PM.

- gone into the house to relax and watch TV around 10:15 PM.

- heard the driver's buzzing around 10:40 PM.

- showered, packed, and begun taking bags out to the front steps by 10:56 PM.

Thus, if he had testified, the defendant could have easily answered the Prosecution's (and most of the pundits') long-awaited big question: "Your lawyers have said that you were chipping golf balls, they've said you were napping, they've said you were watching TV—which is it, you can't have it both ways?"

The answer was and is (true or not) that there is nothing simpler than that these activities may be pursued sequentially without any contradiction whatsoever. True or not, the Defense argument explains how it is that Simpson could have been seen entering the house and emerging five minutes later completely showered and perfectly attired. Simpson was not dressed in bloody black sweats—which were never found and which his maid testified he never owned—but in his travel attire.

We have laid out the thrust of the Prosecution's theory of the crime, together with a few critical questions. We turn now to a more complete look at the mountain of evidence and to other scenarios and timelines that evidence may suggest.

The Source had this to say about all the contradictions and holes in the official timeline:

> *There was a big secret, from day one, and it was like a cancer in this case. And they were warned. But, you see, when you talk about jealousy and stalking and abuse you're talking about one man. ONE! You hear what I'm saying?*

Two

The Defense

The gloves didn't fit. I was there and everybody knew it. The rubber gloves slowed it down but they still didn't fit and it drove the Prosecution insane because they knew O.J. was the man but they couldn't catch him. Someone said, "This man was a great runner, and he still is!" Every time they thought they had him cornered—you know, the knife, the plastic bag, the gloves—he'd twist away. It was weird. They were afraid, upstairs, that Darden was going to try to provoke a physical confrontation in the courtroom, with O.J. or Cochran.
. . . By this time the two factions in the D.A. were: he did it alone, or, he did it with someone else . . .

As the Source says, "it was weird." For every element in the "mountain of evidence" against Simpson, the Cochran team was able to produce a counter theory. In an American court of law, if the jury finds the counter theory plausible, that is all that is required of them to mandate a vote of "reasonable doubt."

The Defense was not forced to present a theory of the crime, or an alibi, or a perfected timeline. Their only burden was to challenge the Prosecution and to suggest reasonable doubt. With Fuhrman, they believed they had found a Prosecution witness whose testimony could easily be called into question because he had openly lied on the stand. But Detective Fuhrman was an outsider to the intimate relationship of O.J. and Nicole. Inherent to any stormy, complex relationship between a man and a woman are the elements of tragedy—blood and passion—elements that cannot be re-

duced to a chart or graph or formula. DNA can be reduced
to a graph, as can the incidence of spousal abuse, but graphs
and charts are not the same thing as bloody murder. Still,
we can measure the stain of blood and passion the Prosecution painted at Bundy against the Defense's Rockingham
timeline, and find out if a credible story emerges.

Defense Scenario:
O.J. Simpson Innocent

The Defense engaged the well-known investigator William
Pavelic, a retired nineteen-year veteran of the LAPD. Within
days the former LAPD detective had discovered, among other
things, that the Coroner's death certificate did not list the
times of death. In short order, he pointed to a set of clues
leading away from O.J. Simpson. He continues his investigation to this day. The following Defense scenario includes
material discovered by Pavelic, material from the trial, and
the Defense's argument for Simpson's actions during the
killing time. You will note that the Defense scenarios do not
include Pablo Fenjves, who heard the 10:15 PM dog wail, but
do include Simpson neighbor Rosa Lopez, who claims to have
seen the Bronco at 10:21 and Robert Heidstra, who testified
he heard voices at Bundy at 10:35 PM.

O.J. Simpson Innocent—June 12, 1994	
PM	
9:35	Simpson and Kaelin return to Rockingham from a visit to a local McDonald's restaurant. Kaelin goes around to his quarters in the guesthouse.
9:42	Nicole speaks on the telephone to her mother about her lost glasses that have been found at Mezzaluna.
10:03	Simpson goes to his Ford Bronco, which is parked outside the gates to his house on Rockingham Avenue. He makes a return telephone call to Paula Barbieri, using the cellular telephone in the Bronco.

10:10	After receiving no reply from Barbieri, Simpson returns from the street to the grounds of the house. He stops in the area in front of the house to practice his golf swing, as was his regular habit.
10:15	Simpson goes back into the house to prepare for his trip to Chicago.
10:15	Rosa Lopez, a housekeeper employed by the owner of the house next door to Simpson, is walking the family dog on Rockingham Avenue. She sees the white Bronco parked outside the gate to Simpson's house.
10:21	Limousine driver Allan Park arrives early at Rockingham for a 10:45 pickup. He has been hired to drive Simpson to LAX for his red-eye flight to Chicago.
10:25	Ellen Aaronson and Danny Mandel are walking toward Aaronson's home and they pass directly in front of the townhouse at 875 South Bundy Drive. They do not see any blood or bodies. Nor do they hear a dog barking. Neither does Denise Pilnack, who is standing across the street talking to her friend.
10:35	Robert Heidstra is walking his two elderly dogs in the back alley across from the Bundy townhouse. He hears a man's voice shout, "Hey, hey, hey!" followed by the sound of two men arguing.
10:40	Park rings the buzzer at Simpson's gate.
10:44	Kaelin comes out of his room with a flashlight after hearing three thumps on the wall.
10:45	Mary Anne Gerchas claims she walked through the Bundy neighborhood looking at rental property. Four men run past her, two Hispanic, two Caucasian. Some are wearing knit caps and holding objects in their hands that could be weapons. The four men jump into a car and race away. Gerchas has the impression that the men are undercover police, driving an unmarked car.
10:50	Simpson comes out of his house to check his Bentley, which is parked inside the gates on a gravel area.
10:56	Simpson goes back inside to get his luggage.
11:00	Kaelin lets the limousine in and Park drives up in the front of the house.
11:00	Simpson and Kaelin load the luggage into the limousine.
11:15	Simpson and Park leave the residence for LAX.

AM | **JUNE 13**

12:00 Rosa Lopez, in her quarters next door to Simpson's estate, hears voices coming from the Simpson property between midnight and 3:00 AM. This causes her to have trouble sleeping.

12:17 LAPD officers arrive at the murder scene on Bundy. The area is sealed off to await the arrival of investigating detectives.

5:00 Detectives Vannatter, Lange, Phillips, and Fuhrman go to the house on Rockingham. They ring the security buzzer at the Ashford Gate but get no reply. They telephone the residence and get no reply. Fuhrman observes what appears to be a spot of blood on the white Bronco parked at the Rockingham gate. He informs Vannatter, who has a criminalist called to the scene. No criminalist has yet been ordered to Bundy. Fuhrman climbs the fence onto the property without a search warrant and lets the others in.

Fuhrman talks to Kaelin in the guesthouse, who mentions the thumps. Fuhrman walks by himself around to the back of the guesthouse and allegedly finds a bloody right-hand glove on the walkway near the guesthouse wall. The Defense will charge that Fuhrman actually planted the bloody glove, after removing it from the crime scene at Bundy.

5:30 The coroner is called and instructed not to come to the crime scene until further notice. Note that between 5:00 AM and 7:10 AM all detectives and criminalists focus on Rockingham rather than the Bundy crime scene where there are two dead victims. The coroner will not arrive at Bundy until about 9 AM.

6:00 Phillips telephones Simpson at his Chicago hotel room to notify him of his ex-wife's death. After the conversation, Simpson becomes very upset and breaks a drinking glass he is holding in his left hand. This produces a cut on his finger.

PM

1:30 Upon his return to Los Angeles, Simpson volunteers to go with detectives to police headquarters where he is interviewed from 1:35 to 2:07 PM. Afterward, he agrees to give a sample of his blood. The blood vial containing Simpson's sample is given to Vannatter, who places it in his pocket.

2:30 Vannatter drives twenty miles, with Simpson's blood, to Rockingham to continue his investigation. He could have booked the blood into evidence at Parker Police Center, less than a mile away.

Hours later, he finally turns over Simpson's blood sample to Dennis Fung, the police department criminalist who arrived at Rockingham at 7:10 AM. The Defense will argue that the police incriminated Simpson by planting his blood on items of evidence and creating the "trail of blood" on the driveway leading into his house. After the trial, Vannatter, a 27-year LAPD veteran who has since retired, publicly states that his procedure was not out of the ordinary, that he would never have risked his reputation to frame O.J. Simpson, that by carrying the blood sample he was preserving the chain of evidence, and that he did not plant any blood.

JUNE 15

Investigating officers impound the Ford Bronco at a storage lot. The vehicle sits virtually unsecured for months; no tests are done until August.

JUNE 17

After a warrant is issued for Simpson's arrest, and arrangements have been made for his surrender, he and his friend A.C. Cowlings disappear from the room in Robert Kardashian's home where they had been awaiting the police. Later the same day, the two fugitives are seen in the white Bronco heading north on a freeway toward Rockingham. The police—according to what Simpson will later explain in his video misinterpret his action as an attempt to flee from justice. Instead, Simpson says, he was being taken to visit Nicole's grave. The Prosecution chose not to include any reference to the Bronco "slow-speed chase" in their case, so Simpson's action and the letter, and what they meant, were never part of the trial.

AUGUST 26–SEPTEMBER 4

LAPD investigators belatedly conduct additional searches inside Simpson's Bronco for biological and trace evidence.

Defense Responses to the Prosecution

Since there were no witnesses to Simpson's alibi from 9:36 PM until 11:02 PM on the night of the murders, the Defense could not prove their client's innocence. They could and did however, conduct an onslaught against the Prosecution's case in an attempt to show that there was reasonable doubt in many areas.

The Clothing Worn by the Killer

The Gloves: The Prosecution tried to prove that the gloves found at the murder scene and near Simpson's guest house were indeed Simpson's. There were, supposedly, two pair of gloves, brown and black, purchased for Simpson by his wife at Bloomingdales. Yet, the D.A. could never produce an invoice, charge, or store employee to prove the gloves were purchased by Nicole. A charge bill that could have covered the cost of two pair of expensive leather gloves was evidence but not proof. And, for their separate reasons, neither the Prosecution nor the Defense ever produced the black gloves, the "other" pair, in court, or any other gloves from the capacious Simpson clothes closet. After the trial, Simpson insisted that he kept his broadcast working gloves in his New York townhouse, and that after the winter season, each year, he gave away the gloves to his doorman and other building employees.

Bruno Magli Shoes: Prints from size 12 Bruno Magli shoes were found at the crime scene. However, no size 12 Bruno Magli shoes (which the D.A. never proved Simpson owned) were ever found. Simpson claimed to have worn athletic shoes that evening and gave them to Detective Lange.

Sweatsuit: No sweatsuit, black or otherwise was found: in short, the jury was left frustrated and confused on the entire matter of what clothing the killer wore and what had become of it.

Blood Evidence

The Defense's blood experts, admittedly some of the finest in the nation, demanded that Judge Ito investigate their discovery that the Prosecution had: Waited three months before producing samples of Simpson's blood for testing; mislabeled the blood samples, thus effectively hiding them from the Defense; and then, secretly sent more samples to another laboratory. As with the search of the Simpson estate in the early morning hours of June 13th by Detective Fuhrman and others, the Defense argued conspiracy and contamination of evidence. The DNA Defense experts pled with the judge that innocent men had been sent to death row on just this kind of careless or conspiratorial handling of evidence. The Defense insisted, in vain, that:

- Blood on the back gate of 875 South Bundy had been collected three weeks after the murders, leaving time for someone to plant O.J. Simpson's blood there.

  According to DNA experts interviewed for this study— any blood drops at Bundy left by any of the four children (Jason, Arnelle, Sidney, Justin) would have been virtually indistinguishable from the blood of their father, O.J.

- The white Bronco's security had been so completely contaminated in the days after the murders that someone had stolen a receipt from the glove compartment. Could not someone just as easily have gained access and smeared the victims' blood on the console?

- The sock stain matching Nicole Simpson's blood had been pressed on the fabric, not spattered as it would have during a brutal fight, and was identified weeks after the sock had been collected as evidence.

- Stains on both the back gate and the socks contained traces of EDTA, a preservative found in vials used by the LAPD to collect blood samples.

- The jailhouse nurse who drew a reference sample of blood from Simpson said he had collected about 8 cubic centimeters. Detective Vannatter took custody of the vial and, instead of booking it into the lab, carried it many miles away to a criminalist at Simpson's estate. On later inspection, the EDTA-laced vial contained only 6.5 cubic centimeters. The Defense demanded of the Prosecution—where was the missing blood? Wasn't it swabbed on evidence long after the murders to make the case against O.J. Simpson?

None of the Prosecution's evidence seemed to hold up, the Defense argued. There was not nearly enough blood in the Bronco or at the Rockingham residence—according to two well-known criminalists, Drs. Baden and Lee—to suggest Simpson as the killer, because these murders would have soaked the perpetrator in gore. Instead, all of Simpson's blood, taken together, amounted to only a few drops.

There were, however, many fingerprints left at the murder scene—seventeen—none of which belonged to Simpson, including those on the Bundy back gate where Simpson's blood was found—three weeks later—supposedly from Simpson's bleeding and ungloved left hand, that would have produced palm and/or fingerprints.

Under intense cross-examination from Defense special DNA counsel Robert Blasier, the chief forensic scientist of the LAPD Crime Lab was forced to concede that blood collected from under Nicole's fingernails could have belonged to someone other than the defendant, as could blood on the victim's back that was not saved by either criminalists or coroners.

Dr. Terence P. Speed, a University of California statistician who often works for law enforcement, testified for the Defense that numbers presented by the Prosecution regarding the incidence of blood type—1 in 6 billion, etc.—were completely misleading because the error rate of the testing laboratory was left out. He suggested that including this error rate brought the probabilities down to 1 in 200.

Summary of Dr. Lee's Testimony

Dr. Henry Lee, director of the Connecticut State Forensics Science Laboratory, is regarded as among the nation's leading forensic scientists. His reputation extends beyond the borders of this country and his work is respected throughout the world. He generally testifies for the Prosecution. Shortly after the murders occurred, Robert Shapiro asked Dr. Lee to assist the Defense.

Like Dr. Kary Mullis (the inventor of a new DNA test used by the Prosecution) and Dr. Speed, Dr. Lee did not personally receive any financial reward for his testimony.

The main points of Dr. Lee's testimony were as follows:

- Ronald Goldman appeared to have put up a long fight with his assailant. *"I cannot tell you how long. It's not a short struggle."*

- The struggle ranged across the small area where Goldman's body was found. He cited the position in which items—the keys, the envelope containing the glasses, and a beeper—were found.

- Asked if the assailant would have been covered in blood from the struggle, Lee answered, *"In theory, the assailant should have some blood."*

- The photographs taken of Simpson shortly after the murders did not indicate that Simpson had recently been engaged in a physical battle.

- Bloodstains in a parallel line pattern on the Bundy walkway and on Goldman's jeans might have been a shoe print. *"I cannot definitely say that that is definitely a shoe print. It could be."*

- This possible shoe imprint did not come from a Bruno Magli shoe. *"If this is a shoe print, it is from another shoe."*

- He refuted the idea that these possible prints could have come from investigators walking through the scene because there was also a print on the victim's jeans.

- He confirmed the testimony of a blood-spatter expert concerning the bloodstain on the sock found in Simpson's bedroom. It appeared that the stain had been pressed into the material and not splashed on it such as might have happened at the crime scene.

• Dr. Lee raised doubts about one drop of blood found on the walkway outside 875 South Bundy that the police identified as the defendant's. The police had collected seven or eight swatches from this single spot on the walkway on June 13. On close examination, Dr. Lee discovered four small patches of blood on the paper packet wrapped around these swatches. The blood swatches could only have leaked onto the paper if they were packaged while wet. Yet, the LAPD technicians had testified that they left the swatches to dry overnight. Dr. Lee found it odd that just three or four of them were wet enough to bleed onto the paper packaging the next morning. *"The numbers don't add up. The only explanation I can give under these circumstances is something wrong."*

• In his book, *Reasonable Doubts*, Defense Attorney Alan Dershowitz includes the following as one of the mistakes made during the investigation:

> *The criminalists did not count the blood samples when they collected them, did not count them when they were put in tubes for drying, and did not count them when they were taken out of the tubes. No documented booking of samples occurred until June 16.[1]*

• The LAPD officers had overlooked three small drop of blood in the foyer of Simpson's home. They did collect and test three other drops but ignored the trio of spatters clearly visible on the gleaming hardwood floor.

• Dr. Lee did not find a single drop of blood on Simpson's door or on the stairs leading up to the master bedroom.

• Ron Goldman's blood-smeared boot appeared to have been put in a brown paper bag while still wet. Such careless handling could cause "cross-contamination" by mingling distinct blood drops on the boot.

Dr. Lee was attacked on his footprint testimony that suggested two people at the crime scene. Unshaken, he said:

> *I stand behind the scientific facts in my testimony. There are imprints on the piece of paper, on the envelope,*

on the blue jeans. There is imprint evidence on June 25
on the walkway. That is true imprint evidence. That is
not workmen's scratches or shoes.

Contested Evidence

Following is a list of some of what the jury heard that invited them to cast "reasonable doubt" on the evidence presented by the Prosecution.

Evidence at Bundy

Left-hand glove: The glove found near the victims did not
have a cut in the area where Simpson later displayed a cut
on his left hand.

Blue ski hat: The hat found at the murder scene included a
hair that did not match either the victims' or Simpson's.

Blood drops leading from the murder scene: Six blood
drops linked to Simpson by DNA tests were either old and
contaminated, or planted by the police.

Second set of bloody shoe prints: Investigators found a
possible pair of bloody shoe prints not matching either the
victims' or Simpson's.

Unidentified fingerprints: Seventeen separate fingerprints
found at the murder scene remain unidentified. No fingerprints found at the murder scene matched Simpson's.

Investigators walked through blood evidence: Blood evidence was contaminated by investigators walking through
the scene without protective "booties."

Blanket from Bundy house contaminated crime scene:
Police covered Nicole's body with a blanket from inside her
home. It may have included Simpson's hair, DNA from his
saliva or semen, and fibers from his Bronco. Such contamination could have falsely implicated Simpson.

Unmelted ice cream: At 12:30 AM, just after the police arrived at the murder scene, a cup of partly melted ice cream was found on a banister inside Nicole's home. This suggests that the murders occurred later than 10:15 PM.

Evidence at Rockingham

Blood drops leading from the driveway into the house: Police allegedly planted this "trail of blood" leading up the driveway into the house. No blood was found on the light switches, railings, or the white carpeting in the house. Three perfect drops of blood were found in the foyer—where police had walked back and forth for hours.

Bloody right-hand glove: Found behind the guesthouse, allegedly planted by Fuhrman. The ground and leaves around and under the glove revealed no traces of blood evidence. Other right-hand glove problems include (1) almost no African-American "limb" hair was found on this well-used glove, but (2) a Caucasian hair was found (3) the blood on the glove contained Simpson's DNA, but only in a minimal amount because, the Defense believed (4) the blood was the result of a lab accident. As stated during the trial, an LAPD criminalist who had been handling the Rockingham glove then accidentally spilled Simpson's reference tube blood.

Bloody socks found in bedroom: Blood from Nicole and Simpson was planted on the socks before they were tested. A June 13 crime lab report stated no blood was apparent on the socks. Only on August 4 was the blood found. Only then, after the blood was noted by the LAPD, was Dr. Lee permitted to conduct his analysis.

False reports emanating from the LAPD prior to the tests on the socks having been run stated that Simpson's and Nicole's blood had been found on the socks. The socks were not sent for testing until September 26. The test results were finally confirmed on November17, identifying DNA from Simpson and Nicole. These events suggest that police could predict the results because they planted blood. Think about it, says Scheck. "Somebody tampered with these socks, they played with the evidence . . . end of case!"

Evidence in the Bronco

Blood found inside the Bronco: The Defense held that blood from Nicole and Ron was planted by a police officer by wiping inside the vehicle with the bloody glove from the murder scene. Alternatively, blood might have brushed off from the Akita-stained animal-control officer from the crime scene when he was in the Bronco. Later, the Defense argued, more of Simpson's blood was planted using the blood sample drawn by the police.

A Prosecution consultant told this study that:

> We tested the back seat of the Bronco, and we found evidence that it had been carefully wiped clean of any blood residue. We were ready to present the evidence in court.

That would have been powerful evidence, indeed, if it existed. And if it did exist, it might have been turned back on the Prosecution: To "carefully" wipe up blood takes time— time that the Prosecution could not spare from their already depleted timeline; to wipe up blood might suggest a second man, or, as we shall see, a second white Bronco. Remember, as well, that the DNA trace found on the wheel did not belong to O.J., Nicole, or Ron. This mystery DNA exists today and can still be tested.

Bronco broken into at storage lot: On June 15, the Bronco was broken into. Items were reported stolen and evidence may have been planted. After the break-in, investigators returned to recover biological and trace evidence. The Defense attacked the evidence handling by exposing the storage of the defendant's white Bronco—unlocked in an open lot for months. After this time, LAPD criminalist Dennis Fung found the blood stains, which Detective Fuhrman had sworn that he had seen on the outside of the driver's door. But Fung found them inside.

How could a jury be swayed to find reasonable doubt in a case where a "mountain of evidence" existed? Point by point, the Defense chipped away at the mountain, and for nine long months of sequestration, the jurors—who spent more time out of the courtroom than in it—had time to consider the elements of the case unfolding impossibly slow day by day by day.

Disputed Blood Evidence

F. Lee Bailey and other Defense staff illustrated why they believed that in each and every case, the LAPD could have either contaminated or tampered with evidence. In many instances, they argued, blood from the LAPD Simpson blood vial—that Vannatter carried out to the Simpson estate instead of booking immediately into evidence as the law requires—could have been planted.

PROSECUTION	DEFENSE
Bloody glove at Simpson estate.	No blood on the ground where the moist glove was found.
Blood in Simpson Bronco.	Criminalist did not test for it until weeks later, and trace DNA (*not* Simpson's) was found on the steering wheel.
Blood on Simpson's socks.	Found weeks later and contained EDTA.
Simpson Blood at Bundy.	Compromised in the collection and storage. Or could have been another Simpson's blood.
Simpson hairs at crime scene.	Contaminated. Not his.
Blood on back gate at scene.	Found weeks later.
Blood at Simpson estate.	From innocent cut or planted.

Coroner's Report

The Defense found that information included in the coroner's report could be interpreted to dispute the Prosecution scenario. (See Coroner's Reports in Appendix.)

Ron Goldman bruised: Goldman suffered massive defense wounds and bruises that suggest he may have struck his attacker. (See Appendix for Goldman's autopsy report) Simpson showed no sign of bruising in photographs taken soon after the murders.

Two types of knife wounds: Some knife wounds appeared to be from a single-edged knife, while others appeared to be from a double-edged knife. Two knives suggest more than one killer.

Time of death not established: The time of death of the victims was estimated at between 9:00 PM and 12:00 midnight. Simpson's whereabouts were known for some of this time period.

Type B blood enzymes and flesh found under Nicole's fingernails: Type B blood does not match with either victim or Simpson. Simpson lost no flesh. This suggests that the assailant was some other person.

The Defense left the jury with these questions:

> *Why was no vegetation disturbed in the area where the glove was found at Rockingham if someone jumped over the fence there? Why was no blood seen initially on the socks found in O.J.'s bedroom? Why was no blood seen on the rear gate at Nicole's residence until three weeks after the murders? Why was Detective Vannatter carrying around a vial of O.J.'s blood? Why was Ron Goldman's blood not discovered in O.J.'s Bronco until months after the murders?*

The DNA Evidence

Still, the media repeated the Prosecution's theme tirelessly—
"There was a mountain of incriminating DNA blood evidence."

One can only speculate on the discussions that could
have taken place within the community of lawyers following
the Simpson case closely when they learned that Dr. Kary
Mullis—the winner of the Nobel Prize for having developed
one of the crucial tests for testing DNA—was prepared to
testify that:

> The DNA tests used in the Simpson case are not suit-
> able for forensic purposes. They are not suitable for
> drawing any scientific conclusions. . . Furthermore, the
> methods of the LAPD laboratory and the California State
> laboratory at Berkeley are seriously compromised. Ba-
> sic scientific principles are being so violated as to leave
> their conclusions worthless.[2]

When Simpson's blood was allegedly identified at the
scene, statistics poured out of the District Attorney's press
briefings and leaks, with DNA statistics quoted that linked
the former champion to the evidence at a near–certainty of
hundreds of millions to one. Such statistical assertions produce figures of astronomical proportions that are often attacked by other experts. In a New Mexico case, an FBI expert testified that the results of a DNA profile used by the
Prosecution showed a match that was a six-billion-to-one
chance. The Defense brought on another statistician who
used the same figures but a different method of analysis to
show a one-in-eighty chance. If you add contamination and
corruption of evidence, as the Defense charged in the Simpson case, the chances may fall to zero, as Dr. Mullis insists.
The accuracy of Cellmark, the testing laboratory, was also
questioned by the Defense. They described the private testing facility in Maryland as having a checkered past.

Simpson's Defense team acquired the services of Peter
Neufeld and Barry Scheck, two New York attorneys who had
made a reputation of using DNA evidence to free seventeen
people wrongly convicted of crimes. Scheck described his

work on *Larry King Live*:

> *We work through the Innocence Project, using DNA to exclude innocent defendants. DNA has the tremendous power to prevent injustice and to overcome the horrible miscarriage of justice based on "eyewitness testimony." Look at David Shepherd, eleven-and-a-half years for rape; Edward Honaker, three life terms for rape and murder. Both innocent! Honaker had had a vasectomy but that didn't stop the Prosecution, we later found out that they had hypnotized the witnesses . . . .[3]*

EDTA on the Socks and Bundy Gate

In late 1994, a law enforcement source alerted an independent researcher to the presence of EDTA in the blood on the socks, and on the Bundy gate. EDTA is the police preservative fluid that would have been present in the tube used to store Simpson's blood sample. The issue was whether the blood found on Simpson's sock got there during the slaying of Ron Goldman and Nicole Simpson, or whether it could have been put there later by the police, using blood from the sample collected from Simpson. The jury will recall that the socks here mentioned are the same ones that the Defense claimed did not appear in the videotape of Simpson's bedroom, where they were found on the carpet. The Prosecution had argued that the socks were simply not seen because of the angle from which the video was made.

The Defense confronted the Prosecution when they learned of the blood-tampering allegation from the independent researcher. Scheck scored a notable point when cross-examining Gary Sims of the Department of Justice Laboratory at Berkeley, California.

> **Scheck:** *Mr. Sims, as you sit here, you don't know how and you don't know when that blood got on the sock do you?*
> **Sims:** *No.*

As for the alleged presence of EDTA on the socks and gate, Rockne Harmon for the Prosecution reacted with disbelief, demanding a test to explode such a ludicrous claim:

> *There's only two possible outcomes to this test. There's either going to be EDTA there or there's not going to be EDTA there. And we're willing to accept the outcome, whatever that is . . . . We agree to accept these results in advance.*

The Prosecution seemed stunned when the FBI tests returned a finding "consistent with" EDTA on the socks and gate. To the Defense, this suggested strongly that the blood had been taken from reference samples of Simpson and the victims and planted. The Prosecution argued that the EDTA could have come from the air or from laundry detergent. Further testing disclosed that there was no EDTA around the area of the Bundy gate, or on the blood-free sections of the socks. It may be useful here, for those considering the Defense's argument as credible, to keep in mind that the blood was not booked until June 16, 1994—four full days after the murders.

The Prosecution, we have learned, was at a loss at this point. The Source said:

> *. . . Bozanich [Peter Bozanich, second to D.A. Garcetti] had already been sent to "Siberia" for blowing the whistle to them that the Rockingham glove was a time bomb, and now the FBI "betrays" them by finding EDTA . . . They were in shock.*

The FBI laboratory, which carried out some of the Prosecution's testing of the blood on the socks, was also not immune from criticism. Dr. Frederic J. Whitehurst, a potential Defense witness, accused fellow FBI Agent Roger Martz of slanting information to favor the Prosecution. Martz testified in the Simpson case that blood found on the sock from the bedroom and on the gate at Bundy was consistent with the presence of EDTA, but that this did not mean EDTA was present. Defense Attorneys Carl Douglas and Robert Blasier signed sworn depositions that Whitehurst would testify that Martz was slanting the evidence on the DNA tests in the

Simpson case to favor the Prosecution. Judge Ito ruled for the Prosecution and withheld Whitehurst's testimony from the jury.

The trial was filled with experts pitted against experts, and testimony that at times became so detailed as to be almost impossible for the average viewer to follow. Still, the Prosecution's "mountain of evidence" line was echoed by most of the legal pundits. After all, how could *all* the blood be planted and contaminated? Is this not a charge that strains credulity? Even those few who recognized that the Prosecution was failing fast in the courtroom contest could not shake off the intuition, the instinct that there was also something wrong with the Defense's story. Their flesh crawled, they could see Simpson's bloody psychological fingerprints all over the universe of the crime. Simpson, the proven wife-beater, who had beaten Nicole so badly in 1989 that she had put away photographs of her bruised face and body in a safety deposit box (photographs the Prosecution had introduced as evidence)—who else but Simpson could be guilty of the murders? Blood and jealousy, this was the volatile chemistry of the Prosecution's theory of the crime. Blood and jealousy was their case and their cause.

The Prosecution and pundits assumed that they knew who these two people were: black male executioner, white female victim. Is that who they were, finally?

The Simpson Subculture

There is a deep problem of perception in these public relationships, like that of O.J. and Nicole, that feed on the blood of the vast consumer society—the Society of the Spectacle, to use a sociological term. Like huge images in the dark on a giant screen, they work their way inside the heads or the fantasies of those who live in Television Land. The hypnotic images of the California Girl and that demi-god, "the Juice"— beamed on the lasers of wish and myth and worship—penetrate the skin, infect the memory, cling to our dreams and nightmares.

Who are these gods of postmodern America?: The jet set,

the beautiful people, the stars, and their minions, in the capitals of the world, the self-invented and reinvented survivors of the political gauntlet, the phallic narcissists wrestling for position, with their perfect *Playboy* paramours along with the women these "Great Men" married when they were young, with their retinue of lawyers, agents, managers, counselors, psychotherapists, plastic surgeons, servants and maintenance men—all in the limelight or near it, famous for fifteen minutes officially, but living on forever in the collective memory of all the fans who buy the tickets and the dream so that an entire new celebrity class can live and die in the style that they have earned.

Is such a free association a truthful criterion for measuring or knowing anyone or anything? Now, it is true that O.J. Simpson was a superb specimen and an heroic athlete, of memory, and that Nicole Brown was an all-American cheerleader and beauty queen, once upon a time, but does anything of meaning follow from that public morgue of stock footage? They were live on tape. They will always be, now, but, in the end, who were they?

Their identities have been split in two: To the tabloid media and the gossip of the gutter, they are two more statistical casualties on the fast lane who, like doomed American royalty, came to a shocking and savage end on June 12, 1994. While for the educated class and their spokespeople, they have become immortal victims of the race and gender wars of our age.

The tabloids produce, out of the carnage of the crime scene, two new bundles of secrets named O.J. and Nicole, with young Adonis Ron Goldman as the third leg of the media triangle. The "serious" media on the moral high ground provides, for serious consumers, boilerplate biographies and trial records. None of this will answer when lives are at stake. It becomes necessary to try to come to grips with the actual victims and their accused and acquitted murderer. To begin over again at ground level, to try to locate Ronald Goldman and Nicole Brown Simpson in time and space. Follow in their footsteps as they walk to their fate.

Return now to that evening of June 12 again and focus on the movements of Ron and Nicole.

Nicole and Ron Perspective
The Evening of June 12, 1994

PM

8:45   Nicole leaves Mezzaluna Restaurant.

8:50   Nicole and children get ice cream cones across the street. (They are accompanied by a young man in his twenties, according to the ice cream clerk. Later the clerk is not certain if the man was with them.)

8:59   The Simpson family returns to 875 South Bundy.

9:00   Nicole readies children for bed; she lights candles in the living room, bedroom, and bathroom, draws a hot bubble bath, and starts a music tape (characterized, later, by police as romantic or New Age). A cup of ice cream is left on a banister.

9:25   O.J. calls to speak to Sydney.

Nicole has "optimistic" talk with friend Faye Resnick concerning purchase of coffee bar or restaurant, according to Resnick.

Eight-year-old Sydney Simpson tells police later that she heard "Mommy crying and fighting with her best friend."

9:37   Juditha Brown, Nicole's mother, telephones Mezzaluna Restaurant to inquire about her lost eyeglasses. They have been found.

9:40   Juditha calls Nicole asking her to retrieve her glasses.

9:42   Nicole telephones restaurant. Ron Goldman offers to bring her mother's glasses to Nicole's after work. Manager John Debello testifies that he told Goldman that he did not have to make "a special trip" to nearby Bundy, but Ron insisted. What is behind this dialogue?

10:30-55   Nicole Brown Simpson and Ronald Goldman are murdered by person or persons unknown.

This timeline is full of events. Almost every minute between nine and ten o'clock throbbing with activity, telephone calls, preparation. It is necessary to break down this hour into increments, look at it in slow motion to make sense of it. Who is in the background? Let's look around—at the candles, the bath. Let's hear the music.

It is clear that, at trial, neither side wished or dared to pursue the question of the identity of Nicole's "best friend." There are several candidates for this role, and the "tears and fight" could have been on the telephone or in person. Could the best friend have been a woman? Or, could it possibly have been Ron Goldman? Were Nicole and Ron more than good friends? Could the "romantic" preparations of the bath and candles have been for him, initiated after Nicole's call to the restaurant about her mother's glasses?

Although at trial the Prosecution finally argued that Goldman arrived at Bundy somewhere between 10:00 and 10:15 PM, their assertions can also bring him there earlier, as follows:

Goldman Early June 12, 1994	
PM	
9:50	Goldman leaves Mezzaluna Restaurant.
9:52	He reaches his apartment in two minutes, according to the Prosecution.
9:52–56	He rushes to change clothes. No shave, no shower, nothing: four minutes.
9:57–10:01	Goldman picks up and drives a borrowed car to 875 South Bundy.

This early timeline will not work—if Simpson is the murderer according to the Prosecution's scenario. According to Darden, by the time Simpson reached Bundy, Goldman would already be inside. Simpson called Paula Barbieri at 10:03 PM and then decided to murder. Even if we posit that Simpson made the telephone call from the Bronco after committing the murders, he would have only the time from 9:57 to 10:02 PM to commit double murder and then get to his cellular phone.

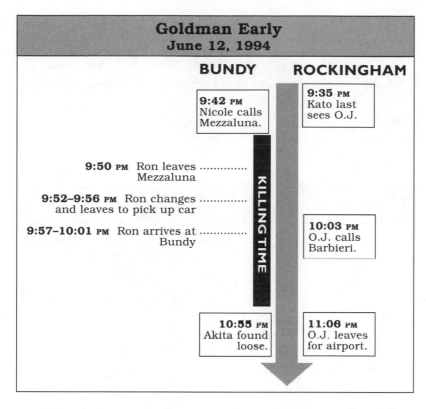

Goldman Early
June 12, 1994

BUNDY   ROCKINGHAM

9:42 PM Nicole calls Mezzaluna.

9:35 PM Kato last sees O.J.

9:50 PM Ron leaves .... Mezzaluna

9:52–9:56 PM Ron changes .... and leaves to pick up car

9:57–10:01 PM Ron arrives at .... Bundy

KILLING TIME

10:03 PM O.J. calls Barbieri.

10:55 PM Akita found loose.

11:06 PM O.J. leaves for airport.

Now let us consider our independently tested timeline for Goldman on that mysterious evening, as he drove to Bundy Drive under a quarter moon—with a borrowed car and his time running out.

Witnesses who worked with Ron at Mezzaluna provided the times for his clocking out and leaving as well as for the phone calls from Juditha and Nicole.

Independent Timeline—Ron at Bundy
The Evening of June 12, 1994

PM	
9:33	Ron Goldman clocks out from Mezzaluna where he works as a waiter, but stops for a drink at the bar.
9:50–55	Goldman leaves Mezzaluna.
9:58	Goldman arrives at his apartment.

10:02	Goldman changes clothes and prepares to go to Nicole's. We have allotted Goldman time here that seems consistent was what friends knew of him. Goldman was known for his studied casual grooming,
10:22	Goldman picks up a borrowed car, drives, parks, and walks to Nicole's.
10:30	Goldman arrives at 875 South Bundy.
10:30-55	Goldman murdered by person or persons unknown.

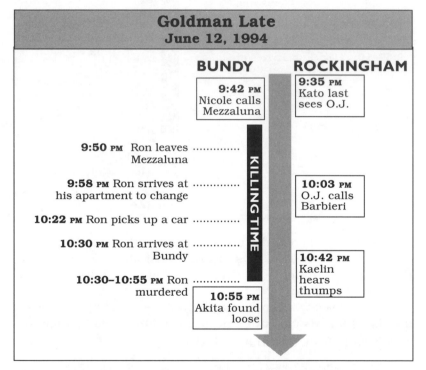

Goldman Late
June 12, 1994

BUNDY   **ROCKINGHAM**

9:42 PM
Nicole calls
Mezzaluna

9:35 PM
Kato last
sees O.J.

9:50 PM Ron leaves
Mezzaluna

9:58 PM Ron srrives at
his apartment to change

10:03 PM
O.J. calls
Barbieri

10:22 PM Ron picks up a car

10:30 PM Ron arrives at
Bundy

10:42 PM
Kaelin
hears
thumps

10:30–10:55 PM Ron
murdered

10:55 PM
Akita found
loose

KILLING TIME

As the jury, you are now able to take a parallax view of two conflicting timelines, neither of which places Goldman at Bundy at a time that fits the final Prosecution scenario: One brings Goldman there too early; the independent timeline, too late—for Simpson to be the murderer in the Prosecution's scenario. We do not know what time Goldman arrived at Bundy—all we know for sure is the time he was found dead. But we do have the Prosecution's timeline into which he must fit for their case to make sense.

Let the jury now turn to some of the earwitnesses of that night, and follow the clocks surrounding the time from 10:30 to 10:45. Omitted here is the earwitness Pablo Fenjves, who was the one witness to testify to hearing a dog barking earlier, around 10:15 or 10:20, and the only earwitness that the Prosecution used in developing its scenario. The Defense chose to look at the many other earwitnesses as well.

Defense Earwitnesses

PM

10:30 — Denise Pilnack finishes a telephone call to her mother. She hears no dog barking.

10:30 — Mandel and Aaronson walk past Nicole's residence. They hear no dog barking, see no blood.

10:30 — Robert Heidstra reaches Bundy, hears no barking.

10:33 — Pilnack and Heidstra hear a dog barking.

10:40 — Heidstra hears "Hey, hey, hey." Heidstra hears a gate (presumably Nicole's) close.

10:45 — Heidstra sees three cars come from the direction of Bundy, one of which "could be a Bronco."

Analyzing the twelve-minute clock when dog barking and sounds were reported: If you accept the testimony of these various witnesses, and that the shouting came from Nicole's yard, you may deduce that Ron and Nicole had been confronted but were still alive at 10:35, and at 10:40 PM. (Remember that it is at about 10:40 PM that Kato Kaelin, at Rockingham, hears the three loud thumps on his wall.)

Hold on to the murder clock, and compare the clocks or timelines of Goldman, Heidstra, and all the other Bundy witnesses (except the Prosecution's Pablo Fenjves) and they fit a common scenario.

In March 1996, the author spoke with Pablo Fenjves, a respected screenwriter. Fenjves could only approximate the time at which he heard the dog wailing. But, he stated, when, on that night of June 12, he was drawn by the commotion to look out his window into the alley behind Nicole's residence, he did not "see a white Bronco."[4]

Heidstra is in the alley at about 10:30 to 10:35 PM. He hears the dog barking furiously, not wailing, not yet. He hears loud voices. Then the fight for life begins. The Prosecution suggests that the death struggle will last only about two minutes. The scientists, Drs. Baden and Lee, posit that the battle must go on for between ten and twenty minutes. Prosecution experts cannot refute this argument.

If we cut the scientific assertion about the duration of the struggle in half, what we are left with is a timelock, based on two individuals—Heidstra and Goldman, on separate sides of Bundy Drive—unable to see each other.

Heidstra/Goldman Timelock

PM

10:33-35 Argument; dog barking; fight starting.

10:35-45 Death struggle; dog barking.

10:47-49 White sports vehicle speeds away; dog wailing.

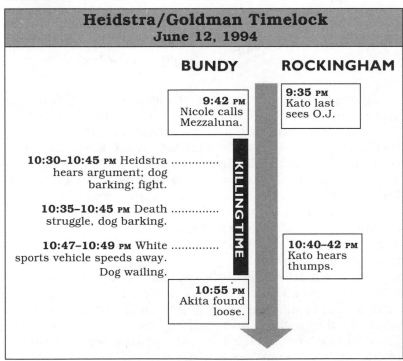

Heidstra/Goldman Timelock
June 12, 1994

BUNDY   **ROCKINGHAM**

9:42 PM Nicole calls Mezzaluna.

9:35 PM Kato last sees O.J.

10:30–10:45 PM Heidstra hears argument; dog barking; fight.

10:35–10:45 PM Death struggle, dog barking.

10:47–10:49 PM White sports vehicle speeds away. Dog wailing.

KILLING TIME

10:40–42 PM Kato hears thumps.

10:55 PM Akita found loose.

After the case was lost, the D.A., in his fury, shouted at critics that it didn't matter. The Source recalls:

> *They said the case was closed, that he did it, and it didn't matter if he killed them as late as 10:50, he could still get home by 10:55, it's only a five-minute drive . . .*

A five-minute-plus drive north from Bundy to Rockingham—note, that Heidstra saw the white vehicle going south—but more to the point: Even if you leave out the thumps and the second glove (and the Defense's argument that when Simpson was seen by the driver entering the mansion at around 10:57, [a] he was re-entering, not entering, because the driver also saw that several travel bags were already packed and placed on the veranda, and [b] Simpson had to already be dressed and groomed for his trip, and [c] the murder weapon and bloody clothes had to have been secreted between 10:45 PM, at the earliest, and 10:55 PM), you still have an entirely new and surreal timeline.

Simpson Acting Alone
Late Killing Time

PM	
10:45	Simpson completes murder of victims.
10:46-48	Simpson slowly walks to alley and back to crime scene. Searches for lost glove and cap.
10:49	Simpson speeds south, then north to Rockingham.
10:54	Simpson skids to a stop (unseen and unheard) at the Rockingham gate, only yards away from a waiting limousine driver on a completely still suburban street.
10:54-56	Simpson races behind house, to bury evidence, as Clark suggested at one time, drops a glove, runs back to the driveway, and is seen entering house at 10:57.
10:58	Simpson answers buzzer.
10:59–11:02	Simpson showers, changes, packs, carries remaining bags out to limousine.

This is the most conservative timeline based on Prosecution assertions, contradictory though they may be. The

Defense did not, and did not have to, spell out these time contradictions, but we have done so to give the Prosecution every benefit of the doubt (a benefit that belongs only to the Defense, in a court of law, under the American system).

Clearly, the defendant does fit into this timeline, because the original Prosecution clock has Simpson at his Rockingham estate at 10:40 PM or shortly thereafter as the source of the thumps.

O.J. Simpson Rockingham Estate

It is time now to take a closer look at the Rockingham estate (see opposite). But remember, maps of Rockingham, like those of Bundy, are highly misleading, giving the impression of space that simply does not exist.

The Testimony of the Limousine Driver, Allan Park

What did the honest limousine driver see? Allan Park's point of view from the Ashford entrance, where he was parked, to the Rockingham gate where Simpson is supposed to have sped to a stop, after the murders—sometime between 10:25 and 10:40 PM—is a very short distance. In fact, the Simpson "estate" is not a large luxury property. It is a substantial home with grounds but the two entrance gates are less than thirty yards apart. Between 10 and 11 PM, on a Sunday night on the dark narrow streets above Sunset Boulevard, it defies common sense to believe that an anxious driver, if he was indeed waiting and watching for Simpson, would not see a white Bronco skidding to a stop and Simpson closing the door and running onto the grounds (as the Prosecution argued).

If the driver, however, was at certain moments inside the limousine and on the telephone, as telephone records show, his ability to hear a Bronco arrive could have been impeded. But, we should remember, Park testified that he had not seen the Bronco when he arrived about 10:21 PM, and neither did he remember seeing it when he left. The ea-

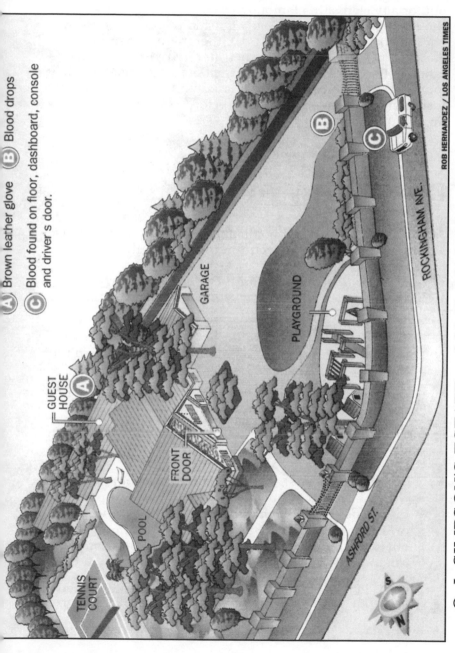

A Brown leather glove **B** Blood drops

C Blood found on floor, dashboard, console and driver s door.

ROB HERNANDEZ / LOS ANGELES TIMES

GUEST HOUSE

GARAGE

PLAYGROUND

ROCKINGHAM AVE.

FRONT DOOR

POOL

TENNIS COURT

ASHFORD ST.

O.J. SIMPSON'S ESTATE— 360 North Rockingham Avenue [5]

ger young driver testified that he was constantly on the look-out for any sign of his famous passenger. If the jury accepts the testimony of Rosa Lopez, who said she saw the Bronco parked on the street at 10:15 PM, then we may assume that Park simply did not see it when he arrived. The jury was taken to Rockingham and drew their own conclusions. They found his testimony important, later on: Park's was the only testimony requested by the jury before rendering their verdict.

Defense Closing Arguments

As the trial wound down to closing arguments, the Defense was able to force the Prosecution to argue that:

- There was police misconduct and, even perjury, but that doesn't mean that Simpson was framed and didn't do the deed.

- There were police and coroner sloppiness and mistakes but that doesn't mean that Simpson wasn't at the crime scene.

- Detective Fuhrman is a vicious racist but that has nothing to do with Simpson's crimes.

   With the Prosecution stumbling, Simpson's "Dream Team" of attorneys argued back:

- There was a "rush to judgment." The four lead detectives left the crime scene to go to the Simpson estate to have Fuhrman, who was "off" the case, climb over the wall to "frame the right man," because it was obvious that Simpson was the killer, because "the husband is always the first suspect."

- "Garbage in, garbage out." All evidence had to pass through the "black hole" of the corrupt, compromised, contaminated LAPD laboratory—so none of the independent lab findings meant anything.

- Several witnesses in the Bundy area contradicted the Prosecution's 10:15 timeline, thus making it impossible for the defendant to be the killer, within the Prosecution scenario.

- The gloves didn't fit and they hadn't shrunk.

Worthy of mention here is the fact that on three occasions the Defense urged the Prosecution to take advantage of the presence of Dr. Michael Baden, Director of the Forensic Sciences Unit of the New York State Police, and Dr. Henry Lee, Director of the Connecticut State Forensic Science Laboratory. These internationally renowned forensic scientists were offered with no strings attached. The Prosecution did not accept the offer. Next the Defense offered to have their client undergo a polygraph test—if the Prosecution would stipulate that the results would be admissible at trial. The Prosecution, again, said no.

Finally, the jury was left to wonder why Simpson's blood was carried by a detective all over the Rockingham estate; why detectives made "reckless" statements in their warrant to search the Simpson estate; why the limousine driver did not see or hear Simpson speed up after the murders, in the bloody Bronco on those quiet Sunday night streets of Brentwood; why Nicole did not change her locks after her keys were "stolen" if she was in fear for her life; why Simpson was busy dating a number of women if he was locked in a deadly obsession; why Nicole had apologized to her husband after some of their fights; why Simpson had not touched Nicole in anger since 1989, including the 1993 taped incident; why Detective Fuhrman was never recalled (after he took the Fifth Amendment); and, always, why the gloves didn't fit and some of the blood samples seemed to contain an LAPD lab preservative, and, why, if Nicole Simpson feared for her life, did she agree to joint custody of the children with O.J. after their divorce?

Defense lawyer Barry Scheck argued to the jury at the end, "When you find a cockroach in your spaghetti, you throw it out, you don't look through it for any more." The jury, in their decision, had found something wrong with the Prosecution's case, and whatever it was, it added up to reasonable doubt, to a person.

The Defense prevailed with the jury and a minority of the population at large, but most of the white public and almost all of the educated and professional classes insist on the overwhelming DNA evidence—despite scientific disputes, the charge of missing blood, and the contamination of the LAPD laboratory; despite the unidentified fingerprints and the unmatched blood and flesh under Nicole's fingernail, and the defendant's unmarked body in spite of the signs of a "ferocious struggle;" despite any and all reasonable doubt—and because of the psychological certainty of Simpson's abusive, possessive, homicidal, jealous rage over the seventeen years of his relationship with Nicole Brown, and the "guilty" actions of Simpson in fleeing in a Bronco holding a gun to his head, having left behind a letter that even his closest advisors interpreted as a suicide note.

For obvious tactical reasons, the Defense was quick to echo the Prosecution profile of Nicole as a kind of angel (D.A.'s and Brown family and friends wore angel pins to symbolize their position). We now know that the Defense held conflicted feelings about the true nature and dynamics of the O.J./Nicole relationship. Many who have since heard Simpson discuss his relationship with Nicole believe he is completely delusional, and is in utter denial over the real nature of their relationship. Simpson in his civil deposition, in his post-trial video, and in his "farewell letter" before driving away with his friend A.C. Cowlings, referred to himself as, at times, "a battered husband." His handwritten "farewell/suicide" letter, that was read to a riveted television audience, points in two directions: guilt and innocence, and perhaps that is why the Prosecution did not introduce it into the trial. Here it is in its entirety.

The Farewell/Suicide Letter

To whom it may concern:
　First, everyone understand I had nothing to do with Nicole's murder. I loved her, always have, and always will. If we had a problem, it's because I loved her so much. Recently we came to the understanding that for now we were not right for each other, at least for now. Despite our love we were dif-

ferent and that's why we mutually agreed to go our separate ways.

It was tough splitting for a second time, but we both knew it was for the best. Inside, I had no doubt that in the future we would be close friends, or more. Unlike what has been written in the press, Nicole and I had a great relationship for most of our lives together. Like all long-term relationships, we had a few downs and ups. I took the heat New Year's 1989 because that's what I was supposed to do. I did not plead no contest for any other reason but to protect our privacy. It was advised it would end the press hype. I don't want to belabor knocking the press, but I can't believe what is being said. Most of it is totally made up. I know you have a job to do, but as a last wish, please, please, please leave my children in peace. Their lives will be tough enough.

I want to send my love and thanks to all my friends. I'm sorry I can't name every one of you. Especially A.C.—man, thanks for being in my life. The support and friendship I received from so many—Wayne Hughes, Louis Marks, Frank Olson, Mark Packer, Bender, Bobby Kardashian—I wish we had spent more time together in recent years. My golfing buddies—Hoss, Alan Austin, Mike, Craig, Denver, Wyler, Sandy, Jay, Donnie—thanks for the fun.

All my teammates over the years: Reggie (McKenzie), you were the soul of my pro career, Ahmad (Rashad), I never stopped being proud of you. Marcus (Allen), you've got a great lady in Catherine, don't mess it up. Bobby Chandler, thanks for always being there. Skip and Cathy, I love you guys—without you I never would have made it through this far. Marguerite [his first wife], thanks for the early years—we had some fun. Paula—what can I say? You are special. I'm sorry we're not going to have our chance. God brought you to me, I now see. As I leave, you'll be in my thoughts.

I think of my life and feel I've done most of the right things. So why do I end up like this? I can't go on. No matter what the outcome, people will look and point. I can't take that. I can't subject my children to that. This way they can move on and go on with their lives. Please, if I've done anything worthwhile with my life, let my kids live in peace from you, the press.

I've had a good life. I'm proud of how I lived. My mama taught me to do unto others—I treated people the way I

*wanted to be treated. I've always tried to be up and helpful.
So why is this happening? I'm sorry for the Goldman family.
I know how much it hurts.*

*Nicole and I had a good life together. All this press talk
about a rocky relationship is no more than what every long-
term relationship experiences. All her friends will confirm that
I have been totally loving and understanding of what she's
been going through. At times I have felt like a battered husband or boyfriend. But I loved her, make that clear to everyone. And I would take whatever it took to make it work.*

*Don't feel sorry for me. I've had a great life, great friends.
Please think of the real O.J. and not this lost person. Thanks
for making my life special. I hope I helped yours.*

Peace and love,   ☺J.

Part of the signature was a simple drawing of a happy
face. Sources in the District Attorney's office now say, in
hindsight, that their ranking officials missed a major opportunity by not introducing the letter. According to our chief
Source:

> *He says he's innocent in the letter but one of the psy-
> chiatrists that works with the office called in and begged
> the brass to understand that the man was guilty about
> something. He's signing off, he's saying goodbye, he has
> a gun to his head. The doctor told them, "Now's the time
> to go to his lawyer, Shapiro the dealmaker, and say to
> him, 'Look, sir, we are only interested in the truth, in jus-
> tice, and if the truth is that your client went berserk for
> some reason, we'll work with you on a plea,'" etc., in-
> stead they went on TV, about how they "were ready for
> him" if he even thought about an insanity plea, and the
> death penalty, etc. They thought they had him but they
> read him and that letter wrong, and, by the end they
> would've sold their souls for a plea, any plea!*

If O.J. Simpson was not guilty about killing two people,
what was he guilty about? Is it any wonder that the sense of
"doubleness" invading the nation should be manifest in the
protagonist of the ongoing drama?

Inevitably, two questions arise: What were the psychodynamics between these two human beings who became the vehicles for a seething cross-cultural drama of sex and race? And, to the point, does it matter who these people were if Simpson is not the killer? Or could there be a third position, as so often in this saga, where life and "lifestyle" converge fatally?

Faye Resnick on O.J. and Nicole

Nicole Simpson's intimate friend, Faye Resnick, produced a book so damning of O.J. Simpson that Judge Ito had to appeal to the television networks not to interview Resnick lest the jury and public be poisoned, altogether, against the defendant and violate his Sixth Amendment right to a fair trial.

Nicole Brown Simpson: The Private Diary of a Life Interrupted, Resnick's instant confessional, paints a picture of Simpson as a charismatic monster, and his wife as a brave, bright mother and wife of strong character. And yet, quite inadvertently, another portrait seeps through the sentimental melodrama of the tabloid book. While there is a constant reiteration of Simpson as abuser, there are admiring references to Nicole Simpson's near-sadistic delight in stoking the aging athlete's jealousy and insecurity.

Resnick relates Nicole's desperation when O.J. pleads with his former wife to leave him alone and not wreck his new relationship with Paula Barbieri:

> *After O.J. realized Nicole wasn't coming back to him, he decided to have nothing to do with her. And he seemed genuinely happy with Paula Barbieri. For once, O.J. was leaving Nicole strictly alone. He refused to speak with her unless absolutely necessary. It made Nicole crazy.*[6]

Sex is described as Nicole's "drug of choice," and, "both a weapon and an opiate." Resnick lightheartedly reveals Nicole as being as jealous and possessive, in her way, as her husband. Describing O.J. fighting with Nicole over her right to see the children, Resnick observes that O.J. is "fucking with a tigress" who will "rip his heart out."[7]

The author also, without meaning to, tells the story of herself, Nicole, and their friends in the Simpson circle in a vocabulary of conspicuous consumption, greed, sex, unremitting narcissism—and, fatefully, narcotics. The players in the Simpson pack—and Nicole and O.J. are definitely the leaders and role models—are described, without exception, as impulse-ridden, addictive, violently or masochistically sexist, as ruthless opportunists—in short, "beautiful people" who are simultaneously praised as loyal friends, lovers, and parents.

This sweet life in the Brentwood discos and Mexican resorts, hundred-thousand-dollar limousines and sports vehicles, rented yachts and million-dollar vacation cottages, the sex and coke binges—all add up to what?

Could it be that this lifestyle of glamorous abuse and alienation, this nihilistic orgy of every kind of excess, while being the natural frame of reference for the murders of June 12, does not absolutely incriminate O.J. Simpson as the Beast who slashed away the life of his Beauty and her youthful friend, or, perhaps, lover or lover-to-be?

Is it any wonder that the police and District Attorney never made the slightest gesture to find anyone else guilty; or that educated white America never, for one instant, presumed the ghetto-born star anything other than guilty? How could there possibly be "something wrong" with this script of O.J. Simpson as the wife-abusing homicidal celebrity golfer?

Most of those surrounding O.J. and Nicole were compromised by one addiction or another—sex, money, narcotics, jealousy—the entire constellation of what psychologists call "narcissistic disorders." Each of "Mommy's best friends" might have been capable of acting out various psychosexual scenarios. Each might fit the profile of either a victim or aggressor in a transaction of violence. Each might be the obvious suspect in any crime committed against any of the others, and, as we shall see, each had something to hide, because each was guilty of a number of derelictions, toward both themselves and others.

Our investigation may contradict or dispose of some of the Prosecution's scenario, with far more than enough questions to create reasonable doubt, and yet leave a clinging doubt for many observers who are neither racist nor police true believers. Because, at the end of the Defense's day, the four tiny drops of Simpson blood at Bundy (collected before Simpson's blood vial contents were available for the planting of evidence), unlike the blood on the back gate, did not contain any EDTA police preservative.

Either the tell-tale drops were contaminated or created in the LAPD laboratory (where Detective Fuhrman was never reported seen), or outright planted there, or they came from Simpson—from the defendant innocently in the past, innocently on the night of June 12, or, finally, as guilty evidence of his involvement in the ghastly act. If O.J. Simpson was at 875 South Bundy after 9:46 PM that Sunday night—then the Defense scenario (O.J. at home chipping golf balls, relaxing, sleeping, packing, etc.) is overthrown in one stroke.

But, as we shall see, if the Defense scenario thus fails, it does not mean that Simpson's presence at the crime scene implicates him as the killer. Then why would he be there if he wasn't stalking or spying or invading Nicole's newly won space? He was always there, why not on this night? Why not, indeed, but to what end? "Motive, means, and opportunity," the Prosecution argued. With the timeline, we are able to confront the "opportunity." For the "motive," we need to look at the slayings from an angle of refraction considerably more acute than the Prosecution's jealous madman horror show.

The Psychological Timeline

Because the Prosecution centered their theory of motive on Simpson's pathological personality, we offer to you, the jury, an expert's extraordinary meditation on jealousy and murder. The following oral commentary is a kind of "free association" by a psychological scientist with a close interest in the case, who must remain anonymous. It is for you to judge the validity of his or her analysis. We present a full excerpt.

> *This is a knotty problem, this entanglement of love, jealousy, envy, possessiveness, abuse. Keep your eye on the relationship. The dynamics of this kind of "malignant*

attachment." In this case you have a sort of Alpha Male and his pride of consorts, all based on superior physical power. In human culture we call this kind of power over others slavery.

Marriage has been, historically, a form of slavery. Women have lived in cultural and actual physical bondage. The simple fact is that men tend to be bigger and stronger than women and children and, so, that is how they have organized their societies, their laws, homes, families and relationships. This is the "fatherland." In the house, or in Nazi Germany, "patriotism" means fatherism.

You see, everybody is hardwired to their past. Everybody has baggage, as they say, bad "objects"—people and the memory of people from their earliest years and feelings.

In an "abusive relationship" you have two abusers, even though one may seem to be only a victim. You have a folie à deux, it's a mutual madness but each one acts out a different role . . . . The man is responsible, because of his strength, the instant he touches her. This is true with children—in any relationship or situation where there is an inequality of power. But she is responsible to get out, to grow up, but that is a personal responsibility—with him there is the added legal mandate to keep his goddamn hands off other people.

We all need others. If we have a compulsion to choose "bad objects," this roots back to some trauma in early childhood. In other words, we are hooked or hardwired into earliest experiences and feelings or types of people— no matter how damaging or rejecting they may have been, how abusive, because whatever they were, they were there and they were ours and we will cling to them whether they abused us or not because without them we are lost.

You talk about Othello. Remember his epileptic fit after he thinks his wife's unfaithful?

Othello: *What hath he said?*
Iago: *Faith, that he did—I know not what he did.*
Othello: *What? What—*
Iago: *Lie—*

Othello: *With her?*
Iago: *With her—on her—what you will.*
Othello: *Lie with her! Lie on her! . . . Lie with her! that's fulsome.—Handkerchief—confessions—handkerchief. . . It is not words that shake me thus:—Pish!—Noses, ears, and lips:—Is't possible?—Confess!—Handkerchief!—O, devil!*

And he falls into a fit at Iago's mercy. Now, in life, Iago is inside us, tormenting us, calling us weak and impotent and old and black or, heaven forbid, not a man's man! and calling out for bloodshed and revenge . . . . There's a deep sexual confusion in all this. Each of these partners in abuse envies and wants not only the other's body but their soul. Part of this is natural: Everybody envies everybody else, everybody wants a phallus and everybody wants a womb, but in the abusive couple it goes beyond fantasy and degenerates into a master/slave situation.

Power can reduce us all to slavery. Power corrupts, lack of power corrupts. The media tells you that these people had everything. Don't believe it. These are wounded children. They've been blinded by the spotlight of publicity. They're running on empty. There's nothing there. That's why they fill each other up. That's obsession. Both of them couldn't live with or without each other. But she is always the potential victim, just like he's always the primary suspect.

In this case, I've seen evidence of a profound struggle by both parties to break the chains of this addiction. There seems to have been some progress. That's the pity of it.

I would never testify one way or the other. You know psychology is a knife that cuts two ways, as the Russians say, and it's a big mistake to try to creep into somebody's head who is dead or somebody who's locked into the rhetoric of a legal defense of "innocence" in a courtroom where the choices are only "Innocent" or "Guilty" . . . because the D.A.'s crackpot brand of psychology never taught them that we're all two people, inside: we all wear masks; male and female; lover and loved; child and mother; murderer and victim—so when he said how much "I loved my Nicole" he was telling the truth as he had lived it, just as Othello did:

> . . . then must you speak of one, that lov'd not wisely, but too well; of one not easily jealous, but, being wrought, perplex'd in the extreme . . .

Well, we're all easily jealous because we've all been children. The man who wrote the letter saying, "Think of me as I was . . ." was not Othello, who said, "Speak of me as I am"—because Othello finally knew who he was, and that's not the man in the courtroom, not yet—who may not actually know whether he did it—or only dreamed it!

This is what might have been. It is a provocative analysis, and because rage is the Rosetta Stone of the Prosecution's case, we dare not evade the issue. But does jealous rage leading to murder define this crime? If not, does it point a finger into the context of the crime and suggest further scenarios? The Source says:

Oh, that Johnnie. He knew things. It's called "signifying." Remember the Colombian drug lords or the four non-African-Americans in stocking caps and everybody laughed? Those were just straw men because he did know something! That's what they think downtown, now. O.J. or somebody knew where to point Cochran. You know, the gate, the socks, the glove, etc. And another thing, you can't hire men like Henry Lee or, that statistician [Dr. T.P. Speed], or Barry Scheck, or Neufeld or Blasier or Dean Uelman just for money. These people were trashed by their friends and colleagues for daring to touch the glitz around this trial. I was told that Johnnie Cochran and Shapiro looked those guys in the eyes and told them—"I want you to know that you will never be embarrassed by this case, never be humiliated, because the man did not do it!"

We have reached the last threshold of credibility for both the Prosecution and Defense timelines. The Defense has only to prove to the jury that there is something wrong with the

Prosecution's theory for the case to be declared technically "open." Did they do it?

Something convinced the jury that there was reasonable doubt. Have you found sufficient cause to agree? And more than that, have you found sufficient cause to believe that Simpson might actually have been not only not guilty, but also perhaps innocent of the murders? Or, are you absolutely convinced that you know who committed the ghastly double murders on the evening of June 12, 1994? We will assume that you will need a greater quantum of evidence before declaring the case truly "open."

A Closer Look at Rockingham

We have discussed the driving time from Bundy to Rockingham. As part of the investigation for this project, researchers conducted the following re-creation:

> At 10:25 PM on a Sunday evening, an investigator stood next to a car at the Ashford gate of Simpson's home; a second researcher drove up to the Rockingham gate— drove up not at speed but, instead, turned off the ignition and coasted slowly up to 360 North Rockingham, with the lights off, and as quietly as possible opened the driver's door, and tiptoed toward the gate.

> **The result:** The first researcher waiting at Ashford was totally aware of every sound of the approaching "silent" and "dark" vehicle, of the door opening and closing, of the footsteps. Everything.

> **Conclusion:** If O.J. Simpson was involved somehow in the murders of Nicole Simpson and Ronald Goldman, he could not have driven his white Bronco up to his Rockingham gate after 10:21 PM (the frozen time of Park's arrival and subsequent telephone calls to his employer) on June 12, 1994, without detection—if, indeed, the limousine driver was fully aware and watching for Simpson—as he testified.

Our analysis isolated the 10:15–11:15 PM timeline at Rockingham as crucial. To drive in the dark, with headlights and motor off—to coast up to 360 North Rockingham for one very long block—is very difficult. First, the machine must be put in neutral, the engine and lights turned off, in order to coast in the dark to a silent stop at the driveway; then, the key must be removed from the ignition to avoid warning signals when the door is opened, the door must be closed firmly in order to lock the vehicle; and the sound the heavy gate to the estate makes when opened must be muted. (Why, you may ask, would Simpson go to these lengths between 10:20 and 10:40 PM, when his usual driver never arrived until 10:45 PM?)

If you drive up to the Rockingham gate at normal or extra speed with the lights on, you will be seen and heard coming for a hundred yards—from where Park sat waiting and watching. The Ford Bronco is a loud, powerful four-wheel-drive vehicle that creates too much automotive sound to avoid attention, especially given the ambient context after 10:00 PM on a Sunday, and the headlight sightlines existing near the corner of Rockingham and Ashford, where Park waited. Even if Park was inside the limousine off and on, telephoning, he could still have a view across the driveway to the Rockingham gate where the Bronco was later found parked.

Our demonstration made it abundantly clear to researchers involved that because the Bronco makes a very loud noise, it would be unlikely that the limousine driver would not have heard or seen its approach. What will you, the jury, find in this case?

Lights in the Simpson Household

From where he sat smoking, the driver could see only one light on in the residence and so he was encouraged by the Prosecution to assume and state that the house was dark. But was it? Is it possible there were more lights on than Park could see? Near the start of his civil trial, Simpson insisted that his attorneys test the sightlines of his estate, to prove to them that from where Park stood, he could not see a number of lighted areas inside the house. Simpson's post-trial video effectively demonstrates the fact that the house can look very dark from the outside and still be fully lit within.

The Air Conditioning Unit and the Three Thumps

Simpson in his video takes the viewer to the location of the air conditioning unit behind the guesthouse where Kaelin talked on the phone. The air conditioning unit protrudes from the building in such a way that a man of Simpson's height would have torn his face open had he run into it. Kaelin had likened the force of the impact to "an earthquake," and said that it shook the picture on the wall. Again, why no sound of footsteps either before or after the three loud thumps? Could the sound have been something else?

Limousine Driver en route to Rockingham

Let us return to the limousine again, and back up in time. Simpson has not yet sped to a stop with his Bronco, managed to get behind the guesthouse, and crashed into that protruding air conditioner making those three loud thumps that shook the wall and scared Kaelin, on the other side of the wall on the telephone; the defendant has not yet dropped the other glove, nor has he raced into the house so he can reappear in a few minutes' time all clean and dressed, ready for the ride to the airport. Let us back up in time to about 10:21 or 10:22 PM, the time Allan Park reaches 360 North Rockingham, to call his employer soon after at 10:25, a telephone timelock. Now, for Park to reach 360 North Rockingham by 10:21 or 10:22, he has to turn north off Sunset at about 10:15, because he will slow down below ten miles per hour as he searches for the address. If Simpson has fled from Bundy at 10:15, and is proceeding immediately back to Rockingham, he will overtake the limousine at 10:20 on Rockingham.

If we are to give the Prosecution any chance to prove

their case as they presented it, we must, therefore, push back Simpson's slow (walking) exit from the crime scene, fast (driving) exit from Bundy to 10:10, in order to avoid the coincidence of the Simpson and Park timelines crashing on North Rockingham.

This would move the killing time back to near 10:05, and Goldman's arrival at Bundy to near 10:01. Thus, Simpson would have to leave the crime scene by 10:12 to be home one minute before the limousine's slow approach and arrival. A 10:12 exit from Bundy means, working backward, that we find the killer parking and entering at Bundy at about 9:57. Next, the killer "lies in wait" until 10:01 when, by chance, Goldman arrives on the scene. Bloody murder ensues with Simpson pausing at 10:02 and 10:03 to telephone Barbieri from his cellular telephone.

What is wrong with this timeline? The Prosecution insists that at 10:03, Simpson is at Rockingham. What if we argue that the Prosecution is wrong, for some reason, and that the murderer makes his call to Paula Barbieri at 10:03 from the alley at Bundy after murdering Nicole and Ron? Then, did Goldman appear at near 9:56 for his fatal encounter?

Let us suppose that it is possible for Goldman to have gone home, changed clothes, walked and driven to Bundy in from one to six minutes. One problem then remains: the clock—the dog. Except for Pablo Fenjves, all the witnesses from both sides put the dog barking later (after 10:20), and the dog wailing much later (after 10:35).

There is no compromise in time, here, because the window of opportunity is exactly eleven minutes and thirty seconds:

Revised Killing Time—Simpson Acting Alone	
PM	**June 12, 1994**
10:03	Simpson on cellular telephone to Paula Barbieri, at Bundy, not Rockingham, as D.A. insisted.
	Murders must take place in the next eleven and a half minutes: the killing time.
10:13–30	The killer has no more than five minutes to travel from Bundy to Rockingham. Remember, the killer must turn

off Sunset onto Rockingham before the limousine—unless an accomplice is involved, or another white Bronco.

10:17–21 Allan Park is slowly proceeding north on Rockingham looking for 360. His rate of speed must go down to less than five miles per hour (according to testimony and independent tests). Park's long limousine crawls to the Ashford gate and Park waits and calls his employer. The time is between 10:20 and 10:25 PM, and the Bronco must be parked at the gate (if Rosa Lopez's testimony is accurate—although Park does not remember seeing the Bronco there when he arrived).

Assume for now the Bronco was there and Park missed seeing it. The driver waits. The sound of a Bronco starting up is, as we have said, loud, and Simpson, therefore, cannot leave the house, get in the Bronco, drive to Bundy, and commit the double murder after 10:21. He cannot be the killer (according to the Prosecution scenario) after 10:30, at the time when all but one of the witnesses heard barking and voices. Simpson, we find, cannot be at Bundy at 10:30 without having (a) left his house after 10:21, driven away, and then, (b) returned, parked and entered at near 10:50—without Park either hearing or seeing him drive away and return. Again, does this not suggest a scenario other than the Prosecution's? Could the scenario involve a second man and/or a second Bronco?

This is an analytical moment of truth for the jury: When the so-called Trial of the Century becomes, in fact, one of the great murder mysteries of all time. No wonder the Simpson jury asked to read Park's testimony before making their decision.

10:16–18 Driver Park enters Rockingham Avenue from Sunset Boulevard.

10:18–19 If Simpson is the killer, then he also is driving north on Rockingham.

10:21–22 Both the limousine and the Bronco will reach 360 North Rockingham at virtually the same minute.

10:23–30 Allan Park is outside his vehicle smoking a cigarette, looking and listening for Simpson.

10:30–40 Park, in the limousine, backs and turns between the Ashford gate and the Rockingham gate—looking for Simpson.

Seemingly, there is no way the Bronco could drive up during this time period, at any speed, without being seen. Each increment of time, speed, space, light and ambient sound for the 10:17 to 10:25 PM time period was tested by researchers, then retested with journalists acting as "devil's advocates."

The conclusion of those involved in this demonstration was that no vehicle could have arrived at or left Rockingham after 10:20 PM without being heard and seen. Therefore, the white Bronco either had to have been parked on Rockingham before, during, and after Park's arrival at between 10:19 and 10:21 PM—or it was not there at all. Perhaps, if it was there, as Rosa Lopez testified, Park simply did not note the presence of the Bronco, and was wrong in this memory—just as he was wrong when he remembered seeing a second auto in the inside driveway that could not have been there.

If you believe now, that there is "something wrong" with both the Prosecution and Defense scenarios, and that each of their half–truths does not add up to the whole truth, then in Holmes's words, we have "eliminated the impossible," and you may be compelled to view the bloody events of June 12 from new, different, and disturbing points of view.

You, ladies and gentlemen of the Jury, are now required to test the validity of a series of independent scenarios for the Bundy murders. Each scenario, at least partially, excludes every other scenario. The common denominator is the killing time crime clock: 9:36 to 10:57 PM, June 12, 1994.

It is important to understand that there are only certain time sequences of events that can fit within the overall murder time frame. Some entries within the killing time, such as telephone calls, are computer-locked. For other entries, the jury will be asked to include some, but not all, of the timeline witnesses, since some witnesses are mutually exclusive. As the jury evaluates the scenarios to come, remember that all actions must fit—without contradiction—within the allotted window of opportunity. Also, realize that each scenario much be accepted on its own terms and duly evaluated.

Our competing action clocks have pushed us into a new arena of possibility. The Rockingham Bronco demonstration compels us to consider the option of two white Broncos.

Goldman's clocks indicate that both his early and late arrival times at Bundy make him a poor fit for the Prosecution scenario—which must bring Goldman and Simpson together in the same killing time.

The moment has come to anatomize this murder case by following the logic of the timeline into new scenarios. Our analyses cannot read the human heart, but they can read a clock and tell us that when and if that clock strikes thirteen then we must turn a cold eye on all that has gone before.

Three

The
Second Man

This case was filled with cars. There were three white Broncos! There was a strange car parked at Rockingham on the night. There were stolen cars, like Paula Barbieri's. At first they [the D.A.'s office] thought there were two Broncos at Bundy—one in front and one in back. Maybe there were. I don't know anymore. Maybe there were two O.J. Simpsons, like the Prosecution said . . .

By trial's end, *Time* magazine was openly reporting the certainty of both the LAPD and the Prosecution that Simpson had a confederate. "There was a clean-up, he had help," a D.A. source assured the weekly news magazine on October 2, 1995.

Time had initiated their coverage of the Simpson affair by billboarding a jailhouse mugshot of the football legend on its cover—only *Time*'s artists, it was soon discovered, had darkened Simpson's skin and beard. When this shocking media manipulation was exposed, the magazine apologized, claiming "aesthetic reasons." In 1963, *Time*'s sister magazine *Life* had committed a similar act when picturing the accused assassin of President Kennedy, Lee Harvey Oswald, on their cover with an enhanced photograph of a rifle in his hands, thus doctoring what some critics already considered a doctored photograph. In Simpson's case, African-American critics pointed to the blackening of the Juice as the start of a dirty psychological warfare campaign to turn the multimillionaire media star into "just another nigger." At any rate, both *Time* and *Newsweek*'s sources echoed the Source:

After the glove foul-up, the word from the 18th floor
was that there was no way to salvage the case unless
either the weapon could be brought into the jury or who-
ever was working with O.J. [could be identified] . . . . The
question was, could they change their story of what hap-
pened in mid-stream?

No. They could not. The Prosecution was shackled by
their obsession with O.J. as a berserk Othello. Some of the
jurors commented, later, that they saw the murder knife as
a symbol of molten passion, while the gloves stood for ice-
cold premeditation. These conflicting symbols of heat and
cold—the knife and the glove—would hang in basic contradiction over the consciousness of both the jury and the nation throughout the trial.

The Prosecution had believed the glove found at
Rockingham to be vital evidence until the day they brought
both gloves into court and asked Simpson to try them on.
First he put on a pair of latex gloves, then the leather Aris
pair, tugging at them and grimacing, showing how poorly
they fit. Some speculated that the gloves were tight because
they had to be tried on over latex. A glove will still fit over a
second sanitary rubber or plastic glove, although it does
take an extra pull to get it on. Even though Simpson got the
gloves on, it was clear they were very tight and did not fit his
fingers properly. Although the prosecution argued that the
gloves had shrunk, this demonstration was a dramatic de-
feat for them. Cochran for the Defense would develop from
this day one of his favorite themes: "If they don't fit, you
must acquit." The glove that had been dropped, according to
the D.A., by the Defendant at Rockingham—the glove that
was the vital link to events at Bundy—had now been "lost"
for a second time, here in Judge Ito's courtroom.

The Prosecution's evidence, in fact, had disappeared at
an alarming rate. Much of what had been reported in the
press never materialized: the ski mask; a sharpened "trench-
ing tool"; the defendant's supposed guilty behavior on the
airplane during his flight to Chicago; a "guilty" golf bag filled
with blood; bloody clothes in the Simpson washing machine;
a "military knife" found in a vacant Chicago lot; various eyewitnesses to guilty behavior in L.A. and Chicago; some of the
uncounted, unlabeled blood samples in the LAPD laboratory.

But at the same time, other evidence was appearing, in the Bronco, on the back Bundy gate, on the Simpson socks.

The Prosecution had believed they had traced the murder weapon—that it was the knife Simpson bought at Ross Cutlery—but then the Defense delivered that very same Ross Cutlery knife to court in a brown envelope. So now the Prosecution had neither the glove nor the knife to use as evidence—and Dr. Henry Lee, the Defense's final expert witness, refused to accept the Prosecution's contention that a second set of footprints found at the scene might have been left by police officers. If they weren't the police's footprints, whose were they? The Prosecution, with its back to the wall, according to sources, including ours, actually had considered naming a co-conspirator in the murders. According to our Source:

> *There would have been a mistrial but at least they could have started over with two accused in another venue and maybe had a chance. But, you know, it was high risk. Too high a risk . . .*

The Second Killer

Who did the authorities have in mind as the second killer? Jason Simpson, the defendant's 20-year-old son by his first marriage? There were some who suspected that young Simpson was the man. They point out that Jason was capable of violence: A court document revealed that in December 1992, Jason had been charged with assault with a deadly weapon, but he wound up pleading not guilty to a misdemeanor charge of disturbing the peace. He was also known to have had brushes with the law involving misdemeanor hit-and-run and driving with a suspended license. He was also passionately loyal to his father, about the same size, and had access to his closet and clothing, gloves and shoes. Further, Jason behaved, after the Bronco chase, at trial, and when the verdict was read, in a manner, perhaps, that seemed odd to some. Could the Second Man have been Jason Simpson?

The Source describes behind-the-scene discussion:

> . . . But yet and still how is the man going to be such a
> monster to put his son up to something like that with the
> clothes and so forth—that kind of planning doesn't go
> with a crime of passion. You're talking about a "hit," or-
> ganized crime, not a jealous husband. That's the way
> they went, back and forth, half the night, it ruined
> Garcetti's health.

Accept the father/son homicide plan for a moment, as
our Source tells us some of the authorities did, for many
months. Jason Simpson was under constant observation
from June 16 on, when it became clear to the police and
D.A. that there might be an evidence problem and that "O.J.
had help." On June 12, the night of the murders, Jason was
working in another restaurant, and so he had an alibi. Still,
the Prosecution watched and waited, believing that the alibi
just might be false. It might. But for this study, we will look
at Jason in relation to the timeline.

Perhaps all of Jason's fellow employees could have been
induced to lie for the young Simpson. In that case, can we
accept a scenario involving father and son as the two murderers? To do so, we must also place O.J. at the scene. Our
later timeline clocks the killings between 10:32 and 10:55
PM. Because we have not been able to fit the defendant into
this time frame, we must also rule Jason out of this particular scenario (father and son from 10:35 to 10:45 PM or later,
wading in blood), but only this one. There are others that he
might fit but only in the almost inconceivable case that an
entire staff lied for this rather ordinary young man who,
from most reports, had a warm, friendly relationship with
his stepmother, Nicole.

Jason was not the only other possible suspect. The
LAPD spent considerable time and effort to ferret out anyone
who might have been involved in the crime. Authorities admit constant observation of a number of potential co-conspirators, including "residence monitoring," which means
having undercover officers move into a domicile near the
target. For that assignment, our independent investigators
learned, police officers who had been active in the notorious
covert operations against the Black Panthers and other mili-

tant rights and peace groups in the sixties and seventies were used in developing the LAPD strategy.

Another candidate for the second assassin slot was the man who seemed to be always at Simpson's side in times of need, A.C. Cowlings. Shortly after the crime, a young lady active in adult films spoke to the tabloids about her sometime escort, A.C. She quoted Simpson's closest and oldest friend as telling her that, "Those were my gloves." and saying that he was told by him [O.J.] to hide a bloody knife. Lawyers for both sides "scoffed at the claims." The Source, too, knew about the D.A.'s suspicion of Cowlings:

> They had undercover people, men and women, all over A.C. They tried to use the Grand Jury against him to shake him up. They tried to set him up. O.J. knew what was happening. He kept in close touch with A.C. Johnnie Cochran told everybody, "Assume that the walls have ears."

Christopher Darden, in fact, was in charge of the Cowlings investigation before being assigned a spot on the Prosecution team in the courtroom. The Source tells us:

> A.C. was their best guess. Size, clothes, plus which he always doubled for O.J. to avoid publicity. Wore his clothes, walked like him. After the funeral, the entire media followed A.C. pretending to be O.J. back to Rockingham.

But Cowlings had an alibi as well, he was with a crowd of guests at a party. And, despite Cowlings's "doubling" over the years for Simpson, and their ancient bond of friendship, and their identical white Bronco sports vehicles, these two running buddies are not there, together, on the timeline. As in the case of Jason Simpson and the other candidates for the "second man," scrutiny led to nothing.

Could the Second Man have been Simpson's adult daughter Arnelle? It appears impossible, and nobody has seriously suspected this young woman, but Arnelle was not home during the time of the murders, and Rosa Lopez, the next door maid, insisted she heard voices raised at Rockingham at about 3 AM—a time when Arnelle was at home.

Neither the Prosecution nor the Defense questioned Arnelle Simpson's alibi that she and a friend had gone to a film, driving in Arnelle's black Saab and returning after midnight. Yet the key Prosecution witness, Allan Park, would not budge from his position that he had seen a dark car parked next to the Bentley in the driveway when he had come to pick up Simpson. An LAPD photograph taken the next morning, June 13, does picture Arnelle's Saab parked behind the Bentley. If the Saab had also been there the night before, as Park stated, this could suggest that Ms. Simpson may have driven to the movies in the white Bronco. Wait.

If Arnelle Simpson was using the Bronco the night of June 12, then where did the blood found in it the next morning come from? Could it have been planted by someone after her return home around 1 AM? But if that were true, why would the Simpsons not have announced this complete alibi on June 13?

The answer is that there was no car parked next to the Bentley on June 12. Why, then, did Park think he had seen a car? Could he have been confused by the Prosecution and their photos and crime scene reconstructions? Confused by the LAPD photo that did show the Saab in the driveway the next day? Did he mix up that scene with what he had seen in the dark the night before? Something of this sort seems to have happened. Remember that Park was driving a stretch limousine, and that such a car could not have circled the driveway if there had been two vehicles parked there.

Recognizing Park's error in this matter, it may be worth considering if other parts of his testimony could also have been in error—including his memory of the mansion being dark; and his recollection about the number and type of bags Simpson had for his trip. There were areas where Park was not exactly clear. An outstanding one is his recollection of the Bronco. Although Marcia Clark had tried to convince him to state categorically that he had not seen a white Bronco parked at the Rockingham curb, he never did. The most he would say is that he did not remember seeing one.

You may ask why the authorities should have looked at Arnelle Simpson as well as Jason. First, O.J. Simpson had hired well-known criminal defense attorneys to protect his older children's interests. Second, the DNA markings of children are extremely close to that of their biological parents.

Who else could have been a confederate? Paula Barbieri, Simpson's girlfriend at the time of the murders, and Simpson's houseguest, Kato Kaelin, were first treated as friendly witnesses and then unfriendly, by the Prosecution. Paula Barbieri a suspect? Remember, there was a third white Bronco. Barbieri had a Bronco; but she also had another vehicle that might have relevance to this case, a car that had been stolen in January 1994. Author Clifford Linedecker and others have reported that in July 1994, the car thief's attorney found a notebook in the thief's belongings, which he turned over to the police because some of the notes referred to Nicole's daily schedule.[1] The log was not one kept by Barbieri. This extraordinary piece of evidence was never dealt with in the trial. We will return to it later.

What connection might there be between Barbieri and her white Bronco and the events of June 12? Or between the log tracking Nicole found in the belongings of the thief who stole Barbieri's automobile? There is also other evidence that Nicole was being spied on or stalked in quite a different fashion from Simpson's open style of making himself visible to her. Who was the stalker, and who did the surveillance? Such questions must wait for another scenario, because the official investigation never went beyond Simpson, himself.

Other suspects? Kato Kaelin's timeline seems to also rule him out: on the telephone, then opening the gate for Allan Park and the limousine. Kaelin was, like Heidstra and Lopez, ridiculed and accused of testifying for money. In the end, Kaelin turned down more than $500,000 in tabloid opportunities and proved to be neither a drug user nor a drug dealer.

Last on the list of candidates for the Second Man was one of Simpson's attorneys and longtime friends, Robert Kardashian. Authorities pressured Kardashian, and went so far as to suggest to the jury that the defendant's close companion and business partner might have disposed of the bloody evidence after Simpson's return from Chicago to Los Angeles. According to the Prosecution, the evidence might have been secreted in Simpson's garment bag and whisked away from Rockingham by Kardashian.

Kardashian did, indeed, on Simpson's return from Chicago, carry Simpson's Louis Vuitton garment bag up to the estate gate, where he was refused entrance (Simpson was being handcuffed at that moment). Kardashian later told the police that when he was stopped at the gate by an LAPD officer that he had then, far from being secretive, attempted to hand the bag to the policeman to take inside. Kardashian's draft stipulation of May 1995 supports this:

> **Kardashian:** *I asked whether the police officers would take the bag onto the property and I was told they would not. I then put the bag in my car and left.*

Unfortunately for the Prosecution, this "farfetched" explanation was validated, because it was captured on videotape by the always-present news media. After all the leaks to the press about Robert Kardashian's being a suspect of some kind, ranging from "co-conspirator" to "aiding and abetting," the authorities never laid a glove on him, or on any of the others.

Kardashian's deposition for the civil suit contains a fascinating insight into the question of the Second Man: On June 15, Kardashian and Simpson drove to LAX to collect Simpson's golf bag. Kardashian would later tell the Goldman lawyers that he took the bag home and asked A.C. Cowlings to help him go through the contents—they "tore it apart." In other words, if we accept this testimony as truthful, two of Simpson's closest friends (both candidates for the Second Man) were not only not conspiring with the Defendant, but were deeply concerned about the contents of his golf bag— which, they found, did not contain any incriminating evidence.

While the Prosecution had the obligation to study a number of people and evidence leads, they had a focus from the beginning on the man who lived at Rockingham, O.J. the ex-husband, with his history of violence directed at Nicole. Lead detective Tom Lange, under cross-examination, was completely candid about the Prosecution's deeply held opinion that O.J. was the killer, Nicole the target, and Ron the innocent bystander:

> **Q:** *Did you ever—as the investigating officer in this case—ever consider any other theory than if O.J. Simpson was the only perpetrator in this case?*

Lange: *I had absolutely no other evidence that would point me in any other direction.*

Lange acknowledged finding a list of women's telephone numbers, including Nicole Simpson's, in a book at Goldman's apartment but was unsure anyone followed up on the names.

Lange: *I didn't see any other leads to follow up on. There was no other evidence to pursue.*

But Simpson, as shown, did not fit the official Prosecution timeline, and similarly, he is a poor fit for the later 10:35 to 10:55 PM murder timeline. As we illustrated in the Bronco demonstration, it is very difficult to figure out how Simpson could have driven the Bronco to or from Bundy during that time—and not have had his vehicle noticed by Park. This does not mean that there were not two killers, nor does it mean that Simpson was not at the Bundy crime scene at some time, nor does it rule out other scenarios.

Simpson at Bundy— Alternative Timelines

The question then becomes: In what capacity could Simpson have been there? Let us now reshuffle and generate new scenarios and timelines. We can only create one scenario at a time, so in each case we vary our choices of information. For the following four scenarios we include Rosa Lopez's sighting of the Bronco at Rockingham.

The first timeline also includes the Prosecution's early assertions that cellular calls were made to Paula Barbieri en route to Bundy Drive and that the white Bronco was parked for several minutes with its headlights on in front of Nicole's condominium. It does not include the Defense's assertion that Simpson chipped golf balls for part of the time he was home at Rockingham.

Simpson at Bundy—Alternative Timeline 1

PM

9:35	**Rockingham Avenue**. Simpson and Kaelin return from McDonald's. Kaelin retires to his guesthouse to make telephone calls.
9:40	Simpson showers and dresses. He does not chip golf balls.
10:02-03	Simpson leaves the house, gets in the Bronco, drives toward Bundy. In transit he calls Barbieri on his cellular telephone. No answer. Tries again. Scrapes his left hand on the telephone. Smears a drop of blood on the upholstery.
10:05	**South Bundy Drive.** Simpson arrives at Nicole's residence. Parks in front with the lights on (the Prosecution claimed they had a witness to this but later eliminated the event—it did not fit their timeline).
10:06	Simpson rings the bell, or enters using his key, or knocks on the door, or looks through the window (a habit). Either way, Simpson sees the lit candles, hears romantic music, deduces the presence of another man, or his imminent arrival, and returns to his Bronco after having made contact with Nicole—or, he simply slips away.
10:10	Simpson drives back home.
10:15	**Rockingham Avenue**. Simpson returns to and enters his house.
10:16	Rosa Lopez, walking the family dog, notices the white Bronco parked at the Rockingham curb.
10:16-20	Simpson dresses and packs for his Chicago trip. TV playing.
10:21	Allan Park, the driver, arrives early, parks, and waits.
10:21-40	Simpson naps. Kaelin, on the telephone, hears three thumps on the wall.
10:45	Simpson is awakened by the driver's buzzing from the gate.
10:50	Simpson brings his bags down to the front door. The driver does not see Simpson exit to collect his golf bag.
10:56	Driver does see Simpson reenter the house.
10:58	Simpson answers the buzzer.

11:02	Simpson exits the house with his last bag for the trip to LAX.

AM **12-3:00**	**JUNE 13** Rosa Lopez hears male voices on or near the Simpson property.

In his post-trial video, Simpson clarified that he only chipped a few golf balls (for fear of denting his Bentley parked in the driveway) and then practiced his swing.[2] But in this scenario, we have him doing neither. And although Simpson has said in post-trial statements that he did not return from McDonald's until nearly 10:00 PM, the clock of Kaelin's telephone record ties Simpson down to returning no later than 9:36 PM. It is at this time that Simpson may have called Nicole's residence to speak to his daughter Sydney. Although he has stated that he may have called before leaving for McDonald's, he would be mistaken in this, because Nicole and Sydney did not return from dinner until about 9:00 PM. No one escapes what the ancient Greeks called "the long foot of time."

Returning to this scenario: If Simpson, at 10:05 PM, did see a man at Nicole's, the odds are that it was not Ron Goldman. More plausible is the hypothesis that he saw either Nicole's preparation for a different visitor, or the visitor, himself. And if Simpson did see Nicole, it is an open question as to whether or not they exchanged any words. Either way, Simpson could easily have returned to Rockingham before Allan Park arrived and in time for Rosa Lopez to have marked the presence of the Bronco at the Rockingham gate.

During his few minutes at Bundy, Simpson could have left a drop or two of blood on the walk. By 10:16 PM, he is back in the mansion and the rest of the scenario/alibi follows, including the nap.

Let us consider a different variation. For the next two scenarios, we have restored one of the Prosecution's Bronco sightings. Why did the Prosecution cut out of its timeline a Bronco seen parked for several minutes, lights on, in front of 875 South Bundy? At trial there were a total of three variations on the Prosecution's statements about this Bronco's movements. First, they reported it parked, lights on in front of Bundy. In their second version, it was first in front and then driven to the alley. In the third, the Bronco was eliminated entirely from being seen out front.

In this version, Simpson practices his golf swing and walks his dog, as he stated in his videotape. In addition to the early Bronco sighting, we also include the Akita barking during a time consistent with the reports of neighbors Robert Heidstra, Denise Pilnak, and others whose testimony was not included in the Prosecution scenario.

Simpson at Bundy—Alternative Timeline 2

PM

9:46	Simpson practices his golf swing and walks the dog.
10:02	Simpson calls Paula Barbieri, as the D.A. posited, but he calls her from Rockingham using the telephone in the Bronco. He scrapes his left hand on the cellular telephone.
10:05-25	Simpson turns on the TV and naps.
10:16	Rosa Lopez sees the Bronco at the Rockingham curb.
10:25-40	Simpson wakes, showers, packs, and dresses for his trip.
10:42	Simpson drives to Nicole's.
10:47	Simpson parks in front of Nicole's residence and hears sounds of "fighting and crying." The Akita is barking furiously.
10:50	Simpson flees the sounds of trouble. He may have seen someone familiar to him, acting alone. Or, he may have seen someone known to him as a professional killer.
10:55	Simpson returns to Rockingham.
10:56-57	Driver notes Simpson entering the house.

In this scenario, Simpson uses his nap as an excuse to cover for his time at Bundy. Let us reflect on what this scenario proposes: Simpson flees a scene where his wife and children, known to be at home, are in danger. Could this be the reason for the athletic hero's later ambivalent and seemingly guilty behavior? This is O.J. Simpson, cultural icon, powerful on the gridiron, and renowned as a celebrity—a man concerned about public image above all.

Simpson had, in fact, run away in the past from dangerously compromising situations involving Nicole, including the 1989 abuse incident when he simply got in his car and left. He had also, as we will see in another chapter, run away from narcotics and narcotics transactions, for fear of ruining his reputation and perhaps endangering his life.

Consider a third scenario.

Simpson at Bundy—Alternative Timeline 3

PM	
9:46	Simpson practices golf swing.
10:02	Simpson tries to call Paula Barbieri, but does not scrape his left hand or bleed.
10:05-25	Simpson turns on TV and naps.
10:16	Rosa Lopez sees Bronco at Rockingham curb.
10:25-35	Simpson showers and packs.
10:35-40	Simpson drives to Bundy.
10:40	Simpson arrives at Bundy, hears danger, sees two assailants, intervenes and cuts his left hand, and then flees and returns to Rockingham.

Two assailants are mentioned here—who could be there for various reasons, perhaps related to drugs, perhaps not. For now we look at the broad outlines of this scenario. Imagine Simpson's guilt in this third scenario: Nicole and/or Goldman would already be attacked or dying or dead, and Simpson, himself, would be in mortal danger. Perhaps he arrived during the attack and intervened but then, instead of heroically standing his ground, he flees, leaving not only Nicole and Ron but also his children inside the house in extreme jeopardy. According to our psychiatric source:

> O.J. Simpson, the man and the myth, would rather be dead or thought a murderer than an unspeakable coward who left his children as hostages to fate; would rather die or go to prison than be revealed as a figure of contempt and cowardice—in other words, not a man.

It is also possible that Simpson parked in front of 875 South Bundy and, while noting sounds and signs of danger, may have seen someone else surveying the area—another vehicle, perhaps, that he had good reason to believe belonged to a unit of law enforcement. Members of the Simpson circle were the subjects of narcotic squad surveillance on an irregular basis. Our independent investigators learned from neighbors who choose to remain anonymous that an unknown vehicle was parked near Rockingham that night around the time of the murders. Consider another variation.

Simpson at Bundy—Alternative Timeline 4

PM	
9:46	Simpson chips golf balls.
10:02-03	Simpson calls Barbieri. Scrapes his hand.
10:04-25	Simpson reads, watches TV, or naps.
10:16	Rosa Lopez sees Bronco at Rockingham curb.
10:21	Allan Park arrives in limousine.
10:25-42	Simpson showers, packs, and dresses for his trip.
10:43-48	Simpson drives to and arrives at Nicole's. Parks in front. Dog wailing, now, the dog Heidstra heard. The dog is an important clock. We have suggested it wails after the murders and after the killer or killers are gone.
10:49	Simpson enters walkway and discovers Nicole and Goldman dead. Panics. May see surveillance vehicle. We now know that there was an LAPD patrol car cruising in the area at exactly this time, according to Prosecution witness Schwab.
10:50	Simpson flees.
10:55	Simpson returns to Rockingham.

Four alternate scenarios that place the defendant at the Bundy crime scene: Do any ring true? One problem with all these scenarios is the fact that Allan Park, the limousine driver, is at Rockingham from about 10:20 to 11:15 PM. As

we have asked before, could he have missed hearing or seeing an arriving or exiting white Bronco, or any vehicle, for
that matter?

Assume, for the Prosecution's sake, that Park does not
hear the going and returning of the Bronco. In this case, our
analysis will allow these four variations. These timelines
permit O.J. Simpson this much involvement (and conse-
quent terror and guilt) but no more—always remembering
that within these scenarios the star is already perfectly
groomed for his trip, and thus the problem of his bloody
clothing does not arise.

What does arise, again, are the gloves and the socks. If
any of the preceding scenarios is accurate, how do we account for the gloves and the socks with the incriminating
blood on them? Could they all have been planted? We will
examine these questions in depth in Chapter Six.

For now, we will make a last observation about those
socks found lying in the middle of Simpson's bedroom rug.
Those who know Simpson find it remarkable that he would
leave a used pair of socks, bloody or not, on his white bedroom rug—dress socks that he had worn the night before
the murders to a charity event. Simpson was a man who
changed clothes completely several times a day and was
known for his neatness. Even acknowledging the simple errors known to expose otherwise "perfect" crimes, it does
strain belief to think Simpson would not have cast a backward glance into his room and noticed the socks. In his videotape, Simpson said that he had thrown those socks into
the dirty clothes hamper (after wearing them the night before the murders).

Then there is the matter of the police preservative fluid,
EDTA, found on the socks. The Prosecution tried to argue
that the EDTA was a result of a laundry detergent. If so,
then EDTA should have been found uniformly throughout
the socks. In fact, as the Defense experts pointed out, the
EDTA was present in the blood traces only, and not on the
surrounding areas.

We will leave it to the jury to take one of the above scenarios further by adding or subtracting information, in order to sculpt a coherent timeline and believable story . . .
while we move on to a different one: Simpson involved in the
murders with a confederate.

Simpson as Co-Conspirator

Note that in this scenario Goldman would arrive in what we have called the "early" time frame. For this scenario to work, Simpson will have to have coordinated with a confederate between the last time he was seen by Kaelin at Rockingham (about 9:35) and his/their arrival at Bundy to commit the murder. Seems difficult, does it not? A lot to do in not much time.

Simpson as Co-Conspirator—1	
PM	
10:03	Simpson calls Paula Barbieri, while driving, to establish alibi.
	Drives to meet co-killer at a designated place.
10:05	Killers arrive at 875 South Bundy to murder Nicole and Ron Goldman.

But the Goldman timeline does not have to deliver the victim to Bundy early at 10:05 or so, as the Prosecution posited. You recall that we also suggested a later timeline for Goldman that brings him to Bundy closer to 10:30 PM, having allowed him time to get home, dress in a more leisurely manner, and borrow a car.

This appears plausible at first glance, and it is, of course, the Prosecution's fall-back position. The problem with this clock is that for Simpson to be one of two killers or the one killer, he must be able to slash and struggle while (presumably) completely groomed and dressed for travel in an ensemble that included a white shirt.

The new scenario could play out as follows: O.J. must, either with a confederate or alone, virtually exsanguinate these two karate-trained friends. Nicole and Ron worked out at the gym together, and also studied martial arts. Ron was a trained athlete (tennis) in his physical prime, much quicker, at this time, than the slow-moving, golf-playing-only O.J., who could not even use his own tennis court because of his crippled knees. There was evidence that the victims did struggle against their assailant or assailants—the ground was torn up around Ron, there were marks on various parts of his body. Nicole's thumb ring (that her friends recall as tight-fitting), found on the steps, was more than likely lost as she resisted one or two murderers. Is it believable that O.J. could have killed both victims, or been one of the killers, or coordinated the killings, without sustaining one bruise on his body (except for a cut on one finger) or getting one drop of blood on his pristine, partly white clothing? Detective Tom Lange testified before the Grand Jury that:

> It was apparent to me that a violent struggle had ensued between a suspect and the two victims, so violent a struggle that it was entirely possible the suspect himself would have been injured.

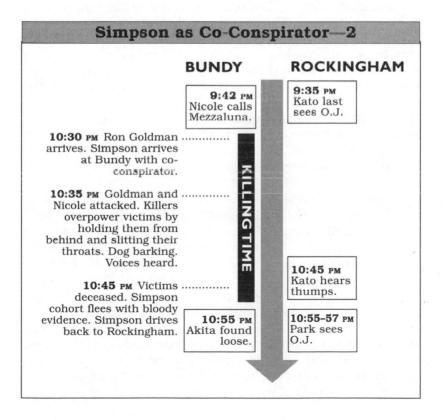

Simpson as Co-Conspirator—2

BUNDY	ROCKINGHAM
9:42 PM Nicole calls Mezzaluna.	**9:35 PM** Kato last sees O.J.
10:30 PM Ron Goldman arrives. Simpson arrives at Bundy with co-conspirator.	
10:35 PM Goldman and Nicole attacked. Killers overpower victims by holding them from behind and slitting their throats. Dog barking. Voices heard.	
10:45 PM Victims deceased. Simpson cohort flees with bloody evidence. Simpson drives back to Rockingham.	**10:45 PM** Kato hears thumps.
10:55 PM Akita found loose.	**10:55–57 PM** Park sees O.J.

KILLING TIME

What about the blood drops left at the crime scene and at Simpson's estate? Assume they come from Simpson. Then the victims did connect with him as they fought back. But how? There was a watchdog on the premises that evening— the Akita. It could have been present during the attack. Could the blood have come as the result of a dog bite? The Prosecution had argued that the dog loved its master O.J., and that is why it wailed instead of barking. And yet, all the witnesses that night who heard dog noises reported that the dog first barked, and then wailed. All the witnesses except for one, that is, the one witness the Prosecution called. Isn't it possible that seeing its mistress being attacked could have changed the dog's behavior toward its master—if it was its master attacking?

Picture a killer with a knife in a struggle against two strong, fit victims and a dangerous guard dog: Cut the dog's throat as soon as possible. But the dog is quick, and it bites the attacker, who pulls back. The knife blade cuts off the dog's tags instead. The fact that the Akita's dog tags were missing when it was found suggests that something like this may have happened.

Imagine the blood that would have come from the victims. Would not some of the rush of blood have stained the killers? Recall Sherlock Holmes' creator, Sir Arthur Conan Doyle, in a real-life case of a man falsely accused: "The most adept operator who ever lived would not rip up a horse with a razor upon a dark night and have only two, three penny-bit spots of blood to show for it. The idea is beyond argument."

Finally, if Simpson is a co-conspirator, you must believe that he could return to his home after 10:40 and not be seen or heard by Allan Park. Unless Simpson was not driving his white Bronco at all. The white Bronco could have been parked all evening on Rockingham, with Simpson driven to and from the crime scene by a confederate. This does not seem probable but it is just possible—if you believe that all the blood evidence in and on the Bronco was planted, or that there were two Broncos in use that night. But for this to be the answer to the riddle of the white Broncos at Bundy and Rockingham, you must find a virtually perfect Simpson conspiracy to murder coexisting with an equally perfect conspiracy on the part of someone else to frame the guilty man.

One more thought: Why would Simpson feel he needed help to murder Nicole all by herself? He could not have known he would find Goldman there. But he did know that Nicole was at home, with their two children, and with another child as a houseguest. Nevertheless, we must accept that he set out with a confederate (or by himself) to perform the bloody deed.

We have raised questions here that merit further investigation. Some may choose to pursue one of these or some variant co-conspirator scenarios, or to develop others, perhaps involving two Broncos in use that night—or even three. But we will forge ahead. As we proceed, we will be guided by an idea expressed centuries ago in ancient Athens by the first drama critic, Aristotle: "A likely impossibility is always preferable to an unconvincing possibility."

Of course it is possible that O.J. Simpson is the killer. And to many, no explanation is needed, so convinced are they of his guilt. But the timeline framework has not so far offered us a completely convincing scenario making Simpson the killer. Given that we have not yet come upon a clear explanation of exactly how he—either alone, or with someone—accomplished the double murders, does not the question before us then become: Was O.J. Simpson necessarily the killer or one of the killers? And if he was not, then who was? Shall we look to a "likely impossibility?"

Unexplored Evidence

A new scenario requires more evidence. Herein follows information that has been uncovered by our independent investigative team in the course of this study of these murders. Some of this material was previously known to the LAPD and to attorneys involved in the trial; but some material is the result of our own interviews and research. In every case, we believe that the material presented below has a bearing on the unsolved murders on Nicole Brown Simpson and Ronald Goldman, and that it is worthy of both consideration and greater investigation, the kind of official investigation that is beyond the reach of this study. As you read through our list you may want to know more. So do we. We include here all that we have discovered to date. Following the presentation of this material, we will construct new scenarios and timelines.

• LAPD logs reveal that an anonymous woman called 911 at around 10:30 on the night of June 12, 1994, to ask police if they had received a report of a "double murder" in the 800 block of South Bundy Drive. This was prior to the bodies being discovered and the murders reported. This stunning official entry has never been explained by the authorities. Did someone—perhaps even O.J.—pass by 875 South Bundy, see what had happened, and then report it anonymously to the authorities? If the person passing by was O.J., could he have asked Paula or his daughter, Arnelle, or his secretary, or some other woman friend to call 911 and report the crime?

• Evidence was gathered by the Defense pointing to a method of entry at Nicole's, possibly used by the killer or killers: through the back garage, using the remote entry instrument from Nicole's Jeep. The device has been missing since June 13.

• Police retrieved a set of bloody car keys from next to Goldman's body and returned them to his former girlfriend, from whom he had borrowed the car he drove to Bundy. This woman told the Defense that the keys were returned to her still caked with blood and, incredibly, that they had not been tested. This unexamined blood joins the untraced fingerprints at the scene as two significant forensics derelictions.

• As reported at trial, blood was found under Nicole's fingernails that did not match any of the principals' blood. Flesh was also found and, we have learned, this also went untested.

• Goldman's knuckles were swollen, strongly suggesting contact with an assailant, and suggesting some mark might have been left on the person receiving the blow or blows. (See Appendix for Goldman's autopsy report.)

- There appears to be a dog bite on the glove found at the crime scene, as well as a knife cut on the same glove, which to some suggests a left-handed killer.

- The Rockingham glove. We suggest you conduct your own experiment: On a night with conditions similar to those of June 12 (temperature was about 60 degrees), take a pair of leather gloves and pour wine or blood from meat on them. Put one out in the night, on the ground, from about 11 PM to 5 AM, and put the other in a closed plastic container. Check both gloves after this six-hour period. We believe that you will find that the glove left outside will be dry, and that the one packaged in the container will be moist. The glove found by Fuhrman at Rockingham was moist.

- The Rockingham socks. While you're at it, try another experiment. We have mentioned the socks found on Simpson's bedroom rug and described the Defense's argument that the socks showed tampering because of the way the blood and the EDTA appeared. This experiment addresses the position of the blood, not the EDTA. The Defense experts argued that the blood found on the socks did not seem to be the result of splatter from the crime scene, but rather of placement, from someone pressing blood onto the socks when they were not being worn. They concluded this because blood was found on both sides of the socks. Douse one sock with wine or blood from meat. Put a second sock on and splatter blood on it. Then compare the two socks. Our result: the one put on will, when removed, have dampness only on one side. The other sock will be wet on both sides because the wine will have soaked through. The socks found at Rockingham had blood on both sides.

- One of Nicole's tightly fitting rings was worked off her finger and found on the ground, indicating struggle.

- The knit cap discovered at the scene was so small that the D.A. never had Simpson try it on his large head at trial. A second knit cap was found inside the residence by Defense consultant William Pavelic, but LAPD refused to book it into evidence. Pavelic stated the existence of this cap in trial testimony.

- Most remarkable: Eight-year-old Sydney Simpson told police that she also heard a man call out, "Hey, hey, hey!" Precisely Robert Heidstra's testimony. Sydney Simpson's earwitness report is unexpected confirmation of Heidstra's testimony that he too, heard, "Hey, hey, hey!"

  Remember that Heidstra testified that he also heard a second voice. If that base voice belonged to O.J. Simpson, how could his daughter have failed to report the fact to authorities? That she did not undercuts the Prosecution's suggestion during the trial that Heidstra had heard Simpson verbally attacking Goldman.

- Defense investigator Pavelic found, further, that Robert Heidstra had told the police that he saw a white vehicle speed away south. Heidstra also confirmed his statement for this study. The police report, however, quoted Heidstra as stating that the sports vehicle sped north. Toward Rockingham, rather than away, to fit the Prosecution's timeline. Heidstra, at trial, tried to correct the statement to what he had actually seen—that is, a vehicle going south, away from Rockingham.

- Nicole's watch was noted by the coroner to have stopped at 10:03—PM or AM? Pavelic has learned that the watch was stopped at 10:03 PM.

- The Bundy gate was locked, but it had been knocked off center by the 1994 earthquake, so that it is possible that Nicole had to go down to the gate, after buzzing Ron in, to help open it. This sometimes was the case, as her friends have reported.

- Lipstick was found on Ron's cheek. This suggests that Nicole kissed him as he came in. We know he had gone home to clean up after Mezzaluna, so presumably the lipstick was not from someone at the restaurant. If it was Nicole's, it would have been placed there before the attack. This would mean that both were assaulted at once, and this strongly suggests two assassins.

New Entries in the Timeline

We have learned the following information in the course of this study:

June 12, 9:15 PM: A girlfriend of Sydney Simpson's had been at the restaurant with the family for dinner and had accompanied Nicole and the children home, intending to spend the night. At 9:15, the girl's parents came to Bundy to take her home because of a change in plans for the next day. (Note: O.J. knew of his daughter's plans and assumed that Sydney's friend was at Bundy for the evening.)

June 12, 10:00 PM: At about 10:00, a neighbor of Nicole's named Lange was walking his dog by Nicole's residence. He saw Nicole out front standing next to an expensive vehicle and embracing a man whose face he could not see. Lange turned away, only to be confronted by another man, possibly a bodyguard, who assumed a threatening martial arts posture. Lange, naturally intimidated, turned and left the immediate area.

June 12, 10:32 PM: A man visiting a neighbor of Nicole's heard a woman's scream at 10:32. Assuming it was Nicole, then she was alive and struggling. Add this witness to Heidstra and to Sydney Simpson: The death struggle, even if it lasts only eight minutes, takes the timeline up to at least 10:40—challenging timelines that include Simpson as one of the killers. (Bear in mind that the term "struggle" in this scenario includes talk, threats, argument, and, finally, deadly battery.)

Many neighbors who spoke with members of our team prefer to remain anonymous. While they feel that they have information pertinent to the unsolved murders, they are uncomfortable knowing that the killer (or killers) remain free. Their interest in having the mystery solved is genuine. We offer, therefore, a summary of what these various neighbors say they saw or heard the night of June 12.

Interviews with Bundy Area Neighbors

Between December 1995 and March 1996, we interviewed neighbors who lived in the vicinity of 875 South Bundy.

One informant, "Jane Jones," recounted the following observations of neighbors from the night of the murders after 10:30 PM.

- Several people saw a white Bronco.
- Two people saw a white Bronco with an African-American driving.
- One heard a dog barking.
- One heard voices.
- One heard a gate slam.
- One heard a scream.
- One man heard a woman scream at 10:32 PM, went to look in the alley, and did not see a white Bronco there.

All the informants believed, at the time of the trial, that O.J. Simpson was the killer. Because they all lived close to the crime scene, they had expected to be called to testify, but the Prosecution did not call any of them to testify at trial.

All these observations, except for the scream, were confirmed at trial by Robert Heidstra, Denise Pilnak, Judy Telender, Francesca Harmon, and Elsie Tistaert.

A word about the recollections of Denise Pilnak, who testified that her friend Judy Telender left her house at 10:21 PM and that the neighborhood had been quiet until

10:35, when a dog started barking, and continued barking for the next 45 minutes. At trial, she showed the jury that she was wearing two watches and described her acute awareness of time. She is a successful businesswoman and maintains impeccable records, files, diaries, journals, and accounts. Her telephone log for June 12 listed her call to her mother at 10:25 PM, lasting three minutes. It was shortly after that time that she heard the barking begin. Whereas some will find Pilnak's focus on time credible, Darden seemed to find it strange. He describes his reaction to Pilnak in his book.

> Denise Pilnak was next, giving the most detailed itinerary I'd ever heard from a witness. . . . How important was time to this quirky witness? At one point, she pulled up her sleeve to show that she was wearing two watches. [3]

The Prosecution also learned that another neighbor, Jamie Titel, was upset by the dog disturbance at 10:40 (he told police), and that a friend of Titel's heard a woman scream at around 10:35. But, in each case, this testimony produced a time equation fatal to the Prosecution's case, and thus these witnesses' observations were not included in the official Prosecution scenario. The time of the noises heard at Bundy overlapped with the time the defendant was supposed to have been making the thumping noises as he ran into the air conditioner outside Kaelin's room.

10:40–10:45 PM at Bundy: Barking, screams, shouts.
10:40–10:45 PM at Rockingham: Thumps on Kato's wall.

Simpson could not have been both places at the same time.

It is compelling to note that, with the possible exception of Rosa Lopez, all of the timeline witnesses who function as clocks to virtually exclude O.J. Simpson from the crime scene and the killing time—believe that he is guilty: Pilnak, Park, Heidstra, Kaelin, Shively, "Jane Jones," and the other neighbors. Except for Park, all of these were declared hostile witnesses by the Prosecution, and none of them could understand why. And yet together, these witnesses are the unwitting components of O.J. Simpson's alibi in terms of his fitting the official Prosecution scenario, the story that the jury was asked to believe in order to find him guilty.

The Independent Killing Time

We believe that our analysis has challenged both the early and late ends of the 10–11 PM killing time: Let's review the various windows within that hour in relation to all the known witnesses—both those who testified at trial and those who did not—who provide information about what they heard and/or saw at 875 South Bundy on June 12, 1994.

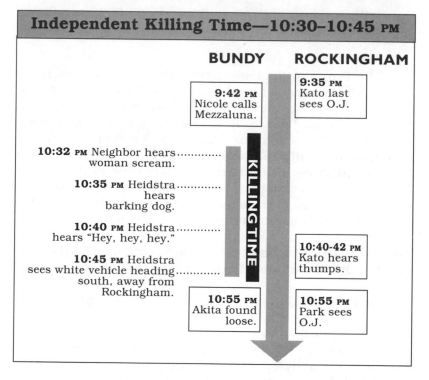

Independent Killing Time—10:30–10:45 PM

BUNDY   **ROCKINGHAM**

9:42 PM Nicole calls Mezzaluna.

9:35 PM Kato last sees O.J.

10:32 PM Neighbor hears woman scream.

10:35 PM Heidstra hears barking dog.

10:40 PM Heidstra hears "Hey, hey, hey."

10:45 PM Heidstra sees white vehicle heading south, away from Rockingham.

KILLING TIME

10:40-42 PM Kato hears thumps.

10:55 PM Akita found loose.

10:55 PM Park sees O.J.

If we place the killing time on the early timeline, between 10:00 and 10:30 PM, we have only one witness—Pablo Fenjves, who was called to testify for the Prosecution. What if we place the killing time later, from 10:40 to 10:59 PM? The logistics of travel, and getting back to Rockingham unseen and unheard by Allan Park, and arriving in time to create the thumps Kaelin heard about 10:45—seem to rule out Simpson. Therefore, we may choose to look in between these two windows, at the time that takes into account Heidstra, Sydney, and that unidentified man visiting a neighbor. We are then looking at a killing time window of about ten minutes, from 10:32 to 10:42 PM or, roughly, 10:30 to 10:45 PM. Heidstra, the unidentified man, Sydney Simpson, the dog = the new independent killing clock.

Bundy and Rockingham are now two islands in an ocean of time. Are these islands connected by a glove and a few drops of blood?

The competing timelines have brought us to the central contradictions in this case. Perhaps Simpson could have made it back to Rockingham under this scenario to make the thumps at the "right" time. Could he also have made it past Park, the limousine driver, and then emerged clean and dressed for his trip to LAX?

Nicole and Ron—Amended Timeline

This scenario brings Ron to Bundy in the early time frame, and includes the sighting of Nicole saying good-bye to a male visitor out front. We have also added the unplanned departure of Sydney's girlfriend, who had planned to sleep over, and the woman's scream heard by a neighbor at 10:32 PM.

Think about the time between Nicole's gentleman caller leaving and her death. It is possible that Nicole was knocked out and bruised inside the residence by an intruder, her gentleman caller, a stalker, a professional assassin, or, even, Goldman—but not by Simpson—until after 10:03 PM (remember, he is on the phone calling Barbieri at that time)—then moved and killed during the next half-hour; executed in a strikingly different fashion than Goldman. Nicole was professionally dispatched while Ron was hacked, slashed, tortured, slaughtered. Although the Prosecution claimed that Nicole's death pointed to someone who knew her, acting in a "jealous rage," others would contend that she was killed more quickly than Ron, in the manner of an execution.

Nicole and Ron—Amended Timeline

PM	
9:15	Sydney's girlfriend, who had planned to stay overnight, is picked up by her parents because of a change in their plans for the next day.
10:03	Nicole's watch is stopped violently at 10:03 PM. Its broken crystal suggests some strong impact.
10:03	Simpson is still at Rockingham or in his Bronco somewhere calling Paula Barbieri.
10:00-03	A neighbor sees Nicole with a man in front as he is preparing to leave.
10:03	Goldman can be at Bundy, especially if he is planning to bathe there, after first returning home and quickly changing clothes.
10:32	A woman is heard screaming by a man visiting a neighbor. We assume this is Nicole, alive but under attack.
10:30-35	Goldman is still alive, fighting for his life and calling out, "Hey, hey, hey!" Heard by both Robert Heidstra and Sydney Simpson.

Think about another bit of evidence—the "slow-moving, deliberate" size 12 Bruno Magli footprints: Could they have appeared later? Did they necessarily belong to the killer or one of the killers coming right back to find his missing hat and glove? To the point: Are we on the verge of discovering two separate actions (a) the murder, and (b) the coverup, or "tidying up," to use the Prosecution's words? There may be more sense in this double action than in supposing that an inflamed killer suddenly decided to stroll slowly back and forth in blood from front to back gate while a dog howled. Would not someone on the scene later, after the murders, (either "tidying up" or planting evidence) move deliberately, because the now-wailing dog had departed the premises after the killer's exit, and was roaming the area?

Does it not seem unlikely that a cold killer, while "tidying up," would note the loss of his glove and hat, look for them, and not find them? Does it make sense that the same calculating criminal would be capable of disposing of all the bloody evidence except the remaining glove, which he decides to toss or bury in his backyard, as the Prosecution suggested? What may make some sense is the concept of a killer planting evidence rather than losing it.

Planted Blood Evidence

The blood at Bundy and Rockingham seems to have been dropped in a kind of forensic timewarp. Reflect on the following questions, generated by a series of tests set in motion by Robert Shapiro, Defense co-counsel. Shapiro and others used eye droppers to test the size of liquid impressions from varying heights. Try it yourself.

The blood drops at both crime scenes display "no direction of travel," the forensic term that can indicate the possibility of planted blood drops. All the Simpson drops reflect an origin of only two feet from the ground. Further, at Bundy, there are drops leading from the killing ground west to the back gate; blood drops to the left of the retreating footprints, but there are no drops following the footprints back, when they return east to the area of the bodies, supposedly to search for the cap and left glove. The killer was bleeding as he left and not bleeding when he went back to look for the missing items?

The left glove is lost at the scene, but there are no bloody fingerprints from Simpson at the scene, in the Bronco, or at his home. No prints on the Rockingham right glove as we would expect if Simpson handled that glove with his bare left hand. No bloody prints anywhere.

The "directionless" blood drops at Rockingham, from the gate to the house, do not follow the path required for the defendant to have gone behind the guesthouse—where he dropped the glove. Yet Simpson states that he did scrape his finger on June 12, so he could have bled on his way to the house, but would have left no drops behind the guesthouse because he had no reason to go there. Are we dealing with true *and* planted blood?

A single killer could be soaked in blood from the death throes of Ron Goldman, especially on the left arm, hand, and side. But there is no blood from Goldman in Nicole's hair, where it should have been found if he pulled back her head to slash her throat after also attacking Goldman.

No blood from the victims at all was found on the Bundy walk where the Simpson blood drops were found, where, presumably, blood from Nicole or Ron would be discovered—unless there was a major cleanup by two killers. But if one of the two was Simpson, why was only his blood found on the walk, yet victims' blood found in the Bronco and on the bedroom socks?

A different timeline, now emerging, favors multiple killers. If we add Simpson to this timeline, in his Bronco in front of 875 South Bundy at 10:10 PM as the Prosecution originally stated, then a synthesis begins to emerge . . . . Hold this composite picture in mind as we now try to develop a profile for the mystery man or men at Bundy on that night.

To review, first, you must judge whether a killer, alone or not, and even armed with a knife or knives, could face and kill two young, quick victims, with a guard dog, and sustain no bloodstains or marks beyond the tiniest of scratches and a cut on one finger. Then, consider, given that Simpson was virtually unmarked (except for the cut on his hand), where did the blood smears in the Bronco come from, and those at Rockingham, and, above all, the blood on the Rockingham glove? These difficult questions were not answered by the lawyers in court, nor were they neutralized by the Defense's arguments, or by Simpson's post-trial statements of innocence in his televised interview, in his video, and during the civil trial depositions.

The most powerful evidence for multiple killers can, perhaps, be found in the autopsy reports found in the Appendix. Nicole's autopsy report describes multiple injuries to her hands as "defense wounds." The report on Goldman describes him as covered with "defense wounds." Read the report and visualize the violent encounters and judge whether there was one killer, or more that one.

A note in summary—based on new and old evidence, we may now be able to comprehend why the Prosecution was forced at trial's end to move up the time of Kato Kaelin's hearing the thumps, from 10:40 to 10:50 PM. The attorneys appeared to suspect, though the public did not, that the murders took place after 10:35—and that Heidstra, Pilnak, and Sydney Simpson were fatal earwitnesses to their proposed scenario and its earlier timeline. And in the case of

Pilnak, because she was speaking on the telephone to her mother just before hearing the screams, the Prosecution accepted her phone records as credible. This computer record also added credibility to her claim that she had seen a figure in the vicinity of 875 South Bundy after 10:40 PM.

This new evidence raises two related questions: (1) If Simpson could not be the source of the thumps on Kaelin's wall, who or what was? And why did Kaelin hear no footsteps after the thumps? Could the thumps have been deliberate, a signal? (2) if Simpson's white Bronco could not have sped (or snuck) back to Rockingham without Allan Park hearing or seeing something, in the stillness, then whose white vehicle was seen at Bundy?

The probability of two killers may now be the more widely held belief by the authorities. This possibility had been raised during the Preliminary Hearing when County Coroner Irwin Golden testified that the wounds to Goldman and Nicole were consistent with two knives. In fact, he restated this in April 1996 in his civil trial deposition. But the Prosecution did not call Golden to testify at the trial. Yet, even at that time, D.A.'s were confiding to former baseball luminary Steve Garvey that O.J. "was behind the murders"—suggesting a conspiracy. Dr. Lee testifying for the Defense also pointed to evidence of two killers.

A final word from the Source:

> The dog, the Akita—there were bloody paw prints going South on Bundy. Sixty feet south. Who was that dog chasing? Where are there any shoe prints going south? There are no photographs of anything except the prints going west, at the residence. But the police all saw the paw prints going south. Not west. South! Two killers!

Let us for now eliminate Simpson as a killer, and reduce his role to that of witness and potential victim, himself. Victim of whom? Who could these other killers be? Are we being insulted with theoretical pipedreams of Colombian drug lords?

Not Colombian, no. American.

Four

All-American Drugs

He [Simpson] would not permit any discussion of any tactic that would tarnish Nicole. He knew things. But he would've rather gone away than win that way, so we let quite a few leads stay very private. Even some of the lawyers really don't know the way this case could've gone, if we'd've had to prove innocence and do the police's work for them— but, hey, we don't. And once we knew we had enough for a "Not Guilty" and, remember, that jury was about to go south, and we wound up leaving out about 40 percent of our case, and we had dynamite.

A bove, is Defense consultant William Pavelic touching lightly on a whispered story going on behind the mass media melodrama. Behind the global wrestling match featuring those two official monsters, Simpson and Fuhrman— Sexual Abuse versus Racial Abuse—Pavelic is hinting at another kind of abuse: substance abuse.

When the Defense, early on, announced that the killings had some of the earmarks of a drug scenario, press, pundits, and police sang a chorus of ridicule. Even so, a number of drug-related stories about the defendant appeared in the press, including a wild tale of Simpson and Kaelin ingesting a cocktail of various illegal substances just before the murders.

The timelines have pointed out the problems in both the Prosecution's official storyline with Simpson as the lone maniacal slasher, and other scenarios that we have developed with Simpson as co-conspirator. We now move ahead into

an area worthy of greater investigation: the world of drugs
and violence surrounding the Simpsons and Goldman.

It is generally known that the victims, Ron and Nicole,
together with a circle of friends enjoyed a lifestyle of gyms,
resorts, discos, and restaurants. Above all, coffee bars and
restaurants. But it is not so generally known that some of
these restaurants were actually fronts for other activities that
come under the police heading of Organized Vice.

The Source:

> *They wouldn't touch _____ [a restaurant] be-
> cause they had outlets in three different areas and ties
> to Vegas, and they were "dirty": porno, call girls, and
> boys, and coke. And there was no way they were going
> to let Pavelic or Cochran open that particular can of
> worms.*

Beautiful young people migrate to Hollywood. One in
100,000 breaks into the entertainment industry. The rest
dream on, drifting into service as waiters, bartenders, and
restaurant personnel. Young, tanned, toned, they find themselves serving and servicing a wealthy clientele, sometimes
with needs and fantasies that involve eager young dream-
ers.

These restless "waiters" may find themselves working
at a bistro or club that turns out to be a recruitment ground
for prostitution and pornographic films, as well as a cover
for drug trafficking. Slowly but surely, these vulnerable
youths may be drawn into the underworld of drugs and prostitution, where the threat of violence may be just a breath
away.

According to Simpson in his post-trial video, in May and
June before the murders he had urged Nicole to free herself
from what he saw as a circle of parasites. "These people are
losers, they'll eat you up," he warned, reminding her that
she was a good mother, had property, money, and a future.
When she developed pneumonia in May, around the time of
her 35th birthday, Simpson came every day to care for her.
But by late May, Nicole would be reporting to her friends that
she had broken up with O.J. and finally felt free. By June 5,
Simpson was threatening to report her to the IRS as having
falsely declared Rockingham her place of residence to evade

taxes. On June 6, he sent her a typed letter stating that she could not use 360 Rockingham as residence or mailing address, also dissociating himself from "any action by you (Nicole) that might intentionally or unintentionally be misleading the Internal Revenue Service."[1]

At trial, Darden had hoped that Nicole's friend Cynthia Shahian would be allowed to testify about Nicole's reaction to the letter: "She's angry, she's upset, she's devastated, she's horrified." By June 9, at Nicole's request, her realtor Jeane McKenna had put the Bundy townhouse up for lease, while Nicole sped up her search for another place to live, one farther from Simpson. On June 10, just two days before being murdered, she had found a house to rent in Malibu.

All that summer of 1994, Nicole and Faye Resnick clung to their hopes for a restaurant or coffee bar of their own. "We wanted to stop being male-dependent, give up alcohol and drugs, and open up a Starbuck's coffee house," Resnick writes.[2] But Resnick was relapsing into her addiction to cocaine, a very expensive habit, and increasingly fearful for her own life as well as Nicole's. Ron also dreamed of opening a restaurant one day. "He had the details all figured out, right down to the doors and the menus. He even had the blueprints drawn up," Sheila Weller reports in *Raging Heart*.[3]

Amid such dreams and dislocations, strange things had been going on all year.

Criminal Activity Surrounding the Murders

Consider the following events, which occurred in the months before and after June 12, 1994. At the least, this information points to new scenarios.

- Paula Barbieri's car was stolen from a Beverly Hills parking lot on January 24, 1994, by a man named William Wasz. Police in Newport Beach who recovered the vehicle found a gun and a crackpipe in it. In July, Wasz's attorney turned over to the police a small notebook found among his client's things. In it were notes tracking Nicole's daily itinerary such as "the gym . . .12:00 noon. Tony Roma's, Ventura Bl. . . . " and other timed entries. However, some press in the L.A. area reported that it was the police who found the log. Although these versions conflict, the point of interest is the log, and the question: Who was keeping it? Wasz in now in jail.

- Someone other than O.J. Simpson was focused on her, Nicole knew, because she reported to friends that she had seen people near her residence and when she was driving, people who seemed suspicious and made her anxious. There were also telephone calls that were obscene both sexually and racially—calls that were so disturbing that she asked Simpson and several friends to drive by her condominium when they were in her neighborhood in the evening hours just to keep an eye on her and the children. This harassment helps explain information that came into the trial regarding Simpson's having been seen at night near her Gretna Green residence, where she lived before moving to Bundy in 1994.

- Two of Nicole's neighbors on Gretna Green Way were Carl and Catherine Boe Colby. The Colbys told the Prosecution that one night in early 1994 they had seen a black man walking in front of Nicole's residence. Thinking it "odd that a man fitting Simpson's description was in the neighborhood at that hour," they called the police. The misunderstanding was cleared up when Nicole explained that she was worried about someone other than her former husband stalking her.

- Prior to his murder, Goldman had received anonymous telephone threats, and one of his managers at Mezzaluna Restaurant had angrily warned him, "If you're fucking her [Nicole], you're in trouble." A witness reports that the manager was furious and was not referring to some threat from O.J. Simpson.

- According to sources and friends close to Goldman and his place of work, Ron was the object of an obsessive and abusive man who was jealous to the point of violence. This man, it is reported, expressed a raging hatred for Nicole and was stalking Ron, and threatening both of them if Ron did not break off his affair with her.

- Defense attorney Robert Shapiro's office was broken into and robbed during the trial.

- Faye Resnick's apartment was broken into in 1994, her journals rifled and stolen (she blamed the Simpson legal team).

- According to journalist Geraldo Rivera, another close friend of Faye Resnick's had been murdered some years before in San Francisco.

- Dr. Jennifer Ameli, a clinical psychologist who had counseled both Ron and Nicole, was in 1994 and 1995 harassed and threatened, her offices burglarized, and case files stolen. A specialist in relationship, marriage, and family counseling, Dr. Ameli also works with drug-related problems and the Tarzana Rehabilitation Center, and has a number of her clients in the entertainment field. In March 1996, she detailed for our interviewer, Ian Bowater, this list of intimidations.

  - Early in 1995, an anonymous telephone caller asked to purchase the files of Nicole and Ron. Dr. Ameli refused. A few days later, her office in Santa Monica was broken into and some files were stolen.

  - Police investigating the break-in removed from the scene other files and a bill addressed to Goldman. Concerned with client/therapist confidentiality issues, Dr. Ameli reported this to the Board of Behavioral Sciences of the Consumer Protection Agency.

  - A few weeks later, an unknown assailant approached Dr. Ameli from behind. He pushed and threatened her, telling her to keep her mouth shut about the Simpson case. She did not see his face or recognize his voice but could only tell that he was tall. During this time, she also received threatening telephone calls.

  - Sometime later, she was confronted near her Malibu home, which houses her second office. Subsequently someone broke into her house and office.

  - Fearing for herself and her family, Dr. Ameli reported all incidents to the police and asked for protection, but found them unsympathetic. She admits that her answers to police inquiries had to be evasive because she did not want to violate client confidentiality. She believes this may have antagonized the police.

Detective Tom Lange investigated the incidents involving Dr. Ameli, but no one from either the Prosecution or Defense teams interviewed her. The *National Enquirer* reported on the harassment and police encounters. Dr. Ameli believes the police treated her badly, describing their behavior as "insulting and victimizing." They even accused her of leaking information about her former clients to the press. In May 1996, Dr. Ameli was deposed for the civil trial, where she reiterated much of this information and dated three break-ins as having occurred between September 1994 and April 1995.

Such extensive harassment and burglary could point toward an organized group rather than a crazed lover. Who was Dr. Ameli's powerful tormentor? Other incidents included a man putting a gun to her back, another cutting her off in traffic—also warning her to keep her mouth shut. An electronic sweep of her home uncovered a number of installed listening devices.[4]

- Both O.J. and Nicole tell Kato Kaelin they have had neo-nazi threats by telephone and letter, 1993–94. The terrorists attack their interracial union, and their ties to Jews.

- O.J. tells a friend he found his kitchen door open, late at night, June 11, 1994, the night before the murders. Inside, he finds a strange message on his answering machine, which seems to be in a foreigm language.

- Simpson had been followed and cornered on a freeway by three cars. (See Appendix for Simpson's statement to LAPD June 13, 1994.)

- O.J.'s friend Charles Minor, a record company executive, is slain in Malibu in March 1995.

Violence Surrounding Ron Goldman and His Restaurant Colleagues

The pattern of violence surrounding Ron Goldman and his restaurant colleagues bears close scrutiny. Two were murdered, and another two are missing. This totals five young men either killed or in extreme jeopardy, all under suspicious circumstances.

- Nicole, Ron, and Faye were steady dancing customers at Brett Cantor's Hollywood nightclub, The Dragonfly. (Ron had worked for Cantor previously). On July 30, 1993, less than a year before Ron and Nicole's murders, Cantor was slashed to death in a knife attack nearly identical to the attack of June 12.

  Cantor, too, had been cut from behind. The killer, ripping from the lower left side of the neck, sliced up and to the right. Like Goldman, this friend was stabbed repeatedly on the arms and chest. As with Goldman and Nicole, the knife used had a long, thin blade, as experts determined from the wounds.

- A restaurant colleague's car was torched in 1994 in Corona Del Mar, California.

- A second friend's life was threatened at his Aspen Colorado night club. Both potential victims have disappeared and must remain nameless while the search for them continues.

- Michael Nigg, a fellow waiter at Mezzaluna, was gunned down in Hollywood by killers unknown, in September 1995. According to authorities in the Aspen and Denver areas, Nigg was involved in the narcotics culture of Colorado.

The Aspen resort is a place name in the story of Nicole, Ron, Faye, O.J., the Mezzaluna crowd, and all the rest of the Simpson circle. Keith Zlomsowitch, Director of Operations at Mezzaluna in Brentwood, held the same title at the Mezzaluna in Aspen and at another California branch. Zlomsowitch testified before the Grand Jury that he and

Nicole had an affair during April and May of 1992.

Brentwood and Aspen . . . restaurant workers and violent crime . . . were Goldman and his fellow restaurant employees at risk? What could they have had in common besides knowing each other through their work? Is it possible
that Goldman could have been the target on June 12? Or
both that Goldman and Nicole were targets?

The Buffalo Drug Connection

Incidents of burglary, spying, threatening, stalking,
and murdering surround the Simpson affair. There is even
more that touches the football great but does not yet im-
plicate him, information that points back in time, to Buffalo in upstate New York, where O.J. started his professional football career with the Buffalo Bills.

- On June 26, 1994, just two weeks after the Bundy murders, Casimir "Butch Casey" Sucharski, 48, was murdered in Miramar, Florida, along with two young women
  companions, Sharon Anderson and Marie Rogers.
  Sharon Anderson, 25, was an aspiring model from Miami who hung around with celebrities including Phillip
  Michael Thomas. Marie Rogers, 25, lived in Pembroke
  Park with her family and three-year-old daughter.[5]

  Sucharski, who had moved from Buffalo to Florida in
  the early 1980s, had a reputation as a playboy and was
  once caught in a drug sting aimed at O.J. Simpson.
  Sucharski had owned a bar in Buffalo in the 1970s that
  was one of many Simpson, then a Buffalo Bills super-
  star, frequented. According to the *Buffalo News,* these
  bars and restaurants played a role in the cocaine ex-
  perimentation of the time. Michael Militello, a club
  owner and longtime O.J. friend, describes cocaine as
  "a big part of the Buffalo night life in the 1970s."

Not surprisingly, Buffalo at that time was the target of
organized crime task forces, both state and federal. Then,
as now, there is a constant fear in big-time sports of illegal

activity on the part of athletes or management—tying drugs to debts to point fixing—that could cost the league and owners hundreds of millions of dollars in lost revenues from an enraged sports public. As an honored guest in these various "connected" clubs and as a prominent athlete, Simpson, too, would certainly have been under heavy surveillance during this period.

According to various sources:

- In 1975, Sucharski was staying at the apartment of a friend, Michael Militello, another bar owner, when police raided the apartment. The investigation was aimed at Militello and O.J. Simpson, who was then playing for the Buffalo Bills and hung out in Militello's bar. A detective told the *Buffalo News* that police thought Simpson used cocaine and supplied it to other professional athletes.[6]

- Authorities were watching others close to Simpson in Buffalo, including the owners of major businesses in the area.

- After leaving Buffalo, Simpson was a substantial investor in a business founded by Los Angeles developer Michael Goland. Simpson had nothing to do with Goland's hiding his control of the Viking Savings and Loan, a crime that put Goland in prison.

- At some time in the 1990s, according to a source close to Simpson, "O.J. considered making a very large investment in a new sports franchise, but pulled out when he discovered mob connections."

The question for the larger jury is whether or not there is a common denominator to this drug culture that ties into the killing time of June 12, 1994. One of the foremost contemporary historians of this murky world of vice and vice squads is Alex Constantine. By early 1995, Constantine had come forward with a report, *The Florida/Hollywood Mob Connection,* which linked the murders to narcotics. Constantine cites mainstream sources for this report, including: the Associated Press; Thomas Burdick's and Charlene

Mitchell's *Blue Thunder* (Simon & Schuster); The *Los Angeles Times*; Mike Rothmiller's and Ivan G. Goldman's *L.A. Secret Police* (Pocket Books); Charles Rappleye's and Ed Becker's *All-American Mafiosa: The Johnny Rosseli Story* (Doubleday); and *The Philadelphia Inquirer*.

Drugs and Organized Crime in Brentwood

One common denominator linking drugs to organized crime in Brentwood is Joey Ippolito, Jr. Here is historian Alex Constantine in his report, *The Florida/Hollywood Mob Connection*, writing about "Joey the Ip":

> *Joey Ippolito is second-generation Mafia, one of several powerful successors of Meyer Lansky . . . . Ippolito's influence in the Combination [organized crime] is felt from Philadelphia to Dade County, Florida, to Southern California. A former speedboat racer, he headed for California in 1988 after completing a 40-month prison sentence for marijuana smuggling. He opened, without flourish, Cent'Anni, a fashionable Italian restaurant in Malibu, and distributed cocaine in Santa Monica and Brentwood.*
>
> *Among Ippolito's distributors was bodybuilder Rod Columbo, his life ended with three shots to the back of the head on January 7, 1992. Columbo himself had been the leading suspect in the murder of cocaine dealer Rene Vega in 1989. He worked in Malibu at Cent'Anni until the restaurant folded in 1991. At this time Columbo began to travel extensively. His body was found slumped over the wheel of a 1984 Cadillac in southern New Jersey. LAPD Detective Lee Kingsford told reporters that the West Coast consensus was that the murder had been drug-related.[7]*

We find both Ippolito and his business ventures connected in various ways with Brentwood people and the Simpson circle.

- A.C. Cowlings was allegedly an occasional bodyguard to Ippolito. When police came to arrest the gangster and found Cowlings visiting, they also questioned him about Joey the Ip's business.

- Ippolito's housemate was Ronnie Lorenzo, owner of another chic restaurant, Splash. Ippolito and Lorenzo were both sentenced to ten years for the distribution of cocaine in Santa Monica and Brentwood. Joey the Ip fled, becoming a fugitive from justice one month before the Bundy Drive murders.

- In February 1995, as the trial got underway, Alex Constantine broke another related story that was picked up by the Associated Press on March 25:

  That Simpson and Cowlings had more in common with Ippolito than point spreads became evident with the arrest of Tracey Alice Hill, alias Amanda Armstrong, a 32-year-old stripper from Santa Monica, in February 1995. Hill was nabbed by police in Dunsmuir, a small town in northern California, with a suitcase containing 40 pounds of cocaine. Police also found a vial of pills in her purse prescribed to Cowlings. Donald Re, his attorney (a former law partner of Howard Weitzman) denied any connection to Hill, but the Contra Costa Times *reported that Hill's computerized address book listed the telephone numbers of both Cowlings and Simpson.*

- The narcotics connection to the case, if there is one, was covered closely only by the tabloid press. *The Star*, for instance, quoted private investigator Barry Hoestler, who did some work for the Simpson Defense, as contending that Nicole and her friends "were over their heads with some dope dealers," and that Nicole and Ron wanted to open a restaurant based on the cocaine trade. Where would the funds for such a venture be found?

- A man Nicole had dated was associated with the world of narcotics. O.J. Simpson confronted the gentleman caller on at least one occasion.

• Faye Resnick, who was by her own report involved with Nicole in restaurant discussions, writes that she and Nicole discussed their plans for some thirty-five minutes by telephone on the murder night between 9:00 and 10:00 PM. Resnick, who originated the call from the Exodus House drug clinic, to which she had committed herself, reported later that their talk had been full of hope for the future.

But recall Sydney Simpson's statement to police that she heard her mother "fighting and crying" with "Mommy's best friend." If Resnick was that best friend on the phone, then their talk touched upon something in addition to those hopes for the future.

Christian Reichardt, Brentwood chiropractor, friend to O.J. Simpson, and Faye Resnick's former fiance, comments on what he believes would have been Faye's state of mind at the time of the call. The following is from his interview with our chief researcher, Ian Bowater. The interview took place at Starbuck's, across from Mezzaluna Restaurant, on February 17, 1996.

> **I.B.:** (Ian Bowater): *Tell me about Sydney's statement about "Mommy crying and fighting with her best friend." Faye says they were having an upbeat conversation with Nicole about opening a restaurant.*
>
> **C.R.:** *Have you ever been to one of these rehab places and seen the people there? Believe me, after four days, and this was Faye's fourth day, they are not "upbeat." I saw Faye on that Sunday. After four days of withdrawal this woman was not upbeat.*
>
> **I.B.:** *Could the argument have been with someone else? Why would Sydney call Faye "Mommy's best friend" and not "Faye"? It's a funny thing for an eight-year-old kid to say.*
>
> **C.R.:** *That's Sydney. She's a bright little kid and very up front. She probably said, "Faye" and when the cops asked, "Faye who?" She'd say right back, "You know, Mommy's best friend." That happens with the cops. They ask two questions, get two answers and splice them together. A lot of that went on in this case.*

C.R.: *The white, middle-class intellectuals are go-ing to have a shit fit when they hear what really went on during this trial. All the people who were leaned on, pressurized to change their testimony, even lie in court.*

I.B.: *Can I quote you? This can all be "off-the-record," if you like.*

C.R.: *I'm going "on-the-record."*

I.B.: *I can quote you?*

C.R.: *I mean I'm already going "on-the-record."*

I.B.: *Oh, you mean a deposition for the civil trial.*

C.R.: *No. Somewhere else. In a few weeks. I've had enough of this. People should know what really went on.*

I.B.: *How did you get to know O.J.?*

C.R.: *I was Faye Resnick's boyfriend. About a year before the murders, O.J. and Nicole were trying to get back together. Part of that was an agreement to share friends and meet other people. Faye and I started going out with them in a foursome. That's how I got to know O.J. We'd talk . . . . I started play-ing golf again. Then things started going crazy with Faye and Nicole. So O.J. and I would talk . . . friends . . . . I was going through some stuff with Faye so we shared experiences. That's how I became close to him . . .*

I.B.: *What do you mean by "crazy"?*

C.R.: *You know on-and-off-again stuff. I kicked Faye out of my house three or four times. It was the same with Nicole. Did you know that O.J. told Nicole that he didn't want her in his life . . . about three or four weeks before it happened?*

I.B.: *When you were all hanging out together did you get to know Ron Goldman?*

C.R.: *No.*

I.B.: *Did you all go to Mezzaluna?*

C.R.: *No. That was the girls' place. When we went out it'd be Toscana or some place in Beverly Hills. The girls kept their stuff separate.*

I.B.: *The girls?*

C.R.: *There was Ron and Cora Fischman in the group too.*

I.B.:   *Cora is in Texas now?*

C.R.:   *No. She's back in L.A. The girls had their own places, dance clubs and favorite restaurants. Mezzaluna was their place. I've been there for lunch or sat outside with an espresso but not with the group.*

C.R.:   *For a start, Faye never kept a diary. In February of that year [1994], Faye had elective surgery. I was against it because I knew she had previous problems with drugs. The painkillers set her off again.*

I.B.:   *Did you think that drugs had anything to do with the "crazy stuff"?*

C.R.   *Oh yes. There was definite drug behavior.*

I.B.:   *What about Nicole? Did she . . .?*

C.R.:   *In Faye's intervention Nicole admitted to using a couple of times . . . I'm dead against drugs. I wouldn't have them in the house. Especially not with her daughter around. Faye was going over to Nicole's place and freebasing over there.*

I.B.:   *Freebasing is like crack, yeah?*

C.R.:   *Sort of, I think.*

I.B.:   *Did Nicole freebase?*

C.R.:   *She was doing some drugs.*

I.B.:   *And Cora?*

C.R.:   *No. Cora did not go with them on all their jaunts round the clubs and places. I don't think she was around the drug stuff.*

I.B.:   *But didn't Nicole lead the intervention that got Faye into rehab?*

C.R.:   *No, that was me. Nicole was against doing the intervention that evening. She said we could hold off. But I insisted and got everybody together. Faye was in a very bad way. Freebasing is no joke.*

I.B.:   *Do you think they ran up debts?*

C.R.:   *They had to. Nicole was using up her money every month. I mean she was spending on the kids too. But Faye had no money, maybe two thousand dollars at the most.*

I.B.:   *She said she lent you money for your practice.*

C.R.:   *(laughter) I gave her a job but had to fire her* *after a few days. I never gave her money and she never had any to give me. Someone told me that if you have a freebasing habit you're going to get through more than one thousand dollars a day! They must run up some debts.*

I.B.: *Where were they getting the drugs? Who was supplying them on credit?*

C.R.: *I don't know. I went through all my telephone records to see if she was calling her dealers from her house. But she wasn't. She knew what I thought about drugs. I think she did it from Nicole's place . . . . Or on her mobile phone.*

I.B.: *There would be records.*

C.R.: *I told the Defense as well as the investigators from the LAPD but I don't know what they did with that. The Defense wasn't so great sometimes.*[8]

A cocaine habit costing over a thousand dollars a day? Resnick told Exodus House, when she checked in, that her addiction was a small matter of about $30 a day. Resnick has vehemently insisted that her commitment to Exodus House does not imply that she had a major drug habit or owed major sums of money that could have somehow been connected to the events of June 12. In her April 1996 deposition before the civil trial, Resnick stated that Christian Reichardt has lied about her many times, that he is a scorned lover, and that he did not become close friends with Simpson until after the murders.

Whatever her habit cost her, Resnick does not deny the cocaine use. Again we must ask, what is the connection between drugs and murder? Robin Williams discussed his $200-a-day cocaine habit in an interview in *The Star:*

. . . I decided to quit cold turkey. After one final sale I told "Angel" [the supplier] that this was my last day. He smiled and shook his head. He knew I would be back . . . . Years later a friend told me who Angel was. He's a professional hit man who kills people for a living. Normally, he would never let someone just walk away from drugs like that. I guess he must have liked me, perhaps I made him laugh. Had I known that at the time, I don't know what I would have done. I just thank God I didn't.

Compare the Bundy murders with the Charles Manson "family" slaughter of Sharon Tate and others in Hollywood in the 1970s. The connection between the ex-con drifter Manson and the film elite he ordered butchered was drugs. Manson had not picked his victims at random. He was a psychotic drug dealer, and to throw the police off the track he planted false evidence that pointed to the Black Panthers as the killers.

A last note on the matter of the telephone conversation between Nicole and Faye the night of the murders. On February 15, 1996, on CNN's *Burden of Proof*, Simpson in conversation with journalist Greta Van Susteren said:

> *Sydney Brooke, my daughter, maybe the last words she heard from her mother was her mother crying on the phone talking to Faye Resnick. Faye Resnick tells the world that she was giggling. Nicole couldn't have been giggling with this woman. And Sydney's a smart girl. She knows if her mother's crying or giggling.*

"From Day to Day I Didn't Know Who She Was"

Was it Nicole Brown Simpson who was out of control after the marriage breakup? Were both O.J. and Nicole "lost?" Nicole had moved out of Rockingham in January 1992, and the divorce was final in November. Weller reports in *Raging Heart* that O.J.'s new life alone was not a happy one: "He was devastated by Nicole's leaving, friends report. As he had after the 1989 beating, he lost a great deal of weight."[9]

But by April 1993, when Nicole did an about face and decided that she was ready to go back to O.J., he was seeing Paula Barbieri, and his sentiments about Nicole had changed. Weller cites various friends who then saw Nicole desperately pursue her former husband. According to Weller, Nicole duplicated the tapes of their marriage and their children's births, sending them to O.J with a final reconciliation plea. He gave in.[10]

Their trial reconciliation began in May 1993, but it was destined to be short-lived. By October their relationship was once again dangerously volatile, erupting on October 25 when Nicole called 911. By June 1994, there were signs that Nicole was again in transition. Her life had started changing dramatically as she came to know other men—after she and O.J. had separated. Unlike Simpson, she had been monogamous during their marriage and she was now fully enjoying her independence.

Nicole's friends Ron Shipp and Kris Jenner are quoted in Weller's book as thinking that she was spinning out of control: "Toward the end," says Kris Jenner, "you never knew in the morning where you'd find Nicole." Ron Shipp called Nicole on her birthday, May 19, and her tone of voice worried him. Weller writes, "It seemed to Ron as if she (Nicole) was now leading a confused and fast-track life."[11]

Here, listen to Simpson's civil trial testimony about the scene he came upon one night at Nicole's in 1992. The man with Nicole is Keith Zlomsowitch, Mezzaluna Director and one of many men Nicole dated between 1992 and 1993. Simpson also talked about this incident—in a much more emotional state—during Nicole's 911 call in October 1993.

> **Q:** *Describe what you saw.*
> **A:** *I was walking to her front door, and her drapes were open on a window. As I was approaching her front door, I saw her, and I looked and saw her with—I didn't know who the guy was because I couldn't see the guy, and she was obviously involved in sex, so I left.*
> **Q:** *Was that oral sex?*
> **A:** *That's what it appeared to be, but I really couldn't see, but that's what it appeared to be.*
> **Q:** *Now, what time of evening was this?*
> **A:** *It was at night. I would say it was midnight to 1:00 maybe, 11:00 to 1:00, somewhere in that area, I would say.*
> **Q:** *Were you invited to Nicole's house that night?*
> **A:** *No.*
> **Q:** *You just went on your own?*
> **A:** *Yes.*

Q: *This was during the time that you were separated and in divorce proceedings. Right?*

A: *That's correct.*

Q: *When you saw her through the front window having sex with Keith or with this man, what did you do?*

A: *I turned around and walked out, and I hit the doorbell as I walked out of her gate.*

Q: *You hit the doorbell?*

A: *Yeah. I just hit it: so they might be aware that they were kind of in the open.*

Q: *You mean that people could see.*

A: *Yeah. If somebody was walking up to the front door, it'd be pretty tough not to see.*

Q: *You didn't knock on the door?*

A: *No.*

Q: *How long were you at a place in front of her door where you were watching or where you could see her?*

A: *Where I saw. Five to ten seconds that I actually saw, yes.*

Q: *And did it bother you when you saw her having sex with this man?*

A: *I was stunned.*

Q: *You were angry?*

A: *No. At the time I was just stunned. Because I had been with her for at that time 15 years, and even if I had not been with her, I think I would have been stunned to see—if I walk up on anybody having sex, that would stun me.*

Q: *Was there any other reason you were stunned?*

A: *I don't think I needed any more reason to be stunned. My kids were there. It was very open. It's just not something you would expect to see, walking outside. You just wouldn't expect to see.*

Q: *The next day did you go back to Nicole's place?*

A: *Yes. I wanted to discuss that, what I had saw, with her.*

Q: *And when she was involved with Keith and other men, you were unhappy about that. Right?*

A: *No.*

Q: *You were jealous about it. Right?*

A: *No.*

Q: *Was Keith the first man after your separation that you knew that she was involved with?*

A: *Well, basically yes.*

Q: *Who were the other men she was involved with?*

A: *A guy named Alejandro.*

Q: *Did he have another name?*

A: *I didn't know another name.*

Q: *So the only two men that you knew Nicole was romantically involved with during that time frame were Keith and Alejandro. Is that right?*

A: *I didn't know that. I saw her with Keith, and she told me right when it was over it was a mistake and a one-night thing, and Alejandro I knew had been around, yes.*

Q: *One-night thing?*

A: *That's what she said. She said it was a mistake. They were drunk and loaded, evidently.*

Q: *What about Joseph Perulli?*

A: *She came to my house to talk to me about Joseph.*

Q: *What did you say to her?*

A: *I told her to just be yourself. You're gorgeous. What is there for him not to like, plus you ain't gonna cost him a dime.*

Q: *Why is that?*

A: *Because she was getting plenty of money from me.*

Q: *So you still wanted to get back with Nicole when she came to talk to you about Joseph.*

A: *I would have, yes. I would have.*

Q: *But you told her to do what she wanted. Right?*

A: *No. I gave her the best advice I can give her. She found a guy who she liked, and if your wife told you that there's a guy that she was crazy about, I think you would move on, and that's what I did.*

Q: *What about a guy named Brett Shaves?*

A: *Okay. Brett Shaves I found out about at one of our divorce hearings. She just told me about him.*

Q: *Were there any other men?*

A: *There was a few guys. I can't recall their names. Marcus Allen, and a few guys, I can't recall their names.*

Note: Marcus Allen was a close friend of O.J.'s, a running back for the Kansas City Chiefs. Although Allen publicly denies having had any romantic involvement with Nicole, many friends of the Simpsons have commented on Nicole's affair with the handsome black athlete, a man some described as "a younger version of O.J."

Q: *When did you find out Nicole's relationship with Marcus Allen?*
A: *I think it was the last week of March of '93.*
Q: *This is before Nicole started pursuing you to resume a relationship with you?*
A: *No. This was in the midst of her pursuing me to resume a relationship with her.*
Q: *And was Marcus Allen married at the time?*
A: *No. He was planning a marriage at my house at that time.*
Q: *What did Nicole relate to you about Marcus Allen?*
A: *That he had been coming around. Originally she was telling me that he wasn't my friend, that he was coming around. She started crying. We were at dinner. And that evidently something had happened at some point.*
Q: *You mean they had sex?*
A: *Yes.*
Q: *Now, Marcus was a good friend of yours. Right?*
A: *Yes.*
Q: *And when you learned this, were you surprised to hear this?*
A: *Yes.*
Q: *Were you upset about it?*
A: *Probably, yes.*
Q: *And what did you do about it.*
A: *I asked for a check.*
Q: *And you guys went home?*
A: *I took her back to her car, and I went home.*
Q: *Did you then talk to Marcus about this?*
A: *The following week.*
Q: *And what did you say to Marcus?*
A: *I told Marcus, do me a favor and ease up on Nicole, because whatever's happening with you guys is really screwing her up. She's like going*

bonkers.
Q: *Did Nicole tell you to do that?*
A: *Yes.*
Q: *What did she say to you?*
A: *Well, when I dropped her off at her car, I said: "So, you know, why you telling me this? Why are you telling me?" And she was saying: "Because he's calling me." And he just called that day, I guess, and wanted her to meet him in Miami, and she thought it was wrong. And I said, "Why don't you tell him you're gonna tell Katherine (Marcus's fiancee)?" And she said she didn't want to screw up his relationship, and that if I told him, he'd stop.*
Q: *Did it stop then to your knowledge?*
A: *I assume so. To my knowledge, yes.*
Q: *What did Marcus say to you when you suggested that he back off?*
A: *He was in a room with people; he said nothing, but the next week, I was taking a nap and he walked into my bedroom and apologized.*
Q: *Now, did you ever learn that Nicole was seeing Marcus again in 1994?*
A: *No.*
Q: *In about March, April or May or June?*
A: *No.*
Q: *Did anybody tell you that they saw his car at Nicole's at Bundy?*
A: *No.*
Q: *Did anybody tell you that he was in town during that time frame, let's say March through June?*
A: *I played golf with him, so I'm sure he was in town.*

Marcus was, indeed, in town and Nicole was seeing him again, according to Resnick, Cora Fischman, and other friends. Resnick's description of the time Nicole told O.J. about Allen plays somewhat differently from O.J.'s recollection. Resnick claims that Nicole told her that while she and O.J. were dining at a chic Santa Monica restaurant, around May 1993, O.J. demanded that she confess about the men in her life; and that when she told him about Allen, he exploded. Resnick writes that a romance with Allen was "strictly taboo," because he was "black and beautiful and a football hero, too . . . a better-model O.J."[12]

If we are to believe the many friends who have placed Marcus Allen back in Nicole's life in June 1994, we now have another man, besides Simpson, who might have been seen at Bundy the night of their murders, although this possibility seems to have escaped the criminal investigation. So, too, did the authorities downplay the presence of the drug culture that lay in and around the Simpson circle. Now, let us see where these new topics can lead us, as we turn the pundits' mocking question on its head—If O.J. did not commit the murders, then who did?

And who was parked that night on Rockingham and, possibly, Bundy; who could have walked deliberately back to the Bundy front gate not to retrieve but to plant one of the brown gloves; who telephoned threats and followed and kept a time log on Nicole; who broke into the quarters of four principals in the case? And who—on the night of June 11, 1994—broke into Simpson's Rockingham home? This latest addition to the break-in timeline became public in 1996, just as proceedings for the civil trial were to begin. O.J. had returned home to find his back door open and a message on his answering machine in a foreign language.

There was some terrible trouble brewing around Nicole Simpson, Ron Goldman, Faye Resnick, and O.J. Simpson all that summer. By June 8, Resnick had relapsed into her cocaine habit for the third time and had committed herself to Exodus House; a few days later, O.J.'s home had been entered; somebody (not O.J., the evidence indicates) had stolen Nicole's house keys and garage door opener; Nicole was receiving threatening calls (not from O.J.); Ron Goldman had been warned at Mezzaluna he could be in trouble if he continued to see Nicole. Before her commitment to Exodus House, Faye describes herself as fearful to the point of paranoia, begging Nicole to leave her children behind and flee with her to another country. Twinning their destinies, Faye was convinced that O.J. had someone following them and that both she and Nicole might be killed.[13] Ron, Faye, Nicole all had serious money problems; narcotic squad surveillance was closing in . . . a crisis was at hand.

Simpson, in his post-trial video:

Why doesn't someone look at her [Resnick's} past? San Francisco. Did another of her friends get murdered? Did she leave the country? . . . Why so many lies after her friend is murdered?[14]

In his deposition for his civil trial, O.J. detailed his state of mind around the time of the murders:

Q: *[Right after the killings] were you feeling you were being attacked in the sense that you believed the press was pointing the finger at you as the person who killed Nicole?*
A: *My pain was for Nicole more than what they [the media] were doing. That was just all a part of it.*
Q: *The loss of Nicole?*
A: *Yes.*
Q: *You loved her?*
A: *Very much.*
Q: *And you loved her on June 12?*
A: *I loved her. Yeah. I didn't want to live with her, but I loved her, yes.*
Q: *How was she acting differently [in the months before the killings]?*
A: *Well, she was just not herself. She was a different person every time I talked to her. When I was in Puerto Rico, she seemed to be having a nervous breakdown; she even said she was, and I suspected it was drinking. I had hoped it wasn't pills or drugs, which I knew her friends were involved in, and I was hoping and still hope to this day that she wasn't involved in that.*
Q: *And how did these problems manifest themselves in her behavior toward you?*
A: *She was erratic. She was—from day to day I didn't know who she was. Then it didn't matter to me because I got out of the relationship.*

Taking O.J.'s viewpoint: He knew only too well how dangerous Bundy had become, between Faye's drug use and Nicole's forays into sex. The Simpsons' friends saw trouble signs as well. O.J. says Cora Fischman had warned him that Nicole was in harm's way, that he ought to "get Nicole and the kids away." Reading between the lines . . . what if the choice he actually had to face involved either taking Nicole back or away, or paying off certain people demanding money? And if Simpson did neither, and death came to Nicole, would not his behavior seem both guilty and innocent? Could the guilt so apparent in his actions after the murders stem not from something he did, but from something he would not, or could not do?

If that was the case, then why the silence about the real killers? Why, indeed. Even life in prison is preferable to a certain death warrant ordered against you or your children by organized crime—if the truth is revealed.

To move our analysis along, let us assume this speculation about the nature of O.J. Simpson's "innocent" guilt, or remorse, is correct. This might mean then, that in a very real way, Simpson was also a target or even the target on the night of June 12. Between the lines of the Simpson deposition and his post-trial video, and against the backdrop of sex and drugs in Brentwood and within the Simpson circle, new scenarios emerge.

Organized Crime and the Bundy Murders

On May 22, 1996, an informant swore in an affidavit, given to Donald Freed, that:

1) O.J. Simpson was suspected by a narcotics kingpin of having informed on him, in order to escape from unrelenting pressure to buy and sell narcotics.

2) The kingpin was arrested and sentenced to ten years in prison.

3) He got out of prison and ordered the murder of Nicole Simpson. He is currently at large.[15]

We must ask now: What, if anything, did the LAPD and the Prosecution know about organized crime's possible ties to the double murder?

On August 23, 1994, *ABC World News Tonight* ran a story by Brian Ross. Notice that running throughout it are the names of people, places, and restaurant/drug/crime themes that we have raised in this chapter.

> (Voice over) *FBI agents moved in on a big cocaine ring operating out of Beverly Hills and Malibu two years ago. The agents found everyone they wanted but the man at the top—Joseph Ippolito, a man state and federal authorities say has longtime ties to the Mafia. Ippolito was later arrested and convicted of drug trafficking. But when agents first went to his Los Angeles apartment, there was a surprise—no Ippolito, but instead a man who says he is one of Ippolito's close friends; a former football player by the name of Alan "A.C." Cowlings.*
>
> *It now turns out that long before Cowlings became known as the man who drove O.J. Simpson in the white Bronco, Cowlings was well-known to law enforcement authorities investigating Ippolito and the world of cocaine and the mob in Los Angeles.*

According to Ross, Cowlings filed a "remarkable affidavit" with the court at the time Ippolito was arrested in 1993, in which he said he had met Ippolito through the restaurant business. He asked the court to release Ippolito on bail because "Joe helped me stay clean," from what Cowlings described as a longtime cocaine addiction.

There is more. Cowling's attorney, Donald Re, is also Joey Ippolito's attorney. At the time Ross's story aired, Re denied that Ippolito was an organized crime figure. But Ross had another informant, organized crime expert Steve Bertucelli in Florida, who said Ippolito had "a 20-year association with top Mafia families." More from Ross:

> *There's now new interest by law enforcement authorities in Joe Ippolito. He escaped from federal prison three months ago, and among the people agents may want to question about his whereabouts is Ippolito's close friend, Alan Cowlings.*

At the time this story aired, the grand jury was investigating Cowlings in connection with his role in the Bronco

chase. No criminal charges had been brought against Cowlings in the FBI move on Ippolito in 1992, and when questioned about his relationship with Ippolito by Ross, in connection with his August ABC News report, he declined comment.

On August 24, 1994, a *Boston Herald* article by Ralph
Ranalli reported that Cowlings had been involved with
Ippolito during the time Ippolito ran a restaurant:

> *Cowlings was a close associate of New Jersey Mafia
> soldier Joseph "Joey" Ippolito when Ippolito was running
> a popular Santa Monica restaurant—and a thriving co-
> caine dealing business—until last year, sources familiar
> with the case said.*

Ranalli's piece brings this connection directly into the
Simpson household:

> *Telephone records for the restaurant, obtained by fed-
> eral prosecutors and the FBI in Los Angeles, also show
> calls from Ippolito's restaurant to O.J. Simpson's Brent-
> wood estate, where the tense freeway drama ended,
> sources said.*

According to Ranalli, the FBI sting that nabbed Ippolito
and Lorenzo was called "Operation Lasima," which stands
for "Los Angeles Sicilian Mafia."

Ippolito was sentenced to 10 years in prison and was
sent to a minimum security prison camp on the grounds of
a military base in Pensacola, Florida. In May 1994, Ippolito
walked away from a work detail and is still at large.

Also in this chapter, we tracked Simpson's career backward to the early days in Buffalo, where we raised the issue
of gambling and sports. These themes are raised anew, again
linked to Cowlings. The following is from a May 6, 1996 *New
York Daily News* article by Michelle Caruso:

> *O.J. Simpson's buddy Al Cowlings was called before
> a grand jury probing one of the largest sports gambling
> rings in Southern California . . . . Cowlings, an ex-pro
> football player, appeared before the secret panel in the
> Criminal Courts building April 23, a date squeezed*

among his three days of questioning last month in the wrongful-death civil suit against Simpson.

According to the article, Cowlings' attorney, Donald Re, said he does not know who is the focus of the probe, but that it is not Cowlings. Caruso continues:

The grand jury also wanted to question Simpson's lawyer buddy Robert Kardashian, according to our law enforcement source. But last week Kardashian said, "I don't know anything about it. I don't gamble."

Our Source has insisted from the beginning:

There were mob fingerprints all over the murder scene. Everyone was dirty.

If this is so, if everyone is dirty, then pulp fiction and real life begin to bleed into each other, and we must dare to enter that dark underworld.

Five

Killer
or Killers
Unknown

There was panic in the office. This is how bad . . .
this is how much trouble they were in. _____
[a D.A.] went to _____ [an investigator] and they
told him that they were sure that O.J. waited for Ron
Goldman to come in the front gate, grabbed him,
with a knife at his throat and told him to call Nicole
out. So he does and then O.J. kills them both. Now,
so _____ says, "How does Goldman get in the
gate and how does O.J. know that Goldman's com-
ing?" I mean, was this his plan? Give me a break.
But the point is, excuse the pun, that someone could
have done that, or two people, but why would O.J.
do that when he has a key? The man had a key!
Why would he wait for Goldman when he had no
way of knowing he was coming to Nicole's?

There are striking similarities between an intriguing detective or mystery story and an analysis such as this: Each
defies obvious or stereotyped predictions, each has the capacity to surprise us. There are, also, major differences, just
as there are between a whodunit and the three greatest
murder mysteries in Western literature—*Oedipus the King,*
Hamlet, and *Crime and Punishment.* In each of these mas-
terpieces, the murderer is known, so that the unbearable
suspense generated by each work is not intellectual but,
rather, moral. Moral suspense is what grips us in a vise as
Oedipus stumbles toward the discovery of his fate. But we
do not know who killed Nicole Brown Simpson and Ronald
Goldman.

This complex, tragic double murder has not yet been

solved. O.J. Simpson was acquitted, but the Simpson matter continues into the civil trial. *The LA Times* reported on May 13, 1996, that it had reviewed some 5500 pages of civil trial deposition transcripts, which "rumble with enough tales of sex, drugs, and partying to fill a bookshelf of paperback potboilers." It cites the onetime best friends who "have tattled tawdry details," the servants who have revealed "explosive confrontations," and the relatives who "let loose vindictive accusations." It is true, as Daniel M. Petrocelli, representing Goldman's father, has said, "the truth is in the details." But, this being the civil trial, whose aim is to once again try to find Simpson guilty under the legal system, the many important details and bits of information, the evidence, the clues, the unstudied markers—that might point away from Simpson—will not be investigated. The charge is yours.

Plunge in: Could Ron Goldman have murdered Nicole Brown Simpson and then, in turn, been cut down by Simpson as he arrived too late on the scene to save his beloved former wife?

Like Othello's Desdemona, Nicole was a "fair warrior." She had stood up to her husband, may even have hired detectives to follow him when he strayed. Weller reports that at one point Nicole became "so obsessed and desperate over O.J.'s infidelity" that she made up a "list of license plates of his suspected girlfriends' cars," in order to have them traced, hoping to find out the identities of the women.[1]

By 1994, the relationship between O.J. and Nicole had changed again. During the restless months of their 1994 separation, Nicole was involved in various romantic liaisons and enjoying her independence. In fact, some of her friends worried about her. Her friend Cora Fischman testified in her April 2, 1996 deposition for the civil trial, that Nicole was leading a dangerous life in her final weeks, one that involved club-hopping and possible drug use, and that she had invited men to join her in three-way sex. Fischman further stated that Resnick had told her that Nicole and Ron were planning to have sex the evening of June 12. A classic mystery novelist like Raymond Chandler could twist this into an endlessly convoluted plot with great ingenuity. Could Nicole have provoked O.J. or a lover into a knife attack on her, on Ron Goldman?

Then, you may ask, could the triangle of death include Ron and another man obsessed with Nicole? Or another man obsessed with Ron? The lone psychopath scenario is, in many ways, a variant on the Prosecution's theory of Simpson as the obsessed split-personality lying in wait. On balance, the scenario of a stalker—someone other than Simpson—may hold up better than the Prosecution's case against Simpson did, but it raises other questions.

Is it a stalker or a serial killer who also followed Nicole and kept careful records of her activities? Did that person steal Paula Barbieri's car? Or, if Simpson was behind the campaign against Nicole—following her, making telephone death threats, and spying at her house—was he also hiring others? Can a Simpson plot explain all of these acts, plus the other break-ins and threats visited on principals in the case?

The Serial Killer

An alleged serial killer has entered the Simpson matter. Glen Rogers, 33, reported by the media to be blonde and handsome, is in custody in Florida for the murder of as many as 70 women and men across the nation—including three in Southern California.

According to a story that ran in the *New York Post*, as quoted in the *Examiner*, Rogers confessed to his friend Tony West that he committed the Bundy murders. In the midst of telling his story to West, Rogers purportedly pulled the murder weapon—a knife—from his boot. This tawdry account is included as part of a larger story headlined, "OJ Wants to Frame Me For Nicole's Murder."[2] Rogers charges that Simpson's Defense tried to frame him for the murders. His attorney, Ernie Louis, states that Rogers categorically denies any involvement in the murders.

What also emerges from this bizarre account is information that ties Rogers to the Los Angeles area. LAPD public affairs officer Tim McBride is quoted as saying that LAPD investigators found no merit in any story involving Rogers in the Bundy murders. But he also noted that the LAPD had investigated Rogers' possible involvement in murders in the Los Angeles area; that they had a warrant for his arrest in a case in Van Nuys; and that they were looking at him in regard to two other cases. Private investigator Bill Pavelic cites reasons for one to consider Rogers in relation to the Bundy murders:

- Rogers worked as a house painter in the Bundy area in 1994, up to the time of the killings.

- Rogers allegedly not only used a knife to kill many of his victims, but slashed their throats to the bone—as Nicole's throat was ripped.

- Rogers allegedly told his attorney that he knew Nicole.

- Rogers allegedly targeted women with blonde hair.

What if a serial killer with smaller hands than Simpson also stole a pair of gloves, that were too big for his hands. Might one glove fall off in the course of killing two people? Unlikely? Is this any more unlikely than the Prosecution's explanation of how the killer lost his glove? Recall their theory that Simpson removed his left glove, after the murder, to scratch his head or check whether his wool cap had fallen off during the two-minute encounter with the victims. The Prosecution argued that the glove and the cap were left on the ground, and that the killer came back to find them, but could not locate them.

Whether or not a stalker or a serial killer was involved in the murders, attempts were made to intimidate Nicole, Ron, and others around the time of the murders. This could point to a sophisticated conspiracy, such as those associated with organized crime. It might also point to an obsessed person using hired agents.

Over time, a spy or stalker would discover, for instance, that Ron Goldman was at 875 South Bundy so often in the evening that neighbors talked of how he played with the children, walked the dog with Nicole, and gave every appearance of being a valued and regular visitor. Neighbor Beverly Newman notes, "I thought they were married." A spy would also know that Faye was staying with Nicole, and that, if one is to believe the reports of her friends, Nicole was deeply immersed in an affair with a famous athlete in the days before her murder.

Two-Killer Scenario

Ultimately, we cannot rule out the possibility that the murderer acted alone that night, and that this person might not have been in any way connected to the other acts of intimidation that make up the prologue to June 12. But this scenario should be compared to a death plan that is more compelling—one that follows details that the LAPD did not notice, chose not to follow, or investigated and discarded.

Two-Killer Timeline	
PM	
8:50	Nicole and children, including a young friend of Sydney's, order ice cream at Ben and Jerry's. A man follows them in and out of store, leading the manager to assume they are together. They are not. But another man is following Nicole.
9:00	Nicole and children arrive home with Sydney's friend. They finish their ice cream and throw away the plastic cups (found in trash), but Nicole leaves her cup, with ice cream in it, on the banister.
	It is probably around this time that O.J. telephones to speak to Sydney.
9:05	A man has followed Nicole home to 875 Bundy. He walks around the building, waiting. This stalker is a killer on the payroll of an LA/Florida crime family.
	He uses a cellular phone to signal a confederate.
	Minutes later, a second killer parks his vehicle in the alley behind 875 South Bundy.
9:15	Sydney's friend, who was to have slept over, is picked up by her parents. Why the unexpected change in plans?
9:15	Hitmen wait in their vehicle in the dimly lit alley behind the condominium.

9:18	Nicole lights candles, draws bath, turns on music. She is expecting a man.
9:20	Resnick calls from her detoxification center.
9:20	Killers inside Nicole's garage.
9:21	Resnick hysterical on the phone; terrified that her drug connection will try to kill her, or may go to Nicole's residence to "collect."
9:25	Killers inside Nicole's Jeep, inside the garage.
9:30	Nicole beside herself at Resnick's information that enforcers from drug dealers could be coming.
9:35	Sydney overhears her mother's screaming and crying, as she confronts her "best friend" on the phone.
9:37	Juditha Brown calls Mezzaluna to check if they have found her eyeglasses.
9:40	Juditha calls Nicole about her glasses.
9:41	Lead hitman uses the remote door device from the Jeep to open the door to the walkway along the side of the house.
9:42	Nicole calls Mezzaluna, asks Goldman to bring the glasses to Bundy after work.
9:44	Nicole's date arrives. He is let in by Nicole, who has changed out of the black dress and wears a robe.
9:45	Killers are on premises. They hear voices from inside the residence. First killer looks in the window and recognizes the man with Nicole on the couch. The killers pull back into the shadows near the back gate.
9:45	Does Nicole tell her visitor her fears?
10:00	Nicole, in robe and barefoot, walks her visitor out to his car.
10:02	Neighbor Tom Lange [not the detective of the same name], sees Nicole embracing a man.
10:05	Nicole reenters her house. In preparation for Goldman's arrival, she slips back into her black dress but does not put on her shoes.
10:10	Killers move toward the front entrance to the residence.
10:15	Nicole hears a noise. She takes out a kitchen knife, puts it within reach. She waits anxiously for Goldman.

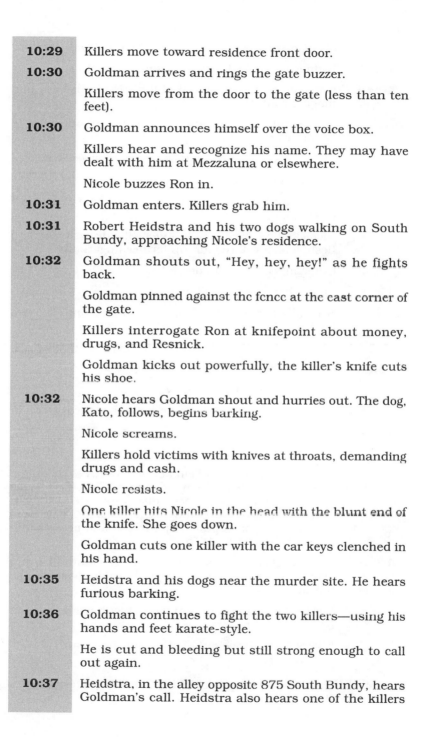

10:29 Killers move toward residence front door.

10:30 Goldman arrives and rings the gate buzzer.

Killers move from the door to the gate (less than ten feet).

10:30 Goldman announces himself over the voice box.

Killers hear and recognize his name. They may have dealt with him at Mezzaluna or elsewhere.

Nicole buzzes Ron in.

10:31 Goldman enters. Killers grab him.

10:31 Robert Heidstra and his two dogs walking on South Bundy, approaching Nicole's residence.

10:32 Goldman shouts out, "Hey, hey, hey!" as he fights back.

Goldman pinned against the fence at the east corner of the gate.

Killers interrogate Ron at knifepoint about money, drugs, and Resnick.

Goldman kicks out powerfully, the killer's knife cuts his shoe.

10:32 Nicole hears Goldman shout and hurries out. The dog, Kato, follows, begins barking.

Nicole screams.

Killers hold victims with knives at throats, demanding drugs and cash.

Nicole resists.

One killer hits Nicole in the head with the blunt end of the knife. She goes down.

Goldman cuts one killer with the car keys clenched in his hand.

10:35 Heidstra and his dogs near the murder site. He hears furious barking.

10:36 Goldman continues to fight the two killers—using his hands and feet karate-style.

He is cut and bleeding but still strong enough to call out again.

10:37 Heidstra, in the alley opposite 875 South Bundy, hears Goldman's call. Heidstra also hears one of the killers

	giving orders to his partner. He hears a gate slam.
10:37	Sydney in her bed, hears Goldman's shouts.
10:40	Goldman failing, now, but still hitting in defense and making contact.
	Nicole still alive, moving, starting to call out, tries to get out front gate.
	Akita barks in frenzy, attacks, tries to save Nicole.
	Dog bites second killer.
	Killer tries to cut dog's throat, misses, and slashes off dog tags.
	Nicole falling, claws out at killer. She draws blood and flesh, which will remain under her fingernails.
	Goldman collapses to one knee.
10:40	First killer finishes Goldman.
	Second killer bleeding; some blood falls onto Nicole's back.
	Dog attacks again, bites glove of Nicole's attacker.
10:45	Goldman down.
	Second killer starts for alley.
	First killer turns to Nicole and slits her throat.
10:46	Dog runs out to street; wailing, now.
	First killer starts after dog.
	First killer sights a woman across the street watching. This could be the anonymous woman who called 911—before the murders had been discovered—to ask about a "double murder on Bundy." Or, the killers may have seen O.J. Simpson pulled up in front and peering into the darkness from his Bronco.
10:48	Second killer returns from alley to get first killer and leave. His are the second footprints leading back to the murder scene.
	First killer signals to him that they have been seen from the street.
	Killers leave. Drive out of alley, heading south.

Will the evidence support this shocking scenario?

Two-Killer Timeline—June 12, 1994		
NICOLE SIMPSON	**KILLERS**	**RON GOLDMAN**
9:00 PM Arrives home.	**9:00 PM** ? ? ?	**9:00 PM** At Mezzaluna.
9:00-42 PM Telephone calls: Juditha Brown; Restaurant; Faye Resnick; O.J.		
9:44 PM Male visitor arrives.		**9:50 PM** Leaves Mezzaluna.
10:00 PM Male visitor leaves.	**10:00 PM** On premises.	**10:00 PM** Showers and dresses.
10:15 PM Nicole hears noise. Brings out knife.	**10:15 PM** In garage.	**10:20 PM** En route to 875 South Bundy.
	10:25 PM On walkway, in shadows.	
10:30 PM Hears Ron at front gate.		**10:30 PM** Ron buzzes at front gate.
	10:31 PM Killers attack.	**10:31 PM** Ron enters.
10:32 PM Nicole rushes out.	**10:32 PM** Knock out Nicole.	**10:32 PM** Stabbed but fights back. Calls out, "Hey–hey–hey!"
		10:35 PM Though slashed, Ron struggles.
10:35–10:50 PM Murdered	**10:35–10:50 PM Murder Nicole and Ron**	**10:35–10:50 PM Murdered**

Evidence for Two Killers

8:50 PM: The police spent no time or effort to identify the man in Ben and Jerry's, to determine whether or not he could be the stalker Nicole had feared. Bill Pavelic for the Defense did find the man and determined that he was not.

9:00 PM: The killers were near and on the premises for some time before their attack. Signs were found in the garage of someone waiting near and in Nicole's jeep, including coins from someone's pocket and evidence of the missing electronic door opener. Authorities did not follow these leads.

9:21 PM: Faye Resnick's telephone call is center stage of this scenario. We turn now to Resnick's recollection of that last conversation and its context:

> Nicole and I shared a dream. We wanted to stop being male-dependent, give up alcohol and drugs, and open up . . . a coffee house . . . . Nicole had $90,000 in the bank. I had $20,000 in "mad money" . . . she vowed that she'd stop all alcohol and drugs completely, right along with me.[3]

Against this highly selective but revealing version of the background of their restaurant plans, Resnick goes on to talk about Nicole's problems, including the man Resnick, Weller, and others, including O.J. in his civil trial deposition, have identified as her second football-star lover: Marcus Allen. According to Resnick, in that last talk with Nicole:

> . . . she'd (Nicole) seen Marcus Allen that day [June 12] or she was going to see him.[4]

Bear this statement in mind.

We may believe the sanitized references to cocaine, and the restaurant plans, and, possibly, the Marcus Allen reference, because it is so often mentioned by Nicole's friends. In fact, in her civil trial deposition, Cora Fischman, a close friend of both Simpsons, said that Nicole and Marcus Allen were having an affair shortly before her murder.[5] Yet, in his deposition for the civil trial, Allen "totally denied" any affair with Nicole Brown Simpson.[6]

But has Resnick described the entire conversation that evening? She has publicly stated that she underwent hypnosis in order to recall everything concerning this final communication, which she insists lasted thirty-five minutes. But something seems to have escaped her: the not-so-happy part of the conversation that Sydney Simpson heard.

Sydney Simpson, as we know, told police in the early hours of June 13 that she had heard "Mommy fighting and crying" with Mommy's "best friend." Can we be certain she is referring to Faye Resnick as this "best friend"? First, recall Simpson's comment about this. Also, after Resnick's book erupted into the middle of the trial, the Brown family expressed their disgust at what they saw as an act of betrayal and rank opportunism. Weller reports that it was then that young Sydney said to her grandparents and Aunt Denise, "I guess Mommy's best friend wasn't such a good friend after all."[7]

10:00 PM: According to Fischman, Resnick, and others, Marcus Allen was allegedly again seeing Nicole. The neighbor, Tom Lange, could not see the face of the man embracing Nicole at curbside, so we can only conjecture about the man's identity. Lange reported that Nicole was wearing a robe as she said goodbye to her visitor. But when she was found by the police, she was in the same black dress she had worn to Sydney's recital.

Other details of interest? Sherlock Holmes, himself, might have been shaken to learn that Nicole's gentleman caller was driving "a white utility vehicle," according to our source. Denise Pilnak and two other Bundy neighbors remember seeing an African-American man in a white vehicle that night. If the man is Marcus Allen innocently driving away from Nicole's residence, then an amazing but simple explanation breaks through the confusion surrounding these white vehicle/African-American man sightings on June 12.

Four light-colored or white vehicles (those belonging to Simpson, Cowlings, Barbieri, and Allen) and three, large, African-American athletic men (Simpson, Cowlings, another): who was at Bundy, who was at Rockingham?

Information introduced into the two-killer scenario may be put into two categories. The first category is evidence supported by the Prosecution and Defense. This evidence will appear in the court transcripts.

- Blood under Nicole's fingernail.

- Blow to Nicole's head.

- Ron's car keys.

- Seventeen unmatched fingerprints.

- Blood on Nicole's back untested.

- No vaginal test for semen.

- Unidentified DNA trace inside Bronco.

- Goldman's hands scraped

- Men's voices heard.

- Coroner Golden suggested possibility of two knives.

- Shoe prints going in two directions.

- One hat, one glove.

The second category is evidence that is less well established or tested. It includes everything from material evidence that was not tested to the recollections of an individual. Each item must be judged accordingly.

- Flesh under Nicole's fingernail.

- Untested blood on car keys.

- Missing garage door opener.

- Knife cut on Ron's shoe.

- Pregnancy test device found in trash.

- Goldman's knuckles swollen.

- Men's voices heard by Heidstra and Sydney Simpson.

- Nicole's scream heard at 10:32.

- Dog bites on glove.

- Untested shoe prints.
- One hat, two gloves.

The reconstruction of the struggle and murder of the two victims is based on known evidence, evidence that was presented in court, and evidence that was never presented in court. There may be disagreements as to the significance of the evidence or about whether the evidence exists at all.

We should note the significance of Sydney Simpson as an earwitness. Remember that none of the Prosecution's witnesses heard the "Hey, Hey, Hey" or the men's voices. Neither did any of the Defense witnesses because, like the Prosecution's dog walkers, all of them passed 875 South Bundy before 10:30 PM— except for Robert Heidstra. When we coordinate Heidstra's timeline with Goldman's and Pilnak's, and add what Sydney heard from a different location than Heidstra, we can produce a new timeline. We leave it to the jury to decide what the overlapping elements here can tell us about when the murders occurred and who might have been the killer or killers.

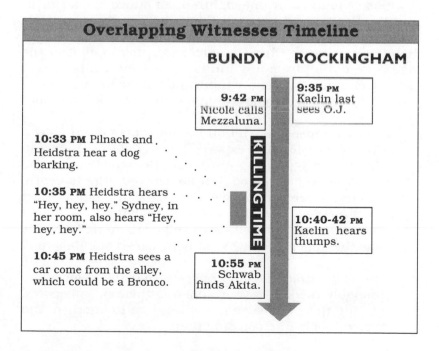

Overlapping Witnesses Timeline

BUNDY   **ROCKINGHAM**

9:35 PM
Kaelin last
sees O.J.

9:42 PM
Nicole calls
Mezzaluna.

10:33 PM Pilnack and
Heidstra hear a dog
barking.

10:35 PM Heidstra hears
"Hey, hey, hey." Sydney, in
her room, also hears "Hey,
hey, hey."

KILLING TIME

10:40-42 PM
Kaelin hears
thumps.

10:45 PM Heidstra sees a
car come from the alley,
which could be a Bronco.

10:55 PM
Schwab
finds Akita.

Killers Unknown

There are also the killers. There are a series of similar characteristics between the Bundy murders and some fifteen other drug assassinations carried out by a professional assassin employed by a Florida/LA drug cartel. A man who trained death squads in Central America, a CIA contract agent notorious as a sadist. This similar M.O. is the opinion of researchers whose field of inquiry is drugs/guns/assassinations/death squads and organized vice. However, in searching for the killer, the authorities rejected any other explanation than that of the jealous husband—who is always "the first suspect."

The utter denial of a narcotics crime becomes incomprehensible when we learn that investigator Bill Pavelic unearthed that, on June 15, 1994, three days after the murders, a call was received by the LAPD from a citizen in the Bundy area reporting that two men had been seen carrying cartons out of the dead woman's residence, loading them in an expensive vehicle and driving away.

Police found only one-eighth of an ounce of cocaine at Bundy. Resnick had stayed there, as her cocaine crisis mounted, from June 3 until June 8. Resnick had a major habit. According to Christian Reichardt, her ex-fiance, she had been cut off from any funds.[8] It is common for heavy drug users to run up many thousands of dollars in debts.

Consider, again, what we know about the killing time;

- Nicole Simpson was hit on the head by a blunt object. The Defense forensic experts discovered this trauma in the autopsy report (See Appendix). Both the Defense and the Prosecution agreed that it occurred prior to death, and that it seemed to have been made by a blunt object such as the butt end of the knife. What was Goldman doing when she was hit, or wasn't he there yet? If Nicole was the target, then why hit her instead of killing her?

- Cuts on Nicole and Ron suggest that the killer, more probably the killers, were holding them at knifepoint, moving the victims from one location to another, and very possibly interrogating them. Why?

A drug-related confrontation would center on both the demand for the whereabouts of Faye Resnick, and the drug cache, and the money that was owed. Arguably, the very scene would materialize that Nicole had feared, the one that had caused her crying and furious reaction, overheard by Sydney Simpson earlier.

- If the killers committed the murders only after the drug-related search, then we have an explanation for the long time frame of the homicides: the silence, then the voices, the barking then the wailing of the dog, the cuts on the neck, the "Hey, hey, hey!", the scream, and, finally, the "furious struggle" with Ron Goldman.

- We are going to have to, later, include Goldman, himself, as the possible target in the murder agenda. We will be looking at incoming evidence that may or may not exclude Nicole Simpson.

- Dr. Irwin Golden, the L.A. Deputy Coroner who had performed the autopsies, stated on direct exam in the preliminary trial that there were "two morphologically different types of stab wounds on the victims." Some, he said, were indicative of a single-edge blade, while others had a characteristically double-pointed or forked end. This meant that the wounds could have been made by two different weapons, which in turn suggests the possibility of two killers.

As we consider what the evidence may suggest, the tight focus of the Prosecution's scenario disappears, and other explanations of events appear. In other words, we know virtually nothing about the events of June 12—because the lead detectives left the crime scene for Rockingham, and because the same detectives did not call the coroner to the killing ground until it was almost unreadable. Afterward, they sought only to prove that the man they arrested was guilty and did not look in any other directions for explanations to the crime.

Detectives, criminalists, and coroners walked away, or were kept away from, Bundy. This turned a potential forensic inquiry of the crime ("the act") into an official scenario of

the "idea of the act," to use an equation of that most controversial of modern philosophers, Friedrich Nietzsche:

> First comes the Idea. Then the Act. Then the Idea of
> the Act. The wheel of causality doth not roll between
> them.

It is your task to study the Act—the crime and crime
scene—not the Idea of the Act, the Prosecution's storyline.

Interview with a Chief Medical Examiner

A chief medical examiner for a county in Southern California spoke to Ian Bowater in January 1996. For obvious reasons, he did not wish to be identified on the record. In the
hour-long conversation, he made the following points:

- There is sometimes a conflict between police investigators and the medical examiner. Police often do not call
  in the coroner's office until later because they feel the
  pathologist gets in the way of their investigation.

- There are always mistakes in autopsies. Things are
  missed but these mistakes can often be corrected by
  further examination. Time of death is very difficult to
  establish except to within fairly wide margins. The de-
  lay in calling the coroner would make the time of death
  estimation far more difficult.

- The official estimate of the deaths occurring between
  9:00 PM and 12:00 midnight is solely based on the discovery of the bodies and when the victims were last seen
  alive. If the medical examiner had been called immediately and arrived at, say, 1:00 AM, and if he had made
  an examination of the victims, taking their internal body
  temperature, then the pathologist might have been able
  to place the time of death closer to either end of the time
  spectrum suggested for the death. Internal body tem-

peratures of the liver and rectum drop uniformly from the normal 98.6 degrees Fahrenheit at about one degree an hour until they reach the ambient temperature. Assuming that the victim does not have an abnormal body temperature, e.g., fever, some estimation can narrow the margin of the time of death.

- Stomach contents are a good indicator of the time of death. A body not under stress will normally clear the stomach in two to four hours. The stomach contents would have been helpful in establishing the time of death, especially because the contents of Nicole's last meal—and the dessert of ice cream—were known. The destroying of the stomach contents by the medical examiner's office was, at the least, a major oversight.

- The visible bruise on Nicole's head had to have been made when she was still alive: Bruising to the body or swelling associated with a blow does not occur after death because then there will be no blood pressure to cause blood to invade the affected area. Often, livor mortis is mistaken for bruising. But, with a major loss of blood—exsanguination—bruising and livor mortis cannot occur, therefore, a prompt coroner's examination might have been able to "read" the bruise to her head to help establish the time and details of the death.

- If Nicole had been knocked to the ground with a force that was enough to make her unconscious and, if she had been left while a single attacker dealt with Ron Goldman, there would be some bruising or swelling. Closer inspection of this contusion might suggest the time this blow to the head occurred.

- The theory that the shoe-shaped bruise on the back of Nicole resulted from the killer placing his foot on her back as he bent down to cut her throat is "very speculative." The body would have to be stomped on to produce a bruise, with time for the bruise to form before the final throat slash took her life.[9]

Once again, these comments point to the fact that the physical evidence in this case, upon which one must base any analysis, is itself open to conjecture at a very basic level.

Who Was the Target?

Defense investigators found evidence—not yet made public—that led them to believe that the target on the night of June 12 may have been Faye Resnick. Resnick was a prime candidate for other roles besides that of victim. When an addict owes sums of money and has nowhere to turn then she may do anything: pimp, prostitute, rob, inform. An addict who turns informer may be writing her death warrant. Resnick's former boyfriend, Christian Reichardt, stated that they were "all afraid of being murdered in their beds."[10] Why—because Resnick had told them all on the night that they confronted her about her drug use, that she was at risk with her connection—and had put them at risk?

Were they all so frightened that one of them, not Resnick, was impelled to contact law enforcement? Her closest friends had to nearly force her into a clinic. Simpson was angry with and jealous of Resnick. Faye and Nicole had been lovers, according to Resnick. It is not unthinkable that Simpson mentioned Resnick to one of his contacts in law enforcement. Goldman, too, was a good candidate for police or DEA surveillance simply because of where he worked and socialized. Goldman was vulnerable. He had declared bankruptcy once and was now reported to be looking for large sums of money for his restaurant. Everyone was a target in some way, it appears. No one an innocent bystander.

Innocent Bystanders

Could the entire cast of characters at Bundy that night have been both "guilty" and "innocent"? There is a curious codependency that binds together all of the principals, Faye, Nicole, Ron, and, finally, O.J. himself. The widespread intuition and unshakable "feeling" that Simpson was there on that murder scene is perfectly understandable: Life and lifestyle brought all of those people to 875 South Bundy that night, in person, or by telephone, or, it may be in Simpson's case, by association.

It is Simpson, the football legend, with all his dependencies—sex, women, money, substances (at times), the compulsive need to be loved—who personifies the lifestyle that Marcus Allen had achieved in Simpson's shadow, and that Ron Goldman longed to grasp. Every one of the principals of June 12 had made love to Nicole: Simpson, Goldman, even Resnick. When others embraced that golden girl, they partook of the myth of O.J. and Nicole. They were one combined dream. Even drug runners and their hired killers are attendant lords in these rites of the rich and famous.

The "presence" of O.J. hung over Bundy like a cloying cologne. The others all bathed in his ambience: Marcus Allen began by wanting to be O.J.; Faye Resnick wanted, and wanted to be Nicole; Ron Goldman wanted to be all of them. So O.J. was at Bundy that night, in the same way that Faye Resnick was, and his ghost will forever inhabit the site.

The cast of characters for the murder night is not yet complete. Remember A.C. Cowlings and Denise Brown. Were they not lovers in years past, running with O.J. and Nicole? Wasn't A.C. purposefully confused with O.J.; wasn't Denise the darker image of Nicole—and wouldn't, couldn't, either of them, but for sheer luck, have been at Bundy that night? So A.C. and Denise also haunt that scene. They were "there" though no computer will ever find them. What about Kato Kaelin? He was certainly "there" in the person of Ron Goldman, who, we may say, symbolizes those hopefuls who circle the Alpha Males and their chosen mates. They were all "there": in person, or on the telephone, in absentia, in effigy. Look past the media mirror at the reality of the people in jeopardy.

- Ron Goldman devoted long hours helping people with physical problems, displaying both tenderness and great generosity.

- Nicole Brown Simpson and Faye Resnick pledged time and effort to their children and their schools and camps.

- A.C. Cowlings had raised hundreds of thousands of dollars for ghetto youngsters and given selflessly to causes and individuals in need.

- O.J. Simpson was famous for his anonymous personal generosity, the funds raised publicly for ghetto youth, and his visits to children's hospitals.

So it is not so simple. Any moral judgment of the cast at 875 South Bundy is only half true. There were no angels or monsters there that night, in person or in spirit, except for the killer or killers—and that story is still beyond the limits of our timeline. The point is this: These people did not come from another planet. They are as American as apple pie.

875 South Bundy on that dark night was an American island of loss, or an infernal machine starting to unwind: Nicole was out of control after her separation from O.J., like a Tennessee William's protagonist, "like a fox with her tail on fire, running to places that had failed her before." She may have been pregnant, she certainly feared she was. She worried about AIDS and had been ill off and on for months. All her money was going somewhere fast. Her co-dependency with Faye Resnick, who, by her own admission, was in a state of crisis, was a vivid danger signal, as was their restaurant fantasy that they shared with Ron Goldman. Goldman may have died trying to save Nicole, or she, him—or both might have died because of, or instead of, Faye Resnick.

Marcus Allen spent the day with A.C. Cowlings. If, in the evening, Allen visited Nicole, he may have gotten away from Bundy just in time. Who can doubt that in another quarter of an hour, he could have been the innocent bystander, the "man in the wrong place at the wrong time."

This is true for all of them—starting with O.J.—they were all in the wrong place at the wrong time that night. In a strange way, Nicole's entire life, and all of her closest cohorts, were "there" with her in the dark between 9:00 and 11:00 that night. They circled around her under the quarter moon, and she spun around in that circle, too, until the music stopped.

There is a touching solidarity among this subculture of lost souls who, in a way, were all ready to die for each other, to be buried together in death as they had been in life. Their time and their timelines, both, were out of joint. Nicole's license plate on the night of her death read "L84AD8." Late for a date.

The victims and the others share a larger culture with the rest of us. We are a jury of peers. All of us are either players or spectators in the American arena with the millennium approaching. We are jurors not judges; actors or audience, off and on stage, in actuality or fantasy. We have all heard the music Nicole Brown Simpson heard—if only from afar—and some of us have danced to it; some of us have only watched the dancers, but all of us are involved.

We live here.

Six

The Fuhrman Timeline

They all knew who Fuhrman was. He collected German war medals. Darden knew, Marcia Clark knew, because they were told by a freelance journalist named Singular, that's his name [Stephen Singular]. This guy tried to tell the D.A. and he tried to tell the Defense, and they, none of them, wanted to buy it. Not even the Defense, 'til later. Much later.

W hat our Source says here about the controversial Mark Fuhrman and his checkered past was later echoed by Christopher Darden in his book:

> *We'd done all we could to keep out the nasty baggage that he carried, to allow the jury to focus on the murder and not Fuhrman's past. We managed to keep out of the trial: a political cartoon from Fuhrman's desk showing a swastika rising above the ashes; unfounded allegations that he'd planted evidence; the 1980 and 1981 psychiatric reports; and a rumor that he had made a comment to a colleague about seeing Nicole Brown's augmented breasts before she was killed.[1]*

The Prosecution was not able to keep Fuhrman's past out of the trial. Ultimately, his racist statements, captured on audio tape, jeopardized the Prosecution's entire case. The question before us: Did Detective Fuhrman, alone or with others, frame O.J. Simpson? To answer this, we need to ask: Who was Mark Fuhrman? He came out of the Los Angeles Police Department and criminal justice system. The jury has only to thumb through the historical record to get a taste of what used to be called "America's Police Force," enshrined on the radio and in comics, books, television, and the movies, from *Dragnet* to *The New Centurions*.

Mark Fuhrman in the LAPD

Before we look at Fuhrman's role in the Simpson matter, let us review his career. After a stint in the Marines, Fuhrman joined the LAPD in 1975.

Mark Fuhrman	
1975	Fuhrman graduates second in his class from LAPD's Lincoln Heights Academy. While assigned to "white" areas of the city, Fuhrman shows promise.
1977	In 1977, Fuhrman is reassigned to the Hollenbeck Division in East Los Angeles, an area populated almost entirely by Angelenos of Latino descent. Fuhrman resents not being promoted when reassigned. His file quotes a superior:

> *He is enthusiastic and demonstrates a lot of initiative in making arrests. However, his overall production is unbalanced at this point because of the greater portion of time spent in trying to make the "big arrest."*

1978	Civil rights attorney Antonio Rodriguez requests an investigation into an incident in Boyle Heights, in east L.A. On November 18, two officers trying to break up a fight there had been shot and wounded by residents. Fuhrman subsequently led the police onslaught against the suspects. An eighteen-month LAPD investigation followed, but no action was taken. In 1985, Fuhrman will boast on tape to a screenwriter that he was the chief target of the investigation:

> *They knew damn well what I did. But there was nothing they could do about it. Most of the guys worked the 77th [Street Division] together. We were tight. We all knew what to say.*

Also this year, a fellow officer is killed by a deranged man. This event triggers Fuhrman's desire to see an LAPD psychiatrist. Dr. Ronald Koegler writes:

> *After a while, he began to dislike the work, especially the "low class" people he was dealing with. He bragged about violence he used in subduing suspects, including chokeholds, and said he would break their hands or face or arms or legs if necessary.*

1980 Fuhrman's second marriage ends. His second ex-wife, Janet Hackett, will in 1996 reveal to *The New York Times* that sometimes Fuhrman's depression was so intense that he "refused to talk or smile for days."[2]

1981 Twice divorced, investigated numerous times for using excessive force or violating suspects' rights, and not being promoted or getting "the big bust," Fuhrman seeks retirement, claiming psychological disability. Because he had not been permanently physically injured or disabled on the job, the only way for him to retire with a pension was to show that he was psychologically disabled.

1982 On paid disability leave, Fuhrman retains counsel in his two-year battle for a pension. Legal briefs portray him as a dangerously unbalanced man.

1984 Charging that Fuhrman was merely a cop trying to get a pension, the Pension Board denies Fuhrman a pension if he quits the force. Fuhrman does not quit. The pension board report states:

> *There is some suggestion here that the patient was trying to feign the presence of severe psychopathology. This suggests a conscious attempt to look bad and an exaggeration of problems which could be a cry for help and/or overdramatization by a narcissistic, self-indulgent, emotionally unstable person who expects immediate attention and pity.*

Fuhrman is transferred from the east side of town to the west side, an area including Brentwood, Westwood, and West Los Angeles. Most of the residents are Caucasian and many are involved in the entertainment industry. Residences include expansive mansions north and south of Sunset Boulevard in Brentwood.

In 1984, O.J. Simpson and Nicole Brown, who would marry in 1985, lived north of Sunset Boulevard in one of those handsome large homes, at 360 North Rockingham Avenue.

1985 Fuhrman meets Kathleen Bell at a Marine recruiting office. In 1994, Bell will write to the Prosecution about her conversation with Fuhrman the day they met:

> *Officer Fermin [sic] said that when he sees "a nigger" (as he called it) driving with a white woman, he would pull them over. I asked what if he didn't have a reason, and he said he would find one. Officer Fermin went on to say that he would like nothing more than to see all "niggers" gathered together and killed. He said something about burning them or bombing them.*[3]

Also in 1985, Fuhrman and his partner respond to a 415, a family dispute call, at the Simpson estate. There they find Nicole and O.J. standing near a Mercedes with a broken windshield. A bat is leaning against a nearby wall. Nicole does not want to press charges against Simpson, so Fuhrman writes no report at the time, but 4 years later he will. His report will state that he saw no bruises or marks on Nicole and that O.J. was agitated, but "not out of control."

In April Fuhrman meets screenwriter Laura Hart, who is working on a screenplay about the police. Over the next four years she tapes their meetings as he gives her inside information on his experiences in the LAPD. The notorious tapes are filled with lurid, violent stories, racial invectives, and inflammatory statements and will become central to the Defense's argument in the Simpson trial.

1987 Joseph Britton, an African-American, sues Fuhrman and several other LAPD officers, claiming they used excessive force, made racial slurs, and planted a knife as evidence when arresting him on suspicion of assault and bank robbery. One of the five or six bullets that penetrated Britton's body came from Fuhrman's gun. Britton recalls that Fuhrman looked at him lying on the ground and said, "Why don't you just die and save us the paperwork?" The City of Los Angeles will later settle this suit for $100,000 during the Simpson trial.

1989

JANUARY

1 LAPD officers (not including Fuhrman) respond to a 415 domestic dispute call at 360 North Rockingham. Nicole is found bruised, dirty, and bloodied, outside at the gate, saying, "He's going to kill me." O.J. eludes arrest by leaving in his Bentley. When the City Attorney's office calls for information about any previous incidents at Rockingham, Fuhrman writes a report about the 1985 incident. He notes:

*It seems odd to remember such an event, but it's
not every day that you respond to a celebrity's house.
It was indelibly pressed in my memory.*

1992   Nicole Simpson separates from O.J. for part of the year
and rents a condominium at 327 North Gretna Green
Way in Brentwood. At about this time, she has breast
augmentation surgery. Sometime before June 12, Mark
Fuhrman allegedly comments to other detectives, on a
number of occasions, about Nicole's breast implants,
and allegedly talks about an affair with her.

1994

JUNE

13   **Sunday:** Detective Fuhrman, now a nineteen-year
veteran of the LAPD, is called to 875 South Bundy
where Nicole Brown Simpson and Ronald Goldman
were murdered the night before.

JULY

Fuhrman testifies at the preliminary hearing and is
questioned by Marcia Clark. Soon after, Kathleen Bell
writes to the Prosecution about Fuhrman's terrifying
remarks to her in 1985.

SEPTEMBER

Deputy D.A. Lucienne Coleman tells Clark and her
boss, William Hodgman, that Fuhrman's past behavior with blacks and Latinos could lead to serious problems if he is a witness at the trial. She tells Clark that
Detective Walter Purdy told her and Deputy D.A. Julie
Sergujian that in 1987 Purdy found numerous swastika insignias painted on his locker at the LAPD station. Purdy said the matter had been investigated in-
ternally and that Fuhrman's fingerprints were found
on the inside of the locker.

OCTOBER

D.A. Clark is informed that Deputy D.A. Ellen Burke
knew of an officer who had been told by Fuhrman at a
barbecue a few years before that he had just seen Nicole
Simpson's new "boob job up close and personal." This
Fuhrman story and the Purdy swastika story are also
detailed in a book proposal by Stephen Singular that
the Prosecution learns of before the trial. This is all part
of Fuhrman's "nasty baggage" that makes the Prosecution so uneasy.

1995

FEBRUARY

Fuhrman, still in touch with the screenwriter, tells her about his importance in the Simpson trial:

> I'm the key witness in the biggest case of the century. And if I go down, they lose the case. The glove is everything. Without the glove—'bye, 'bye.

In a pretrial meeting, Fuhrman tells Christopher Darden that he collects German war medals, saying "The craftsmanship is incredible." Darden is wary of Fuhrman and tells Clark "Putting this guy on will get me killed. I can't. I won't." [4]

Johnnie Cochran warns Darden not to put Fuhrman on the stand.

2

Numerous TV programs, including *Good Morning America*, report that Mark Fuhrman has purchased property in Sandpoint, Idaho, an area that has become a sort of retirement center for members of the LAPD.

13

When Coleman tries again to warn Clark about Fuhrman, Clark tells her that she is tired of other D.A.'s trying to muscle in on the case. Coleman still urges Clark and Hodgman not to put Fuhrman on the stand.

MARCH

8

Fuhrman testifies for the Prosecution. Clark treats him gently, asks how he feels about testifying. He says "nervous." Clark introduces Kathleen Bell's letter. Fuhrman denies its contents. Clark then takes him through the events of June 13 and his discovery of the glove and other evidence at Rockingham. After his appearance, Fuhrman receives several dozen bouquets from people and police all over the country.

12

Cross-examination of Fuhrman by F. Lee Bailey for the Defense begins.

14

Bailey asks Fuhrman if he has used the word "nigger" in the last ten years. Fuhrman states that he has not.

> **Bailey:** So that anyone who comes to this court and quotes you as using that word would be a liar, would they not, Detective Fuhrman?
> **Fuhrman:** Yes, they would.

With this line of questioning, Bailey paves the way to exposing Fuhrman as a liar. Bailey also establishes that

Fuhrman was alone when he found the glove at Rockingham and suggests that he planted it so that he could stay on the case.

JULY

Defense consultant Bill Pavelic discovers that Fuhrman was taped by a screenwriter and that in the tapes Fuhrman used the word "nigger" and defamed Latinos, and also discussed falsifying evidence, brutalizing suspects, and his distaste for women in the LAPD.

Cochran verifies the existence of the tapes.

A trial begins in North Carolina to compel Laura Hart McKinny to turn over the tapes as evidence in the Simpson trial.

AUGUST

7   A North Carolina judge rules McKinny must turn over the Fuhrman tapes. On this same day, Fuhrman retires from the LAPD, this time entitled to a twenty-year uncontested pension. He moves with his wife and children to Sandpoint, Idaho.

29   Judge Ito orders 61 excerpts from the McKinny tapes played in court without the jurors present. Fuhrman uses the word "nigger" 42 times in the tapes.

SEPTEMBER

5   Kathleen Bell and others testify about Fuhrman's racist remarks.

6   Defense lawyer Gerald F. Uelman asks Fuhrman the following questions:

> *Was the testimony that you gave at the preliminary hearing in this case completely truthful?*
>
> *Have you ever falsified a police report?*
>
> *Did you plant or manipulate any evidence in this case?*

To every question, Fuhrman responds: "I wish to assert my Fifth Amendment privilege."

26–27   Clark and Darden close for the Prosecution. Darden argues that Simpson was a "burning fuse," that his need to control Nicole and fear of losing her drove him to murder her and Ron in a "rage killing." Clark argues that the evidence proves Simpson is the murderer, as she fills in a projected picture of his face with pieces of the evidence. She acknowledges tha Fuhrman is a liar, describes him as a vile racist human being, asks, "Do we wish no such person were on the planet?" and answers her own question, "Yes." Nevertheless, she asks that the jury believe his testimony about the events of June 13.

27–28 Scheck and Cochran close for the Defense. Scheck rebuts the Prosecution's forensics evidence point by point, arguing, "Somebody played with this evidence." Cochran argues that the Prosecution's message can't be trusted. He makes a plea to the jury to "Stop this cover-up," pointing out that even the prosecutors agree that in Fuhrman:

> There's a lying, perjuring, genocidal racist and he's testified willfully false in this case . . . . You are empowered to say we're not going to take that anymore . . . . You're the ones who send the message.

Cochran also discusses Fuhrman's "genocidal racism" in relation to Hitler's views, a reference that some (including Defense attorney Shapiro) find offensive and call "playing the race card."

1996

MARCH

2 A *New York Times* article describes Fuhrman as "a complex, paradoxical man" and suggests that there is little evidence that Fuhrman committed the acts of violence he boasted about on the tapes. But this article also quotes his second wife, Janet Hackett, talking about Fuhrman's 1977 assignment in East L.A .to crack down on Hispanic street gangs. His mission, he told her, was to "harass anyone who looked like a gang member, and obliterate them." [5]

This article also reports that three investigations of Fuhrman are now underway: a civil rights investigation by the FBI; an inquiry into whether he committed perjury on the stand, by the California Attorney General's Office; and a full-scale "biopsy" of all of Fuhrman's cases, by the LAPD.

Now living with his family in Sandpoint, Idaho, Fuhrman, according to friends, "is often depressed—in fact, devastated—by the way people have made him into a Nazi-like figure." [6]

Fuhrman has vocalized a desire to return to law enforcement, somewhere, somehow.

Detective Mark Fuhrman, LAPD
"You do what you have to do . . ."

Focusing now on Detective Fuhrman and the Simpson case, we take up again the central issue: Was he someone whose past overtook and destroyed him—but who actually may not have done anything illegal in the Simpson case? Or, did he tamper with or even plant evidence for reasons that may be found in his personal and professional background? To evaluate the second possibility, we need to consider both motive and opportunity. First, we look at what we can extract from his background that might pertain to motive:

- The belief held by many policemen that a "team player" does what is necessary to ensure conviction of a guilty party. This might include anything from sharpening or omitting a detail, to simplify things for the District Attorney, the judge, and the jury, to tampering with or planting evidence, or even committing perjury.

- Racist tendencies and a hatred of interracial couples. He had bragged about these feelings on the tapes and to Kathleen Bell; and Defense Attorney Bailey stated at trial:

    We intend to show in incident after incident that Detective Fuhrman was willing to violate the Federal civil rights statute to unfairly prosecute black men who he found in the company of white women and that this pattern was consistent right up to until shortly before this incident.

- His chance at the "big time." Early in his career, Fuhrman's superiors had described him as longing for "the big arrest." In his conversations with McKinny, he had painted himself as the most competent cop around, the one who always knew what to do, who had to take charge—and yet nothing in his career had placed him in the limelight. The incident at the Simpsons may have been his one claim to fame. Recalling the 1985 incident at the Simpson estate, he testified at trial:

I had never been to a celebrity's home before on a family dispute. Simpson was a very famous man, and once I walked in, I recognized him. Those two things would make it a memorable incident.

- Personal feelings for Nicole that motivated him to ensure O.J.'s conviction. Information reported by Stephen Singular in *Legacy of Deception*, by *Los Angeles Times* staff, by Christopher Darden, and others suggested that Fuhrman may have had some personal relationship with Nicole. Reportedly officers at a local bar joked that Fuhrman was "Nicole's cop;" some reported he had talked about Nicole's breast augmentation, and that he had hinted at an affair with her.

- "The white knight." Singular's thoughts about the possibility that Fuhrman realized he had not saved the fair maiden when he could/should have. Singular suggests that, if Fuhrman did plant evidence, there may even have been a note of gallantry in his act. Describing Fuhrman as "a fervid cop . . . whose job it is to help people and protect them from all the horrific things that go on in the night," Singular imagines Fuhrman blaming himself when he arrived at Bundy and found the bodies:

  Nine years ago he'd seen what O.J. was capable of. Why hadn't he done something back then or in the time since, when he could have intervened and changed the situation? Why hadn't he done something to save her?[7]

Can you find a motive or motives suggested by Fuhrman's past, and by his own words? From the tapes:

In almost twelve years on the [police] department, I never felt guilty for one day . . . . Even if you get the wrong guy, he's done something wrong before, or he's thought about doing something wrong.

I've been on several calls in West L.A. where I'm in the third or fourth call—third or fourth car—and I end up handling the whole situation . . . . Then you go to court and I'm the only one who knows how to testify.

It's like my partner now. He's so hung up on the rules and stuff. I get pissed sometimes and go, You just don't fucking understand. This job is not rules. This job is a feeling. Fuck the rules; we'll make them up later. He doesn't know how to be a policeman. I can't be . . . . Oh, you make me fucking sick to my guts. You know you do what you have to do to put these fucking assholes in jail!

And, bragging to McKinny in 1995:

I'm the key witness in the biggest case of the century. And if I go down, they lose the case. The glove is every-thing. Without the glove — 'bye, 'bye.

A final look at Fuhrman as Darden describes him in the days before he testified:

He was driving us all crazy. We weren't preparing him to testify, just holding his hand. He seemed to care noth-ing about the case, about justice, about the victims. He was just worried what was going to happen to him.[8]

Who is this man Mark Fuhrman? A scared cop? If so, why? Is he the worst that the LAPD has to offer? A geno-cidal racist? A glory seeker reaching for the brass ring in other people's tragedies? Did he see himself as a gallant knight? Or was he a victim of circumstances? He would ulti-mately become the person both sides—Defense and Prosecu-tion—would demonize. He became the person everyone could blame.

You are the jury. Driving toward Bundy, in the dark, what was going through Mark Fuhrman's mind? Could he have sensed destiny's crude call, pulling him into the heady mix of bit players in the world of O.J. and Nicole?

We'll go back to Bundy, now, to the early morning hours of June 13. Focus on Detective Fuhrman as the crime scene unfolds.

LAPD Timelines

*It is close to midnight at 875 South Bundy. The area is silent,
no dogs barking except perhaps in the distance. A car may
drive by. A neighbor hears a prowler, she thinks, and calls
911. Another neighbor and his wife walk along Bundy with
Kato, the Akita, its paws still bloodied, hoping this dog will
lead them to its home. It brings them to 875. Sukru Boztepe
and Bettina Rasmussen peer into the dark walkway and see,
amid the ground cover and ferns, a woman's body in a fetal
position, her blood trickling along the tiled walkway.
Rasmussen goes to call 911. Soon the scene begins to fill up
—cars, police, flashing lights. In the darkness, the investigation into this double murder begins.*

    Here follows the broad overview, with times and de-
scriptions that are based on testimony and police logs. Be
mindful that even records may show a few minutes' vari-
ance, and that we chart here the activity of some, but not
all, of the police at the scene. We will return to the scene
again to isolate Fuhrman and analyze his movements.

LAPD—Bundy Timeline	
PM	**JUNE 12**
11:50	Boztepe and Rasmussen discover Nicole's body. Nicole's dog turned over to them by Steven Schwab has led them to 875 South Bundy. Rasmussen calls 911.
11:50	Neighbor Elsie Tistaert calls 911 to report a prowler.
AM	**JUNE 13**
12:17	Officers Riske and Terrazas arrive. Riske discovers second body, Ron Goldman, and sees blood drops to the left of the bloody footprints. Riske at trial testifies that he established the crime scene parameters, so that after him, no officers entered through the front gate. They proceed south on Bundy and west on Dorothy, then north into the alley behind the condo—to enter from the rear. Riske also will testify that he saw a cap and a single glove under a plant. He calls for backup and he and his partner go room to room in the house.

12:20	Officer Cummings arrives and establishes the time log. Officer Hussey also on the scene.
12:30	Riske finds children asleep. He reports it, using Nicole's phone. He sees melting ice cream in cup on bannister.
1:05	Detective Mark Fuhrman, sleeping, gets call at home from Detective Ron Phillips.
1:25	Fuhrman drives to West L.A. Police Station.
1:50	Phillips and Fuhrman meet at West L.A. Station and pick up a homicide unit vehicle, which has a homicide kit in the trunk.
2:10	Phillips and Fuhrman arrive at Bundy. They meet with Rossi and Riske, are briefed and taken around the crime scene.
2:30	Phillips and Riske go to corner of Bundy and Dorothy. Fuhrman sits on couch inside and writes first notes. Outside more officers are arriving. Some are securing the crime scene, others are knocking on neighbors' doors, and blocking traffic.
2:30	Lieutenant Frank Spangler, Fuhrman's superior officer, arrives at Bundy. Talks to Rossi, views the crime scene with Phillips. Phillips tells Fuhrman that Robbery/Homicide detectives are coming to take over the case. Fuhrman finishes his notes.
2:50	Fuhrman is at corner of Bundy and Dorothy awaiting the lead detectives. He testifies that because he is no longer in charge, he does "no detecting" between 2:50 and 4:00 AM. However, during this time, Spangler asks him to view the crime scene with him from the pathway near the fence by the victims. After this, Spangler testifies, they return to the corner.
2:50	Photographer Rolf Rokahr gets call to go to Bundy.
3:00	Robbery/Homicide Detectives Philip Vannatter and Tom Lange are called to report to Bundy.
3:25	Rokahr arrives at Bundy.
4:05	Vannatter arrives at 875 South Bundy. Phillips gives him Fuhrman's notes, briefs him, and takes him on tour of crime site. Vannatter takes no notes himself. Vannatter finishes tour and goes to Bundy and Dorothy where he joins Captain Dial, Lieutenant Rogers, Fuhrman and others.
4:25	Tom Lange arrives at Bundy. Phillips shows Lange around. Phillips tells Lange that Commander Bushey

has ordered "personal notification" be given to O.J. Simpson. After tour of crime scene Lange joins others at corner of Bundy and Dorothy.

5:00 Phillips asks Fuhrman if he can lead Lange and Vannatter up to Simpson's Rockingham estate, since they do not know the way. Fuhrman checks the exact address with Riske, because he has not been to the estate since 1985, he will testify. The four detectives leave in two cars, Phillips and Fuhrman leading. Vannatter testifies that all four go because he believed the other two detectives could "assist in the disposition of the children and handling of the situation."

We now leave the Bundy crime scene with the four LAPD officers and head for the Rockingham estate of O.J. Simpson, a short five-or-six-minute drive away.

LAPD—Rockingham Timeline

AM **JUNE 13**

5:05 The four detectives arrive at 360 North Rockingham. At the Ashford gate, they ring the outside gate entry bell 10 to 15 minutes, get no answer. Seeing a sign for Westec security, Phillips calls them on his cellular phone.

5:20 Fuhrman, flashlight in hand and alone, begins checking out a white Ford Bronco parked, as both Vannatter and Fuhrman would testify, "a little askew" on Rockingham. Vannatter joins him and Fuhrman points out a stick lying on the pavement that Vannatter testifies "didn't seem to fit in the area." They also see items inside the Bronco, a box addressed to "Orenthal Productions," and a shovel and large piece of plastic in the rear cargo area.

5:30 Vannatter tells Fuhrman to run a check on the Bronco license plate.

Back at the Ashford gate a Westec unit has pulled up. Vannatter returns to the gate, as Phillips is requesting the telephone number for the estate.

Fuhrman calls Vannatter back to the Bronco. On this dark residential street, with only his small flashlight for illumination, he has found a spot—much smaller than the size of a dime—above the driver's door handle. They both think it looks like blood.

Vannatter testifies that at this point, he felt they could have there "an extension of the Bundy crime scene where someone could have been killed or hurt or injured." A police car that just reported to the location is asked to call for a criminalist—to do a presumptive test on the spot on the Bronco. No criminalist has yet been called to Bundy.

5:45 The detectives discuss their findings and the situation. By now, they have the phone number of the residence and have called but gotten only a machine. They have also learned there is supposed to be a live-in maid. They know that the Bronco is registered to Hertz, and, knowing Simpson is a Hertz spokesman, they assume the vehicle is his. Vannatter testifies that he and his partner Lange conferred and made the decision that they needed to enter the estate "and find out if everything was okay." At trial, Fuhrman states he said to Vannatter, "We have an emergency here. There may be people bleeding to death inside." Fuhrman volunteers to go over the wall and open the gate to admit them.

The detectives go to the front door. No answer. They follow a walkway around to the rear, meeting a docile, friendly dog, who does not bark or attack. They come upon the guesthouse. Phillips knocks, awakening Kato Kaelin, who directs them to Arnelle Simpson's room.

6:00 Fuhrman stays with Kaelin and questions him alone. Fuhrman learns about the "thumps" of the night before, then takes Kaelin inside the house and leaves him for the other detectives to question.

6:05 Arnelle helps the detectives locate her father. Phillips calls Simpson in Chicago to notify him of events.

6:05 Alone, Fuhrman goes around to the side of the guesthouse to the area behind Kaelin's room. In the darkness, he shines his light on the ground and discovers a moist-looking bloody glove. After checking out the area for 15 minutes, looking for a victim or a suspect to go with the glove, as he testifies at trial, he returns to the house. One by one he brings the others out to view the glove.

6:45 Vannatter sends Fuhrman and Phillips back to Bundy to see if the Bundy glove is similar to the one found at Rockingham. Lange returns in a separate car to take charge of the Bundy crime scene. Vannatter stays at Rockingham.

7:00 Phillips and Fuhrman return to Bundy. Phillips directs Fuhrman to get the photographer, Rokahr, and have him photograph the Bundy glove, and then return with him to Rockingham to photograph the second glove.

When Fuhrman returns to Rockingham and reports the gloves look like a pair, Vannatter declares Rockingham a crime scene and begins writing a warrant.

7:10 Criminalist Dennis Fung arrives at Rockingham. He goes to Bundy after completing work at Rockingham.

8:00 A call to the Coroner's Office is made. They arrive at Bundy about 9:00 AM.

10:10 Criminalist arrives at Bundy.

PM

1:35 At Parker Center, Vannatter and Lange begin their interview with Simpson, who has returned from Chicago. Interview completed at 2:07 PM. Simpson's blood sample is taken. Vannatter carries this sample to criminalist Fung at Rockingham hours later. At trial, the Defense argues this is highly irregular procedure. In post-trial interviews Vannatter will state he did so to preserve the "chain of evidence."

6:30 Fuhrman leaves Rockingham, having remained all day with other police "keeping the location secure."

We have walked through the Bundy and Rockingham crime scenes, focusing on Fuhrman's activities. Notice the many places where Fuhrman is first, alone, or has the opportunity to be alone:

- He and Phillips are the first detectives to arrive at Bundy.

- Fuhrman explores the Bronco by himself, finding the stick on the pavement and the blood spot on the door.

- He has relatively free access to Rockingham during the first half-hour inside the estate.

- He is alone when he finds the Rockingham glove.

- He is photographed with the Bundy glove.

- He remains at Rockingham until 6:30 PM and is there when Vannatter returns with O.J.'s blood sample.

- He testifies at trial that at Bundy he found "a partial fingerprint and two additional blood drops on the back gate" that had not been seen earlier by Riske.

F. Lee Bailey for the Defense would argue at trial that the jury would:

. . . have to evaluate the question as to whether or not this officer, incensed at being kicked off the biggest murder case in the history of this state, decided to keep himself in it by coming an indispensable witness as he surely has done.

The Fuhrman Timelines

With Fuhrman's history and his taped comments ("you know you do what you have to do to put these fucking assholes in jail,") in mind, consider a second timeline. This includes information from testimony plus explosive allegations raised in Singular's *Legacy of Deception*. Information from the book is marked with the symbol "+" and italicized.

The Fuhrman Timeline—1	
AM	
1:05	Fuhrman, sleeping, gets call at home from Phillips. He learns there has been a double homicide at 875 South Bundy and that the female victim might be the ex-wife of O.J. Simpson.
1:25	Fuhrman drives to West L.A. Police Station.
1:50	Phillips and Fuhrman meet at West L.A. Station and pick up a homicide unit vehicle, which has a homicide kit in the trunk. At the station Fuhrman learns that Simpson is on a trip to Chicago. This has been reported to the station by Sydney Simpson.
2:10	Fuhrman and Phillips arrive at Bundy. Fuhrman is wearing a light jacket with tie. Lt. Spangler at trial testifies that when he arrived at 2:30 AM Fuhrman was wearing his jacket but that when he asked him to view

Goldman's wounds with him about 3:00 AM, he was not wearing it.

2:20 Fuhrman tours crime scene grounds and inside residence, where he writes his notes. About 2:30 he is told that Robbery/Homicide is taking over the case.

+*Outside, Fuhrman sees the blood-soaked Akita playing with a uniformed cop who is a friend of Fuhrman's.*

+*In the back alley, Fuhrman breaks off a sliver from a wooden fence.*

+ *He inspects the bodies up close. He picks up one of the gloves with the sliver of wood.*

+ *He transfers the glove to a blue evidence envelope in the trunk of his vehicle.*

3:00 Fuhrman testified that at about 3:00 AM., after leaving the condo and before going to stand on the corner of Dorothy and Bundy to await Robbery/Homicide, he had removed his jacket and placed it in the car. He also stated that from 2:50 to 4:00 AM he was standing on the corner at Bundy and Dorothy with others waiting for the lead detectives to arrive. But, in Singular's scenario, Fuhrman leaves Bundy during this time.

3:00 +*Fuhrman drives to 360 Rockingham, accompanied by another officer.*

+*Fuhrman plants the glove in the walkway of the Simpson estate. (At this time, Fuhrman may have planted blood evidence inside the Bronco.)*

+*He has a dispute with the other officer about this. Their voices and agitated barking are overheard by Rosa Lopez, who is sleeping in her room on the other side of the fence. In the course of the dispute, Fuhrman drops a torn piece of the blue evidence bag near the walkway.*

+*Fuhrman also drops the sliver of wood on the road next to the white Bronco.*

3:20 +*Fuhrman returns to Bundy crime scene.*

4:00 Fuhrman is back in the middle of the murder scene when lead detectives Vannatter and Lange arrive at Bundy.

+*Fuhrman tells Vannatter that he had once broken up a spousal dispute between Nicole and O.J. Simpson in 1985 and that there could be murder evidence at Simpson's house.*[9]

Lange's testimony indicates that Phillips told him before the four detectives left for Rockingham that Fuhrman had mentioned an earlier domestic violence incident that had resulted in Simpson's arrest.

Could this have happened? There were more that a dozen LAPD police and detectives at the Bundy crime scene at its height—in the confusion, could two of them have slipped away to plant the glove at Rockingham?

There could also be other explanations for how the glove found its way to Rockingham. Perhaps Fuhrman found it on the street: Could the dog have carried it there? Remember the bloody paw prints going south on Bundy, toward the corner where Fuhrman waited for the lead detectives.

Or, perhaps the glove lay hidden beneath a bush and had not been visible to the officers who initially only had flashlights to help them penetrate the darkness. Recall that the people who came upon the bodies had not noticed Goldman's body at all. Could Fuhrman have seen the glove when he viewed the bodies and tucked it into his pocket, knowing it was important evidence, and planning to "find it" at an appropriate time?

Perhaps he did not even think about framing Simpson, but only about doing something to put himself back in the center of the investigation. Darden described Fuhrman before testifying as not thinking about justice or the victims, but only about himself. Recall Fuhrman's boasts to McKinny about being "at the center of the biggest case of the century. If I go down, they lose the case. The glove is everything."

Did Fuhrman carry the glove with him to Rockingham and then "find it" outside the guesthouse after learning about the mysterious thumps? Is it not also possible that the source of the thumping noise was not the person responsible for the glove?

These are just some of the many scenarios that could help to explain how the mysterious glove wound up at the Simpson estate. We now offer more information that the jury may wish to consider. We note that some of what we have discovered in our research contradicts Fuhrman's testimony during the trial.

The Fuhrman Timeline—2

AM

2:30   Lieutenant Frank Spangler, Fuhrman's superior officer, arrives at Bundy. Talks to Rossi, views the crime scene with Phillips. Phillips tells Fuhrman that Robbery/Homicide detectives are taking over the case. Fuhrman finishes his notes. At trial, he will tell Defense lawyer Bailey that "he was disappointed in losing a case that looked very interesting and complex."

2:50   Fuhrman is at corner of Bundy and Dorothy awaiting homicide. He testifies that because he is no longer in charge, he does "no detecting" from 2:50 and 4:00 AM. However, during this time Spangler asks him to view the crime scene with him from the pathway near the fence by the victims. They do so and Fuhrman identifies the wounds as being made by a knife, not a gun. Spangler testifies that Fuhrman is the only officer present to 1) enter the crime scene and 2) identify the wounds as knife wounds.

3:25   Photographer Rokahr arrives at Bundy.

4:40   An LAPD photograph is taken of Fuhrman pointing to a glove lying near Goldman. Fuhrman, later, will erroneously state that the photo was taken after his return from Rockingham, about 7 AM.[10] The police photographer testified that he found Fuhrman alone and near the glove, before taking the photograph of Fuhrman pointing to the glove.

5:00   Phillips asks Fuhrman if he can lead Detective Lange and Vannatter up to Simpson's Rockingham estate, because they do not know the way. Lange testifies that Phillips told him before the four detectives left for Rockingham that Fuhrman had mentioned an earlier domestic violence incident that had resulted in Simpson's arrest.

5:13   Fuhrman runs the license plate of the Bronco, just minutes after arriving at the Rockingham address.

5:25   Other officers arrive in a police car from Bundy—yet Vannatter testified that the four detectives had gone to Rockingham to make a death announcement and ask Simpson to pick up his two young children at the West L.A. station. Why did the police car follow them a few minutes later, and more than ten minutes before Fuhrman and Vannatter say they entered the Simpson property?

6:05 Police photographs also show part of a blue evidence bag near the glove. Note: Defense and independent blood experts insist that for the Rockingham glove to still be wet with blood at this time, the glove must have been concealed or covered in some kind of container for several hours.

6:49 Detectives at Rockingham refuse to let the coroner go to the Bundy crime scene until later.

A police car from Bundy arrives with a uniformed officer, a friend of Fuhrman's, who has been playing with Kato the Akita at Bundy. The officer may have picked up blood from the dog's legs and paws. He and Fuhrman "investigate" the Bronco. The door is unlocked or broken open by Fuhrman (at this time or earlier). The uniformed officer reaches into the Bronco and opens the hood.[11]

Could the bloodstains in the Bronco—not mentioned by Fuhrman prior to jumping the wall to the Rockingham property—have been left at this point by the officer who may have gotten blood on himself from playing with the blood-soaked Akita?

In *Legacy of Deception*, Singular relates a conversation about this with his source:

Source: *All the blood in the Bronco is suspect.*
Singular: *What do you mean?*
Source: *You should question every bit of it.*
Singular: *How did it get there?*
Source: *I don't know how it got on the console, but I can tell you a few things and you can draw your own conclusions. Don't you find it curious that if the four detectives, who went to Simpson's house at five o'clock in the morning of June 13, wanted a good and plausible excuse for jumping O.J.'s fence without a search warrant, they would have mentioned the bloodstains?*
Singular: *What if they didn't see them? It was still fairly dark outside.*
Source: *You saw pictures of the smears, didn't you?*
Singular: *Yes.*
Source: *Didn't they seem pretty obvious to you?*
Singular: *Much more obvious than the tiny speck of blood that Fuhrman said he saw on the outside of the*

truck. Are you saying that the smears appeared inside the Bronco later?

Source: *At the preliminary hearing, did Fuhrman testify about seeing these smears?*

Singular: *No.*

Source: *Did Vannatter?*

Singular: *No.*

Source: *Did anyone else?*

Singular: *Not to my knowledge.*

Source: *Has anyone talked to the people in the LAPD fingerprint shed? The truck was taken there after it was hauled away from Simpson's house.*

Singular: *You're saying that the stains were placed there later?*

Source: *Draw your own conclusions.*[12]

We are reminded that the Bronco was broken into at least once at Viertel's impound yard, and that when criminalist Dennis Fung returned to the Bronco on August 26, 1994, he discovered more blood in the vehicle than had been previously recorded.

Continuing with the Fuhrman Timeline:

AM

8:30   Fuhrman questions Rosa Lopez, the maid at the Salingers' home, on the other side of the walkway behind the Simpson guesthouses. Lopez tells Fuhrman she heard men making noise and speaking loudly on the Simpson property at around 3:00 AM. She says she knows Simpson's voice and that Simpson was not one of the men. The tenor of their voices frightened her. Lopez also says she walked the Salinger family dog at around 10:15 PM and saw the white Bronco parked outside the Rockingham gate.

Fuhrman writes down none of Rosa Lopez's observations and tells her someone from the LAPD will be in touch later. Fuhrman walks around the Salinger property "as if looking for something," according to Lopez. No officer or detective from the LAPD will ever contact Rosa Lopez.

We note that when Mark Fuhrman climbed over the fence after 5 AM, and entered Rockingham with the other detectives, the dog lay in the driveway and made not a sound. As in Sherlock Holmes' case of "The Dog That Didn't Bark," could Chachi's silence here indicate that the dog knew the "stranger" Fuhrman?

9:30 Video taken of Simpson's bedroom reveals no bloody socks on the rug. Fuhrman is outside at the time. Later, Fuhrman goes upstairs in the Simpson residence to look for clues and evidence, and afterward comments to other detectives about a letter from O.J. to Nicole that he had seen in the bedroom.

The bloody socks are found by other officers—after the video was taken and after Fuhrman went upstairs.

Planted Blood Evidence

Now, the questions we must ask are:

- Did Fuhrman plant blood evidence at Bundy?

- Did Fuhrman plant blood on or in the Bronco?

- Did Fuhrman plant the Rockingham glove?

- Did Fuhrman deposit blood on the Rockingham driveway ?

- Did Fuhrman put blood on Simpson's socks?

Our timeline suggests that Fuhrman had the opportunity to plant the sliver of wood by the Bronco, the blood on the outside of the Bronco, the glove at Rockingham, the blood on the socks, and the blood elsewhere at Rockingham. Fuhrman probably could not have planted the Bundy blood—although this does not mean that this evidence could not have been tampered with or contaminated later.

Bundy Blood Swatches 47, 48, 49, 50, 52

The Bundy blood: these blood samples were collected by in-training criminalist Andrea Mazzola and labeled with her initials. These same samples of evidence came out of the LAPD lab on unmarked swatches.

Dr. Henry Lee was focusing on the handling of these swatches when he stated, "Something wrong," suggesting tampering.

Blood on the Bronco: Blood Smears 30 and 31

LAPD criminalist Dennis Fung had been ordered to collect blood from the Bronco in mid-June by Clark, in order to back up Fuhrman's original claim of sighting blood streaks on the Bronco door.

When Fung returned to the Bronco on August 26, 1994, photographs picture more blood than was there in the first place. And the blood smears were inside the vehicle. Recall that Fuhrman had sworn that the Bronco was locked when he came upon it June 13.

On June 13, the Bronco was not locked, we now know, because Fuhrman's friend—a uniformed officer who may have gotten blood from Bundy on himself after holding Nicole's Akita—entered the vehicle and flipped open the hood for inspection.

LAPD Detective Kelly Mulldorfer testified at trial that Blood Samples 30 and 31 had not been present when the Bronco was taken to the fingerprint shed on June 13.

Back Gate Blood

Blood from the Bundy back gate, while observed on June 13, was not collected until three weeks later. During this time, the site had been unsecured.

The gate blood contained signs consistent with the presence of EDTA (police preservative fluid), as did the dress socks from Rockingham. In February of 1995, D.A. Rockne Harmon wrote to the FBI asking them to run tests "to refute" the charge that blood evidence had been taken from Simpson blood samples.

Blood Tests, August

On August 4, 1994, all of the blood from Bundy and Rockingham, plus the blood samples from the victims and Simpson, were brought out and put together in the LAPD lab. This is the day that the blood on the socks was found; more blood from the Bronco was identified; the Bundy blood that Mazzola had not initialed was packaged; and all of the blood evidence went out to the various testing laboratories the Prosecution used in this case.

Rockingham Glove

The Defense will skillfully exploit Fuhrman's credibility and charge that Fuhrman actually planted the bloody glove, after removing it from the crime scene at Bundy. When cross-examining Fuhrman at the trial, on March 12, 1995, Defense Attorney F. Lee Bailey retraced Fuhrman's steps at the Bundy scene on the morning of June 13th. When he was done, many legal experts believed he had established that Fuhrman had five to fifteen seconds alone with Goldman's body, when he presumably could have picked up the glove.

No one has proven this Defense theory, but some may believe that our timeline analysis and the circumstantial evidence lend credibility to their allegations.

Blood on the Socks

A major media leak that occured on September 1994 also threw some of the blood evidence into question. Traci Savage, KNBC-TV reporter, broadcast that DNA tests on the socks found in Simpson's bedroom identified the blood as Nicole's. At the time of her announcement, however, the blood on the socks had not yet been sent to Cellmark for testing. Thus, the Defense argued, when the tests indicated Nicole's blood being present, that the results could be known in advance because the blood was planted.

The Black Dahlia Murder Case

Is it conceivable that an official conspiracy could falsify, frame, and plant all of the evidence? If Mark Fuhrman is guilty and not acting alone, do his co-conspirators include hundreds of officials and thousands of police? Of course not. A State plot may involve only one or two conspirators, and a larger number of passive, unquestioning, or Code-of-Silence individuals. (The 1991 Rodney King beating included 25 police witnesses.)

Illegal behavior by the authorities is often the work of a very small confederation or even one person, while the cover-up of the violation can spread over an entire layer of bureaucracy. As an example of such a circumstance, consider the sensational "Black Dahlia" murder case. It occurred in L.A. in the late 1940s and never went to trial.

- Elizabeth Short, a beautiful part-time actress, who also worked as a waitress, was brutally murdered.

- Short had drifted into a Hollywood sex and drugs ring, run by various nightclub owners.

- A police psychiatrist found the killer and brought him "downtown" for interrogation.

- The press waited for the arrest—which never came.

- The killer was released and disappeared.

- The psychiatrist was fired.

- The murder remained unsolved.

- Independent investigators—of that day—learned that a brutal psychopath had been allowed to run free because, (a) he had been a small-time hood employed by the well-connected nightclub owners, who were involved in sex and narcotics traffic and who were, (b) paying off a number of corrupt LAPD detectives and high-ranking police officials.

- The D.A.'s office covered up for the LAPD.

- The L.A. press kept the facts from the public.

• The public lost faith in the police. The Chief and high aides were fired. The LAPD virtually collapsed.

LAPD Media Timeline

Could a Los Angeles-based jury be predisposed to believe that police might perjure themselves or falsify or plant evidence? The Simpson trial did not exist in a vacuum. The Rodney King incident had occurred only a few years before, in 1991. In fact, Fuhrman had been one of the forty-five police officers identified in the Christopher Commission Report, the city's response to the Rodney King beatings.[13]

Charges against the LAPD probably would not have been a surprise to any members of the jury. Throughout the trial and right up to weeks before the civil trial, local papers carried stories pointing to LAPD misdeeds, some at high levels.

A selection of 1994–96 news accounts:

1994–Sheriff's Department–Los Angeles County: The Sheriff's Department pays a record $611,000 for the 1990 beating of four "suspects" who appeared to be guilty of drinking beer on the pavement outside their home.

1995–Los Angeles: Detective Teague—another Christopher Commission "problem officer"—and his partner are charged with forging a confession in a shooting case. Teague, after eighteen years of service, is dismissed from the force along with his partner. In a postscript to the case, the D.A.'s office concluded that no charges should be brought.

1995–Sheriff's Department–Los Angeles County: A deputy in training resigns after accusing her training officer of planting drugs and other evidence on innocent Latino suspects. This was alleged to be a regular practice because the deputies earned overtime for testifying in such cases at trial.

1995–Santa Monica Police Department: The Santa Monica Police Department is sued in Federal Court by the ACLU for the violation of the Miranda Rights of suspects. Under interrogation, suspects were told that attorneys were expensive, time-consuming, and would "just get in the way."

1995–Inglewood, California: A state-employed courier has a flat tire while driving in a rental car from LAX to downtown Los Angeles. While he is out of the car checking the tire, someone goes into the car through a partially open window to steal his jacket and a manila envelope he has carried from Sacramento. An insignificant street crime—except that the envelope contained photographs of the assassination of Robert F. Kennedy.

The photographs were being returned to their owner. He had sued the State for their return after the official files were released in 1988. For seven years, the State had said the photographs were "lost" until they mysteriously appeared in a filing cabinet in Sacramento,only to soon fall prey to what a city attorney calls, "a run of bad luck."

March 1, 1996: The *Los Angeles Times* reported a new scandal in a story headlined "LAPD Drug Officer Being Investigated." The charge involved the Field Enforcement Section of the LAPD Narcotics Group. This unit was under the command of Captain Constance Dial—who had been one of those in charge of the Bundy crime scene on June 12,1994. The story began: "Authorities fear detectives may have lied on court documents . . . ." On the same day, another story in the same paper is headlined: Deputy Accused of Planting Evidence Surrenders.

Finally, one must not overlook the total setting for the Simpson trial: The Los Angeles D.A.'s office had experienced a string of stunning losses at trial, including the McMartin sexual molestation cases, the Rodney King scandal and trial, and the Menendez brothers debacle. They needed to win this one, and it had not started off well. The entire LAPD had been publicly disgraced by allowing Simpson to escape in the Bronco chase spectacle.

We do not mean to suggest that the District Attorney actively combined with conspirators lower down on the law enforcement ladder. We simply place the Simpson case in its local political context.

In the last analysis, Mark Fuhrman may be as much a scapegoat as a rogue. The LAPD and Prosecution knew everything about Fuhrman because he was their creature, their offspring—they taught him, promoted him, turned over cadets in training to him. The judge knew about him too—Ito's wife, Captain Margaret York, had investigated Fuhrman. Darden and others made it very clear that some within the LAPD had serious reservations about letting Fuhrman testify at all. And yet, the Prosecution's office chose to put him on, although they were aware of his "nasty baggage."

Darden reveals in his post-trial book that he and the D.A.'s office were also aware that the Defense might argue evidence tampering. He writes that a man who was "a very good source" called him in early November 1994 to report that the Defense would claim that the blood stain on the gate was taken from Simpson's blood afterward and planted. He informed Darden that a woman in the police lab was helping the Defense. She claimed that a supervisor told her to put some of Simpson's blood onto a clean swatch. Darden learned that the information actually came from an independent author named Stephen Singular, who claimed to have talked to the woman while researching the Simpson case.

Darden took his notes on the conversation about Singular to a meeting with Marcia Clark and Bill Hodgman, who dismissed the matter. But Darden decided to look into it further. In reviewing the Defense's discovery requests, he found one for:

> *Two empty test tubes, tops and seals, used by the nurse who drew blood from the defendant O.J. Simpson on June 13, 1994 . . . thirty unused clean swatches from the same batch . . . .*[14]

The implication was that Simpson's blood reference samples were not secure and were being tampered with by staff within the Scientific Investigation Department. Darden writes:

> *This was Brady material . . . and we were required to turn it over to the defense because the manuscript. . . might contain certain information that would conceivably exonerate their client.*[15]

A few days later, Darden and Clark met in Judge Ito's chambers to tell the Defense, on the record, about the Singular manuscript. Soon after that, an investigator for the Prosecution found the Singular proposal and gave it to Darden. At once, Darden grasped that it contained information that could, if true, destroy the Prosecution's case. The proposal described the information that Singular had given the Defense in August 1994, shortly after the murders:

- Fuhrman had known Nicole Simpson since 1985 and had been her "special cop."

- Fuhrman had used a stick to pick up one of the two bloody gloves near Goldman.

- Fuhrman put the glove in a blue plastic evidence bag, drove to Simpson's and jumped his fence. He dropped the bloody glove and hid the stick and bag nearby.

- Fuhrman briefly had access to the blood sample drawn from Simpson and had dropped the blood on the Bundy sidewalk and the gate.

Singular said that a police lab preservative, EDTA, would be found in the last blood sample. Darden was shaken:

I was basically looking at a blueprint of O.J. Simpson's defense, months before it became operational . . . . Singular was writing about information that hadn't been made public at the time he wrote his treatment.[16]

As explosive as this information was, the prosecution did not investigate any of it further.

Finally, common sense demands to know: If Simpson is not the killer, what link or relationship could possibly exist between a police conspiracy (involving one or more people) to frame Simpson and, let us say, a narcotics murder? The answer is that there need be no connection between them whatsoever.

The next section will provide you with more information and leads to consider before you begin to weigh the evidence and reach your verdict.

Seven

The
Open
Timeline

. . . I don't know anymore._____[a D.A.]
even said to me he thinks maybe Ron Goldman
wasn't alone, that he came with someone or some-
one forced him to—used him to get at her. I don't
know. . . For a while they thought there were two
of the Broncos in use because—one in front of
Bundy, one in back. It's possible because—you
want to hear something strange—they [the D.A.]
believed Rosa Lopez. I'm telling you. That's why
they went after her. They believed her and
Heidstra—and that's the end of their case, because
of the time . . . Fuhrman? If that strange person
wasn't just bragging about an affair with Nicole
Simpson—if they ever reopen this case and find out
Fuhrman was connected . . .

B̲efore summing up and declaring the case closed or open, in the name of probity let us glare into the face of the facts one last time and ask—"What if the Prosecution's timeline was false, couldn't O.J. Simpson still be the killer?"

To answer this, we can look once again at Simpson's opportunity in its broadest sense. He was seen by Kaelin at Rockingham at 9:36 PM and not seen again until 10:55 PM. A time of approximately 80 minutes, with Bundy just a brief five or six minutes away. Time enough to get to Bundy and back, time enough to kill. All that is known of Simpson's movements within that period is that he placed calls to Barbieri at 10:02 and 10:03. Once the jury frees itself of the rigid restrictions of the Prosecution timeline, it becomes apparent that in terms of opportunity, Simpson had the time to commit the murders.

This investigation suggested a number of possible scenarios that fit that window of opportunity; some include Simpson and some do not. We have considered ear-witnesses, eyewitnesses, evidence, logistics of transportation, and the social identities of both victims. The task before the jury is now to do the same: Looking at the window of opportunity, create a credible timeline and scenario. For this purpose, we include a timeline template in the Appendix. This book is the beginning of your database. But it is only a start.

The Simpson jury found reasonable doubt when they deliberated. No one from our team has yet been able to answer the question that we asked from the start: Who murdered Nicole Brown Simpson and Ronald Lyle Goldman between 10:00 PM and 12:00 midnight on the night of June 12, 1994?

O.J. Simpson: The Interview

When the O.J. Simpson post-trial video was finally released, the media gave it little weight, saying there was nothing new in it. It is true that Simpson's discussion of the trail of blood is substantially what was heard at trial. However, for the first time the public is taken into the Rockingham estate, including the area of the air conditioning unit behind Kaelin's guest room. This is what the viewer sees, as Simpson leads:

- He walks along the narrow path. It is thick with brush, berries, and vines.

- He passes two doors that allow entrance into the house. He identifies these as leading to a garage and a laundry room.

- The air conditioning unit protrudes from the wall and fills the width of the path, at head height. Anyone running into it would in all probability sustain a wound to the head and face. Anyone crawling beneath it—the only way to pass—would certainly get dirt and debris from the ground on his clothes.

If Simpson, or someone, had climbed over the fence from the adjoining property, he would have had to turn to the left, on the path, going away from the unit, to enter the house. No need to navigate the air conditioner, unless he dropped to the other side of it.

- This area, as noted, has dirt, leaves, and other debris. It is here that the glove was found, wet with blood and folded over. And yet, the glove had none of the leaves or dirt or debris that one would expect. Seeing the location makes one wonder all the more why was there no debris on the glove.

- In another part of the tour, Simpson illustrates how it is possible for the interior of the house to have many lights on and yet for it to seem dark when viewed from the outside, as Park would have seen it.

The coda to the tape is an intense declaration concerning Simpson's feelings of guilt that he did not "take Nicole and the children away"—as he was warned to do by their mutual friend Cora Fischman—ten days before the murders. Simpson calls, again, for a real investigation and pledges his cooperation. He swears by his God that he did not commit the murders.[1]

The Bundy Murders: a Forensic Puzzle

On the eve of the civil trial, Simpson continues to profess his innocence. Where has our investigation taken us? Some may believe that we have worked our way to the edge of two conspiracies: the killing, and the Fuhrman scenario. The killers who stalked and threatened, who murdered "restaurant" waiters, who broke and entered—on the one hand—

and those who planted or covered up evidence on the other. Some may find that we have demonstrated the inadequacy of the official Prosecution timeline and the need to create a different, credible timeline if Simpson is to be shown to be the killer. But on some things it may be possible to agree:

- As we have explored the timelines and considered the physical evidence with care, the mountain of evidence linking Simpson to the crime seems to have shrunk.

- Our dependence on interviews, impressions, and reports has grown.

Sometimes the latter can help to unravel complicated crimes, just as the Zapruder film forever changed our understanding of the assassination of JFK. Sometimes science overrules eyewitnesses, as in cases where DNA evidence has exonerated "criminals" convicted by eyewitness testimony and answers given under oath.

For now, the Bundy murders are still pieces of a scattered forensic puzzle. Only when physical timelines and report evidence fit into a credible scenario with motive and opportunity, will we be able to say that the murders have been solved. To reach this point might require one additional element as well: a credible confession.

Now that you, as a juror, have returned to the scene of the crime again and again, perhaps you agree with Dr. Lee's statement: "Something wrong."

Leads to Pursue

As you begin to develop your own scenario and timeline, you may want to consider some of the following leads:

- Defense investigators found the recipient of two pairs of Aris Isotoner gloves from Nicole Simpson. The recipient, contacted the D.A.—silence. Was this two more pair, or the only two pairs?

- There were gloves in Simpson's closet that neither side introduced into evidence. Vannatter handled a single brown glove at Rockingham that was not covered with blood. Where is this glove?

- Why would no present-day Aris Isotoner executives testify at trial?

- Was Nicole Simpson pregnant? We have learned that she believed she was. Is it possible that the coroner's autopsy could overlook this important question?

- Acquaintances of Ron Goldman were allegedly involved in mob-connected pornography and prostitution. Was Goldman pressured by organized vice? Did he expect to borrow money from certain "leisure industry" sources to finance his new restaurant?

- More on the murder of Goldman's friend, Michael Nigg, from a September 9, 1995 *Associated Press* story out of Los Angeles, that ran with the headline: Friend of Ronald Goldman Killed.

  The story reported that Nigg, 26, was killed Friday night as he and his girlfriend were going to a restaurant. Police spokeswoman Cherie Clair is quoted as saying that Nigg had just stepped out of his car when two thieves approached and demanded money. When he refused, he was shot in the head, while the woman with him, Julie Long, was not injured or robbed. The thieves fled in a car driven by a third suspect.

  According to the article, Nigg was from Colorado and had previously worked at Mezzaluna in nearby Brentwood, where he and Goldman were good friends. It also reported that Nigg quit Mezzaluna in May 1994, just a month before Goldman and Nicole Simpson were slain.

  Was the Nigg murder, in fact, a random crime? There are telling indications to the contrary: no robbery; a second person left unharmed; a getaway car; the killers who just "walked" away.

- We have learned that the stocking cap found at the murder scene was one of two belonging to the family, and that the children often wore this cap.

- What connection, if any, is there between the crimes of June 12th and a murder our Source reports occurred in the Bundy neighborhood in 1993?

- An investigator for the Defense asserts that the contents of Nicole Simpson's stomach were not "lost," as the coroner testified to in court, but stolen. Coroner Golden was made the scapegoat for its absence. Is this being investigated?

- A New York photographer who claims to have photographed Simpson in Florida wearing Bruno Magli shoes—the brand linked to the bloody footprints at Bundy—is to be deposed for the civil trail. The controversial photograph was supposedly taken sometime before the murders. For the Prosecution, this new "evidence" could more strongly link Simpson to the crime scene. The Defense is likely to argue that the photograph was doctored.

- On June 7, 1996, a story by Stephanie Simon in the *Los Angeles Times* reported that Detective Philip Vannatter went to the coroner's office on June 15, 1994 and picked up blood samples of Nicole Brown Simpson and Ron Goldman. Criminalist Gary L. Siglar revealed this information during his May 2, 1996 deposition for the civil trial. The samples were used to compare the victims' genetic makeup with blood splotches on pieces of evidence, including the socks found in Simpson's bedroom and the gloves found at his estate and at the Bundy crime scene.

  Siglar said that all other evidence was sent directly to the LAPD's Scientific Investigation Division. Simpson lawyer Daniel P. Leonard asked Siglar how often he had seen samples handed directly to a detective. He replied that he had "seen it occur a few times" during his twelve years with the coroner's office. However, the headline for the story reporting this was: Simpson Detective Deviated from Usual Practice, Expert Testifies. According to Simon's account, LAPD Police Captain WIll Garland defended Vannatter's actions, saying there were good reasons for Vannatter to pick up the blood himself: to save time and to keep close tabs on the vials.[2]

Remember that LAPD did not record or log in the blood evidence from the crime scene until after June 16, 1994—three days after the collection by police criminalists, and one day after Vannatter took the victims' blood from the coroner's office. Thus, between June 13 and June 16, Detective Vannatter had in his possession, for some period of time, samples of all the principals' blood.

In legal terms, this development is likely to be bigger for the Defense than the fact that Vannatter also hand-carried Simpson's blood sample on June 13, 1994 to Rockingham instead of booking it into evidence downtown. This act was critical to the Defense's charges of conspiracy and that blood was planted.

• On June 12, 1996, two years after the murders, the *LA Times* reported that the blood swatch from the Bundy back gate has been lost.

• On July 1, 1996, a source close to the Chicago Police Department said that _____, a 14-year-old boy, saw three Caucasian men in the alley behind Nicole's Bundy townhouse after 10:30 pm on June 12, 1994, the night of the murders. The boy's parents informed the LAPD. The boy was never questioned. The parents were threatened by an anonymous telephone caller to "keep quiet" or "be killed." they are now debating whether to come forward.[3]

• Police officers informed the Defense that Fuhrman was among those officers conducting a search in Simpson's bedroom on June 28, 1994. At the time, Fuhrman had been off the case since June 13.

- Criminalist Dennis Fung was promoted during the course of trial. The Police Protective League is once again defending Fuhrman to the media. Vannatter is now active in media appearances, defending his actions and criticizing the LAPD for not defending him and Lange during the trial. Vannatter and Detective Tom Lange are said to be interested in writing a book.

The Media

From the day the bodies of Nicole Brown Simpson and Ronald Goldman were discovered at Bundy, the tabloid press staked their claim as the premier news arbiters in the case. The jury cannot turn up its collective nose at the story from the gutter or the supermarket or the television tabloid: Like our personal night terror they tell us that there is something wrong. Though often reviled, the tabloids spent fortunes during the Simpson trial to maintain their lead over the respectable press.

It is common knowledge that in its coverage of the trial, the *Enquirer* often broke stories before the establishment press. In a recent conversation between John Kennedy Jr. and *Enquirer* editor emeritus Iaim Calder, Calder discussed the paper's coverage of the Simpson trial:

> . . . *we were working alongside—and in the same court-room as, the* LA Times, The New York Times, Newsweek, Time, *and the television stations. Very quickly, the* Enquirer *became a hot item in the courtroom on a Monday morning. And not only was the* Enquirer *breaking stories that were really exclusives, but we were also not going with many of the stories that the other press were running.*[4]

For the purpose of this study, no basic distinction could be made between the tabloids and the establishment media. Both dealt in sensation rather than analyses. Both relied on legal and legalistic assertions and opinions of the trial, and almost never reported on the actual substance of the evidence at the crime scenes. Both based their syntax or meaning of the murders on the Prosecution's alphabet of blood and jealousy. The tabloids emblazoned these signs in their headlines, while the respectable media more subtly incorporated them into their boilerplate. For both media, the givens were the same: one killer (O.J. Simpson), one victim (Nicole Simpson), one innocent bystander (Ronald Goldman). To The *Star* or *Globe* the crime was a redaction on the myth of *Beauty and the Beast*, for *The New York Times* or *Los Angeles Times* the metaphor of choice was *Othello*.

Whether the reportage or the commentary shot up from the gutter or flowed down from the ivory tower the intention was the same—profit. Thus, despite millions of minutes and words devoted to the crime, the public never was aided in their attempt to distinguish between the spousal confrontations of 1985, 1989, 1993, and 1994, or the context of the blood evidence both within and between the two crime scenes of Rockingham and Bundy. Both the *Enquirer* and the *LA Times* fit linguist Marshal McLuhan's definition of the instant media—"They live only in the present, like wild beasts."

You will, of course, point out that the profit motive is attached to all of the books written about the murders—including this one. Precisely the point: Only you, alone, as jurors, have no motive other than the search for truth and justice, only you have no secondary gain. Like the jury in the courtroom, you, alone, represent all the people. You are the thirteenth juror.

Post-Trial Media

Here follows more material that appeared after the criminal trail. Give it due weight when you deliberate.

Miami, January 1996: In a *Globe* "World Exclusive," Simpson's former NFL All-Pro friend, Eugene "Mercury" Morris, claims that his old football rival admitted to him in a December 1995 telephone conversation that he was at the murder scene but did not commit the crimes.

According to the article, The *Globe* had the tape of the interview analyzed by Ray Casto, who has developed a voice-stress analysis machine, Verimetrics. This truth-testing computer is regarded as more reliable than the polygraph "lie detector." Casto confirmed that Morris was telling the truth.

Morris also discusses his own drug use and claims that drugs played a big part in Simpson's life during his playing days. Morris cites an incident during his [Morris'] last year with the San Diego Chargers when they were in Buffalo to play the Bills:

> After the game, Juice took me to this guy's house who was supplying him with cocaine. He bought three grams of coke and gave one to me. Juice was on speed, cocaine, and he was taking steroids.

Morris ends with this,

> I'm finished with drugs. But Juice may never have gotten his wake-up call . . . . Just track him from the 70s into the 80s and then the 90s and look at the stories about his drug use. That whole pattern has brought him to where he is today.[5]

Los Angeles, January 1996: *The Globe* reports a sniper attack on Simpson's Rockingham home. Several .177 caliber slugs were found, which Simpson security guards believe may have come from a high-powered air rifle. The incident occurred shortly after Simpson had left the property. When told of the attack, Simpson ordered an extra $25,000 in high-tech security equipment.

A source close to the Simpson household is quoted in the article:

> When O.J. was told what happened, he froze. He told me: "I've been waiting for some crazy to take a shot at me." Now, O.J.'s scared to death that a lunatic will assassinate him even in the safety of his own heavily guarded home. Juice is afraid a sophisticated plot to kill him may have been launched.[6]

Does Simpson know his potential assassins?

Los Angeles, January 1996: *World Weekly News*, a journal noted for its bizarre revelations, reveals that Nicole Simpson's grave is empty. Francis Winnover, an author based in
San Diego, claims that he got the story from a "high-level
source" in the LAPD. According to the article:

> *Police have interviewed witnesses who say they ob-
> served a group of four or five people at the grave site on
> the night of November 17, 1995. The witnesses reported
> they saw lots of activity around Nicole Simpson's grave
> for a period of two hours or so, after which the unidenti-
> fied people left carrying a large object. Police believe that
> object was Nicole's corpse.*[7]

Setting aside all the editorial spin and speculation of
"lone nuts," "stalking husbands," and "empty graves," there
is another thread running through these stories. The history
of drug pressures and use in Simpson's circle; his alleged
presence at Bundy on the night of the murders; Nicole's fear
in the month prior to her death; and a plot to silence Simpson himself.

The conventional wisdom in the tabloid culture is to
link stories to O.J. Simpson's guilt. However, the subtext in
the stories would be even more consistent with the involvement of a person or persons as yet unknown in the murders
of Nicole Simpson and Ronald Goldman. Former Simpson
Defense Attorney Gerald Uelman still contends that the
murders were more consistent with drug-related murders
than with domestic violence. When asked by Geraldo Rivera,
on a show that aired in July 1996, if "as a man" Uelman believed Simpson to be innocent, Uelman answered, "Yes."

There are others who have publicly supported Simpson's innocence, and who also find a drug-related murder
scenario to be credible. An article by Henry Louis Gates that
appeared in The *New Yorker* quotes novelist Ishmael Reed
talking about the media:

> *... wealthy white male commentators who live in a world
> where people don't lie, don't plant evidence—and drug
> dealers give you unlimited credit . . . . Nicole you know,
> also dated Mafia hit men.*[8]

The same article quotes the social critic Cornel West:

> *I think he's innocent, I really do. . . . I do think it was linked to some drug culture of violence. It looks as if both O.J. and Nicole had some connection to drug activity. And the killings themselves were classic examples of that drug culture of violence. It could have to do with money owed, it could have to do with a number of things. And I think O.J. was quite aware and fearful of this.*[9]

If and when the case is forced open, the stereotyped logic may be dropped and some of these stories may be respun in the press as "exclusive" predictions of the truth.

Rest assured, ladies and gentlemen, that the London gutter press is already closing in on a story circulating on the Internet: Nicole, Ron, and Faye—desperate for money—conspire to murder O.J. Their plot includes leaving a trail of abuse evidence against Simpson, and a series of provocations to establish the stalker/cuckold image. The Juice is lured to Bundy. Two knives are in readiness. The alibi, carefully crafted, will be "self-defense." The plan goes wrong. O.J., like a stag at bay, turns on his tormenters. Once again he is the child of luck. He is Agamemnon saved. So it is that the fabric of our lives crosses into myth.

The tabloids of the twenty-first century will continue to tell and retell this tale, in all its carmine variations, unless the twentieth century lives up to its mandate—to bury these slain ghosts of June 12, by searching out the truth. This is what happens when people feel that they have not been given the entire story—whether in Dallas or Los Angeles—they speculate and obsess forever.

The Simpson Alibi

O.J. Simpson's complete alibi began to emerge during his deposition for the civil trial. Once again, the *Globe* and the tabloid press beat the competition. No jury had ever heard this story before. We provide excerpts of it as found in Simpson's deposition.

The Simpson Alibi

1994	
PM **11**	**JUNE 11** After a Saturday night date with Paula Barbieri, Simpson dropped her at her apartment and returned to Rockingham. When he arrived home, he found that the alarm was not set and the kitchen door was unlocked. *I found this strange because neither Arnelle or the nanny were at home. There were also three messages on my answering machine. The messages seemed to be the taping of a conversation between two people in a foreign language.*
PM **6:00**	**JUNE 12** Simpson leaves the dance recital. He is invited to join the family for dinner. *Somebody mentioned they were all going to eat dinner and wondered if it would be okay if O.J. came too. I declined and drove straight home.*
9:35	Simpson returns home from a visit to McDonald's. He has seventy-five minutes to prepare himself before he is due to leave for Los Angeles International Airport. *I went inside. Maybe turned off the TV. I was killing time. I went out to the garage and grabbed my three wood, started hitting with my three wood. I talked to my dog, Chachi. I looked in my Bentley at what clubs I had in there. I took my pitching wedge and a couple of balls from the trunk. I chipped a couple of balls but was afraid I was going to hit and dent my car.* *I put the pitching wedge back in the trunk where there were some other balls and then went out the gate. I went out to the Bronco to get my blue jacket. Chachi ran out. I let Chachi relieve herself in Stanley Sheinbaum's ivy across the street.* Simpson goes back to the Bronco and makes his call to Paula Barbieri. *I left a message in which I tried to make up. I spoke of filling the house with babies which was her dream.*
10:00	After the call, Simpson says he put his golf club back in the garage and returned to the house.

I turned off the TV's. I went upstairs. Sat down on the bed. I went to my Louis Vuitton bag, which was on the bed next to the phone, and looked at my travel folder. I may have turned the TV back on. I wasn't doing much of anything.

10:36 Simpson remembers looking at the clock, so he is precise about the time.

My driver, Dale, usually arrives fifteen minutes early, and I used his arrival as a gauge by which to get ready to go. I took my book and used the toilet. The phone rang a couple of times and then stopped. I knew the caller was not Dale at the gate because the phone rings for eight or nine times when someone is at the gate. I got into the shower. The phone rang while I was in the shower. I believed the caller must have been Dale so I started to rush.

I jumped out of the shower. I looked at my golf outfits in my closet. I wondered where my black golf shoes were. I thought they might be in the Bentley so I put on my robe and went out to the Bentley. I got my shoes out of the Bentley. I saw the limo in the driveway outside the gate. I put my shoes in the golf bag which was still sitting on the bench in front of the house.

10:56 Simpson comes out of the house to meet the limousine driver, Allan Park.

I yelled at the driver to get my (golf) clubs and then threw the clubs over the gate.

11:00 Simpson is stopped by Kato Kaelin coming out to investigate the thumps he heard at the back of the house. Kato wanted him to get a flashlight. This is when Simpson says he cut his finger.

I may have noticed that my finger was cut and bleeding on the counter. Kato looked in the cupboard for a flashlight and I looked in the washroom where there is a door that leads outside. I asked Kato if he'd found a flashlight but then realized what time it was. I then said I had to go.

11:05 Kato and the driver help Simpson to load the car.

I remember telling the limo driver not to put the golf bag on top of the suit bag. Kato asked me if the bag, which contained the green windbreaker and golfing equipment, belonged to me. I said it did.

11:15   Simpson and his driver leave for the airport.

In the limo, I asked the driver to turn off the air conditioning because I hate air conditioning. I was sweating because we had been rushing around so much.

11:30   En route to the airport, Simpson calls Kaelin to ask him to set the alarm in his house because he remembered Kato had been frightened about hearing noises. This made Simpson think about the strange incidents from the previous night: the kitchen door open, the messages on the answering machine.

A close inspection of this alibi reveals that it does not substantially differ from the version of events that Simpson's lawyers presented in their opening statement at trial. It is simply a more detailed and explanatory rendering of Simpson's movements on the night of the murders. Every moment is accounted for in its most banal detail: talking to his dog Chachi, checking bags, idly turning on a TV, looking over his travel plans, reading on the toilet. The only thing this person is killing is time.

It appears that Simpson may be still willing to take a polygraph test concerning his alibi. A tabloid paper claims to have recorded Simpson asserting his innocence on a recent TV appearance, and to have given it to their expert to evaluate. The expert promptly announced that since the Simpson statement did not reveal stress, Simpson must have been carefully coached and that he therefore was actually "lying." However, the original inventors and exponents of the P.S.E. (Psychological Stress Evaluator), Colonel Allan Bell and Charles McQuisten, judged that the absence of stress in a respondent's answer indicates a truthful response.

Simpson's alibi certainly has the "ring of truth"; a fair juror must decide whether the details are true of the murder night or whether they are only a composite drawn from many innocent travel evenings. One must also evaluate the credibility of the new material regarding a possible break-in on June 11. Simpson describes coming home June 11 to strange voices on his answering machine. Could they be related to the voices allegedly heard by Rosa Lopez late at night on June 12, or early in the morning June 13?

Simpson on Domestic Abuse

What Simpson said about domestic abuse in his deposition for the civil trial evoked the collective wrath of the press at large. By February 3, the major media could no longer hold back. *Los Angeles Times* ran a huge front-page headline: Ex-Wife Fabricated Domestic Abuse Charges, Simpson Says. Here follows a lengthy section from that deposition:

Q: *What kind of thoughts did you mean when you told them that you had had weird thoughts about Nicole?*
A: *I don't know at that particular time if there was anything specific in my head, but from time to time you do have thoughts, yes.*
Q: *Now, one of those weird thoughts that you had in mind when you said that to [LAPD detectives] Vannatter and Lange was the thought of killing Nicole. Right?*
A: *No, that's not correct.*
Q: *And your point in telling them that you were having weird thoughts was that the weird thoughts might somehow come out in the lie detector test. Right?*
A: *My point was I didn't understand a lie detector test, and once I had a better understanding, which I did, I would be happy to do one.*
Q: *Did you do one?*
A: *We offered one.*
Q: *Excuse me?*
A: *We offered it to the prosecution, yes.*
Q: *And what did they say?*
A: *They declined.*
Q: *You didn't take a test on the 13th. Right?*
A: *Correct.*
Q: *And you didn't want to then. Correct?*
A: *I had to talk to my lawyers about it. And then they didn't want me to either.*
Q: *You were concerned that the weird thoughts that you have had about Nicole might somehow affect your polygraph test. Correct?*
A: *Yes.*
Q: *Now, these weird thoughts that you had had about Nicole, they were weird thoughts about violence. Correct?*

A: *In a sense, one, yes . . . . I kinda at one point thought it would have been nice if [Simpson's housekeeper] Michelle, when Nicole punched her ... if Michelle would have punched her back.*

Q: *Is that the only thought of violence that came up when you said you were having weird thoughts about Nicole concerning violence?*

A: *I don't know if it was violence. Something happened in January, and I at one point thought it might have done her some good if she would have been injured during this incident, or caught.*

Q: *[You] told me so far about Nicole striking [the] maid. I want to know . . .*

A: *About Nicole striking a human being, a person. I don't look at them as maids. As a person, she struck a small woman in my house. I thought it was wrong, and at the time I had thoughts that I had wished the lady would hit her back.*

Q: *Is what you're saying is that you thought that the maid had killed Nicole?*

A: *That's ridiculous . . . . I don't think—that person is such a kind person—that this person could harm anybody. I don't think this person could be physical with anybody, and I don't think this person should have been subjected to being punched in her face in my house.*

Q: *That's a despicable act, isn't it?*

A: *Yes, it was.*

Q: *Something you would never do. Correct?*

A: *I would not do that, yes.*

Q: *Never did. Correct?*

A: *Never punched anyone, other than when I was a teenager, in their face, yes . . .*

Q: *And you never hurt your wife, either. Correct?*

A: *No. I hurt my wife, yes.*

A: *Yes.*

Q: *Did you ever bruise her?*

A: *Yes.*

Q: *Did you ever make her black and blue?*

A: *Yes, I saw her bruised, and I felt responsible for those bruises. If it came from me or if it came from when she fell outside, in any event, I was responsible for it.*

Q: *You made her face black and blue, didn't you?*

A: *If her face was black and blue the next day or two days later, I was responsible for it. No matter how it happened that day, I was the person responsible for it.*

Q: *And you cut her lip, didn't you?*

A: *That's incorrect.*

Q: *What did you do to her?*

A: *I rassled her.*

Q: *What does that mean?*

A: *That means I had my hands on her, and I was trying to force her out of my bedroom. We rassled. I know she was outside. She fell when she was outside.*

Q: *You had your fingers around her throat. Correct?*

A: *I could have touched her neck, yes.*

Q: *And you made marks on her throat, didn't you?*

A: *I didn't see them, but I'm told there were.*

Q: *You were in such a rage that you don't remember what you did. Is that right?*

A: *I remember exactly what I did.*

Q: *You were enraged when you had this act of violence toward her, weren't you?*

A: *I don't know if that's totally true, but I was angry, yes.*

Q: *OK. When she came back, did she strike you?*

A: *Yes.*

Q: *You didn't see her coming?*

A: *I might have seen her coming.*

Q: *Where did she hit you?*

A: *I don't know. She was just—it was just a swing, kind of. I was on the bed, and it was just a thing that she did . . . . At that point I was just trying to get her out of the room, and she was—Nicole is Nicole. She didn't want to be put out of the room.*

Q: *How did you actually get her from the bed out of the room?*

A: *I grabbed her and I kind of rassled her and I kind of pulled her. I may have at that point had her around her waist sort of, and I believe I was behind her at that time, because I didn't have much problem getting her out of the room.*

Q: *In your entire relationship with Nicole and the entire time that you knew Nicole, you never once hit her with your fist. Is that true?*

A: *Never once did I ever hit her with my fist, ever.*

Q: *You never once slapped her with your hand.*

A: *Never once have I ever slapped Nicole.*

Q: *Never once did you strangle her.*

A: *Never.*

Q: *Never once did you choke her.*

A: *Never.*

Q: *Never once did you beat her.*

A: *Never.*

Q: *Never once did you physically hurt her.*

A: *Never.*

Q: *And if Nicole said you did those things to her, she would not be telling the truth.*

A: *Correct.*

Q: *She would write notes to herself or journal entries about your beating her when that didn't occur?*

A: *Yes, that's correct.*

Q: *Why would she do such things?*

A: *Because she wanted me to tear up my prenuptial agreement, and I gather her lawyers and her came up with that as a scheme.*

Q: *So you are saying Nicole would in effect have tried to defraud you?*

A: *Not under oath she wouldn't, because she refused to testify to that under oath, which she told me.*

Q: *So she told you that she made up all these incidents of battery by you just for the purpose of voiding your prenuptial agreement with her at the behest of her lawyers?*

A: *But you must understand, they never used it. She would never let them use it. It was sort of a threat, but it never went anywhere.*

Q: *But in carrying out this fraud, you believe that she went so far as to write down on paper a number of incidents that you believe she made up out of whole cloth?*

A: *Yes.*[10]

This is Simpson's understanding of his marital relationship. The dominant reaction of press and pundits has been that Simpson is delusional and grossly downplaying his past history. Is there denial? Possibly very much. Then, again, read divorce action statements at random and compare the raging rhetoric of former mates with that of O.J. and Nicole. Simpson, facing a tremendous media attack now that he was speaking, fought back by calling in to a radio talk show to say:

> You know, I never called it stalking when Nicole followed me home, or on the golf course, or even to Mexico . . .

Ongoing Investigation into The Bundy Murders

There is an ongoing investigation into the murders that is based on Ron Goldman as the target and Nicole Simpson as the "innocent bystander." If Goldman was the primary victim, then an ominous new angle of refraction appears.

What follows is a summary of a long interview with a highly motivated researcher who is looking into this fresh dimension.

> We are following the money. The police and district attorney walked away from this case. The answer to the murder could be found today—if we had official interest, if we had a Jim Garrison at_____ [the name of a restaurant].
>
> We believe that Ron Goldman owed money, as much as $100,000 we're told, and he was in trouble. He was like so many young people who fall into the black hole of these bistros and dance clubs and restaurants—like the speakeasy during prohibition—and then a manager says, "If you need some money. . ." etc., and the young man finds himself into sex and drugs. We believe there is real evidence that this happened in this case.
>
> We know that Ron Goldman and some of his friends, who were murdered, were on the spot. We believe that Goldman was under terrible pressure from someone connected to restaurants who was also involved with prostitution and pornographic films. Some of the people were in Mezzaluna that night, we're told, while Nicole Simp-

son and her family ate dinner. One of these connections, a man, according to our sources, was extremely jealous of Goldman's relationship with Ms. Simpson.

The story we get is that there were two murderers in the alley at Bundy and two in front . . . . The point is there are L.A. Vice Squad and D.E.A. people who know how to crack this case today! They know who to drag in front of a Grand Jury. We've given them a name who's connected to organized narcotics and to Ron Goldman. We're not saying that Ron Goldman was not a victim—he was—we're saying that he was the target that night, and that the entire Simpson circus was a sideshow![11]

In March 1996, Deputy D.A. Darden published his version of the Simpson trial, in which he largely blames the judge and jury, along with himself, for the Prosecution's loss. Along with that, *In Contempt* contains some telling new information about Fuhrman:

"Item 13" of Fuhrman's crime scene report indicates that he knew "where dog was kept." How would Fuhrman know this?

"Item 15" indicates that Fuhrman found a "possible fingerprint" on the back gate at Bundy. This is the one Fuhrman also testified to finding. What happened to it? Was it wiped off?

"Item 17" refers to a "ski mask." This erroneous designation may link Fuhrman to the skimask leak to the media.

Judge Ito's wife, Captain York, confronted Fuhrman for allegedly snickering when she told officers that someone scrawled KKK across the date of Martin Luther King's birthday on a police calender.

Fuhrman confided to Darden that he, Fuhrman, collected German World War II medals.[12]

The Long Foot of Time

On February 25, 1996, came the first official view into the skirmishes within the Prosecution in the days before the trial, reported by Bill Boyarsky of the *Los Angeles Times*. Peter Bozanich had been the District Attorney's highest assistant until the week of June 24, 1994. By July, Bozanich had been demoted and transferred to an outlying area. What happened was this: In late June, Marcia Clark presented the first draft of her case to Garcetti, Bozanich, and the rest of the high echelon. When Clark's narrative reached the glove found at Rockingham, Bozanich said:

> *There is something wrong with the glove . . . . What's it doing there? That doesn't make any sense. How did the glove get there? Was there any evidence of blood along the path? . . . There were no answers for me and by the time we got to the trial, there were still no answers.*[13]

Bozanich later confronted his boss, Garcetti, warning him, urgently, that there was something wrong with the glove. To no avail.

On the same day that Boyarsky reported the Bozanich story, Mark Fuhrman's Idaho house went up for sale and the former detective was rumored to be leaving the country.

Meanwhile, the verbal riot of most of the experts has continued, as Simpson is universally pointed to by the press and talk show commentators as the guilty man who got away with murder. Simpson is, quite simply, *persona non grata*. He is banned from some clubs and restaurants (although he denies the extent of this official hatred), and unable to advertise his video in any major media outlet, including the tabloids who have coined fortunes from the case—as have all the media and some of the key participants, beginning with the lawyers. Simpson has seemingly been banished forever into a twilight zone of fear and hatred. Simpson's commentary on this:

> *I spent 460 days behind bars and I can't have a homecoming party, I can't put an 800 number on TV to sell my tapes, to earn money for my family—when the*

*prosecutors are making millions [Clark and Darden]—
and the Goldman family gets free air time to raise a for-
tune to prosecute me . . . . If you don't like me, leave me
alone! I have a few people working on the case—what I
can afford—because there's still killers out there!*[14]

Will there ever be an end to this saga that, by now,
reaches into every home in the land? Will O.J. join J.F.K.
and Elvis in the Greek Islands, where they now live, according to certain tabloids—will Nicole be there, too (because it
was a double who died that night)? Will O.J. and his Nicole—
the "Juice" and the California Girl—ever find rest, or will
they wander forever through the halls of fame?

And now television oracles assassinate the character of
the jurors, along with that of the defendant and his advocates. Police, Prosecution, Defense, media, authors, jurors,
attorneys, judge: Nearly every principal in the Simpson Matter has accused another of bad faith, opportunism, bias, and
moral blindness. These charges may all be true, in their own
way, and yet it may equally be the case that each competing
advocate was, and perhaps still is, searching for justice.

Therefore, instead of searching for who is to blame, this
study has attempted to pursue the facts, and develop a way
to reach the truth. For the "facts," we have offered a summary of the trial and some of what our investigation has
learned; for the way to the truth we have offered our competing scenarios and timelines. The rest we leave to you, the
jury. The search goes on.

Simpson, too, is now searching, wandering, lost in the
strangeness of his present state. Here, he is quoted in a
Linda Deutsch Associated Press story of July 1, 1996:

*I walk around the house some nights and I get an-
gry. I get angry with Nicole . . . . I've been to the grave
and I've just gone off at her . . . . Nicole was a good person, maybe a little lost in the last years of her life. But
she was a good person.*[15]

Doubleness.

Members of the jury, this case is bigger than O.J. Simpson. Two lives were lost, and no one has been found legally

accountable. Whatever happens to Simpson—in the real and ruthless world—whether he is reduced to selling neckties in front of football stadiums, or wrestles Mark Fuhrman in the Coliseum—his story and that of Nicole Brown Simpson and Ronald Lyle Goldman, are now a corner of our cultural canvas. The events of June 12, 1994, will forever remain a part of our national nightmare—unless, or until, you, the jury, seek demystification and a comprehensive search for the killer or killers.

You are the conscience of the community; the final arbiters of Justice; citizens with critical faculties the equal of any computer: You are the jury!

What is your verdict?

O.J. is Guilty as hell!

Appendix

Timeline Template

This timeline template contains only the basic facts that have been "time-locked" by a number of reliable clocks. Using this information, create your own timeline: You are the jury.

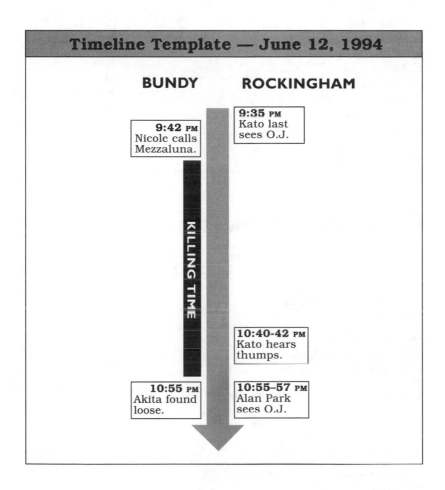

The Lawyers

The Prosecution Team
Marcia Clark
Christopher Darden
Gil Garcetti
Hank Goldberg
William Hodgman
Lisa Kahn
Cheri Lewis

The Defense Team
F. Lee Bailey
Johnnie Cochran Jr
Alan Dershowitz
Carl Douglas
Peter Neufeld
Barry Scheck
Robert Shapiro
Gerald Uelmen

Prosecution Witnesses

January 31
Sharon Gilbert–LAPD 911 Dispatcher
Det. John Edwards–LAPD
Det. Mike Farrell–LAPD
February 2
Ron Shipp–friend of O.J. and Nicole
Mike Stevens–LAPD investigator
Terri Moore–911 Dispatcher
February 3
Sgt. Robert Lerner–LAPD
Catherine Boe–neighbor of Nicole
Carl Colby–neighbor of Nicole
Denise Brown–sister of Nicole
February 6
Denise Brown–sister of Nicole
Candace Garvey–friend of Nicole
Cynthia Shahian–friend of Nicole
February 7
Tia Gavin–waitress at Mezzaluna
Stuart Tanner–bartender at Mezzaluna
Karen Crawford–manager at Mezzaluna

Karen Goldman–sister of Ron Goldman
Pablo Fenjves–neighbor of Nicole
February 8
Eva Stein–neighbor of Nicole
Louis Karpf–neighbor of Nicole
Steven Schwab–neighbor of Nicole
Sukru Boztepe–neighbor of Nicole
Elsie Tistaert–neighbor of Nicole
February 9
Sgt. Robert Riske–LAPD
February 14
Sgt. Robert Riske–LAPD
Sgt. David Rossi–LAPD
February 15
Sgt. David Rossi–LAPD
Det. Ronald Phillips–LAPD
February 16
Det. Ronald Phillips–LAPD
February 17
Det. Ronald Phillips–LAPD
Det. Tom Lange–LAPD
February 18-March 8
Det. Tom Lange–LAPD
March 9
Det. Tom Lange–LAPD
Det. Mark Fuhrman–LAPD
Patti Goldman–Ron Goldman's stepmother
March 10, 13-16
Det. Mark Fuhrman–LAPD
March 16
Lt. Frank Spangler–LAPD
Det. Philip Vannatter–LAPD
Darryl Smith–*Inside Edition* cameraman
March 17, 20-21
Det. Philip Vannatter–LAPD
March 17, 21-23, 27-28
Brian "Kato" Kaelin–O.J.'s houseguest
March 28
Rachel Ferrara–friend of Kato
Allan Park–limo driver
March 29
Allan Park–limo driver
Judge Delbert Wong–Special Master
James Williams–skycap at L.A. International Airport
March 30
Sue Silva–Westec Security Inc.
March 31
Charles Cale–neighbor of O.J.
April 1

Gregory Matheson–chief chemist
April 3-5, 11-14, 17-18
Dennis Fung–LAPD criminalist
April 20, 25-27
Andrea Mazzola–LAPD criminalist
May 5
Gregory Matheson–chief chemist–LAPD
May 5
Bernie Douroux–towtruck driver
May 8, 9-15
Robin Cotton–lab director, Cellmark Diagnostics
May 16-22, May 31-June 1
Gary Sims–Calif. Dept. of Justice
May 23–24
Renee Montgomery–criminalist, Calif. Dept. of Justice
May 24
Collin Yamauchi–criminalist, LAPD
May 25-31
Collin Yamauchi–criminalist, LAPD
June 2-15
Dr. Lakshmanan Sathyavagiswaran–L.A. Chief Examiner
June 15
Brenda Vemich–merchandise buyer, Bloomingdale's
Richard Rubin–former Isotoner Glove executive
June 15
Richard Rubin–former Isotoner Glove executive
June 19
William J. Bodziak–FBI shoe print expert
June 20
Samuel Poser–shoe department manager, Bloomingdale's
June 21
LuEllen Robertson–custodian of records, Airtouch Cellular
Kathleen Delaney–lawyer for Mirage Hotel, Las Vegas
June 22-23, 26
Bruce Weir–population geneticist
June 26
Denise Lewis–criminalist, LAPD
June 27
Denise Lewis–criminalist, LAPD
Susan Brockbank–criminalist, LAPD
June 28
Susan Brockbank–criminalist, LAPD
June 29, July 6
Douglas Deedrick–FBI Special Agent

The Rebuttal Witnesses
September 11
Mark Krueger–photographer at Bears game in Dec. 90
Bill Renken–photographer at Bengals game in Jan. 91
Kevin Schott–photographer at Bills game in Nov. 93

Stewart West–photographer at 49ers game in Dec. 93
Michael Romano–photographer at Bills game in Jan. 94
Debra Guidera–photo assistant at Giants game in Dec. 93
September 12
Richard Rubin–glove expert
September 13
Gary Sims–Calif. Dept. of Justice Lab
Stephen Oppler–Investigator, D.A.'s Office
Teresa Ramirez–videographer, D.A.'s Office
September 14
Teresa Ramirez–videographer, D.A.'s Office
Douglas Deedrick–FBI Agent,expert on hair and fiber
William Bodziak–FBI Agent, expert on shoeprints
September 15, October 18
William Bodziak–FBI Agent, expert on shoeprints
September 21
Comm. Keith Bushey–LAPD

Defense Witnesses

July 10
Arnelle Simpson–O.J.'s daughter
Carmelita Simpson-Durio–Simpson's younger sister
Eunice Simpson–Simpson's mother
Carol Connors–songwriter, met O.J. & Paula Barbieri on June 11
Mary Collins–interior designer, redoing O.J.'s house
July 11
Shirley Baker–O.J.'s older sister
Jack McKay–golf partner of O.J.
Danny Mandel–walked by Nicole's at 10:25 PM
Ellen Aaronson–on a date with Danny that night
Francesca Harman–at dinner party on Dorothy
Denise Pilnak–Bundy neighbor
Judy Telander–Bundy neighbor
Robert Heidstra–Bundy neighbor who heard "Hey, hey, hey," dog
barking and saw white sports-utility vehicle at Bundy
July 12
Wayne Stanfield–pilot, O.J.'s flight from LA to Chicago
Michael Norris–Network courier saw Simpson at airport
Michael Gladden–asked Simpson for his autograph
Howard Bingham–spoke with Simpson on the flight
July 13
Stephen Valerie–on flight just ahead of Simpson
Jim Merrill–Hertz employee–met Simpson at Chicago
Raymond Killduff–Hertz VP–drove Simpson to O'Hare airport–

Mark Partridge–attorney, sat next to Simpson on trip to L.A.
July 14, 17, 18
Dr. Robert Huizenga–O.J.'s doctor
July 18
Juanita Moore–O.J.'s barber for 16 years
Donald Thompson–police officer who handcuffed Simpson
July 19
John Meraz–towtruck driver; stole items from Bronco
Richard Walsh–trainer for the Simpson video
Willie Ford–LAPD photographer
July 20
Willie Ford–LAPD photographer
Josephine "Gigi" Guarin–O.J. Simpson's housekeeper
Det.Kelly Mulldorfer–Los Angeles police detective
Det. Bert Luper–Los Angeles police detective
July 24
Dr. Fredrich Rieders–Defense EDTA expert
July 25, 26
Roger Martz–FBI expert on EDTA
July 27, 31August 1
Herbert MacDonell–tested blood stains on socks
August 1
Herbert MacDonell–tested blood stains on socks
Thano Peratis–LAPD Nurse, drew blood from Simpson on 6/13/94
August 2-4. 7
John Gerdes–Director of Denver laboratory, testified about
contamination in the LAPD Crime Lab
August 7-8
Terence Speed–professor at the U of Cal., statistical expert
August 10-11
Michael Baden–former NYC chief medical examiner
August 14-15
Michele Kestler–head of LAPD Crime Lab
August 17
Gilbert Aguilar–fingerprint Specialist, LAPD
August 21
Larry Ragle–former head Orange County crime lab
August 22
Christian Reichardt–former fiancee of Faye Resnick
Kenneth Berris–Chicago Police Department detective
August 22-23, 25, 28
Dr. Henry Lee–forensic expert
August 29, September 5-6
Laura Hart McKinny–screenwriter, audio tapes of Fuhrman
September 5
Kathleen Bell–says Fuhrman used racist language

Natalie Singer–says Fuhrman used N-Word in 1987
William Blasini Jr–says no blood in Bronco on 6/21
Rolf Rokahr–LAPD photographer
Roderic Hodge–says Fuhrman called him the N-word in 1987
Det. Mark Fuhrman pleading the fifth
September 19
Philip Vannatter–LAPD detective
Michael Wacks–FBI Special Agent
Larry Fialto–reputed mob figure
Craig "Tony the Animal" Fialto–reputed mob figure

Rebuttal Witness
September 18
Herbert MacDonell–defense expert who conducted shrinkage
experiment on gloves

Simpson Arrest Warrant

Felony Complaint for Arrest Warrant, Case No. BA097211
    The undersigned is informed and believes that:

COUNT 1: On or about June 12, 1994, in the county of Los
Angeles, the crime of murder, in violation of Penal Code
Section 187 (a), a felony, was committed by Orenthal James
Simpson, who did willfully, unlawfully, and with malice
aforethought murder Nicole Brown Simpson, a human being.
    Notice: The above offense is a serious felony within the
meaning of Penal Code Section 1192.7(c) (1).
    It is further alleged that in the commission and at-
tempted commission of the above offense, the said defendant,
Orenthal James Simpson, personally used a deadly and dangerous weapon, to wit, knife, said use not being an element of
above offense, within the meaning of Penal Code Section 12022
(b) and also causing the above offense to be a serious felony
within the meaning of Penal Code Section 1192.7(c)(23).
COUNT 2: On or about June 12, 1994, in the county of Los
Angeles, the crime of murder, in violation of Penal Code
Section 187 (a), a Felony, was committed by Orenthal James
Simpson, who did willfully, unlawfully, and with malice
aforethought murder Ronald Lyle Goldman, a human being.
    Notice: The above offense is a serious felony within the
meaning of Penal Code Section 1192.7 (c)(1).
    It is further alleged that in the commission of above
offense, the said defendant, Orenthal James Simpson, personally used a deadly and dangerous weapon, to wit, knife, said
use not being an element of the above offense, within the
meaning of Penal Code Section 12022 (b) and also causing the

above offense to be a serious felony within the meaning of
Penal Code Section 1192.7(c)(23).

It is further alleged as to Counts 1 and 2 the defendant
has in this proceeding been convicted of more than one offense
of murder in the first or second degree within the meaning of
Penal Code 190.2(a)(3).

Further, attached hereto and incorporated herein are
official reports and documents of a law enforcement agency
which the undersigned believes establish probable cause for
the arrest of defendant, Orenthal James Simpson, for the
above-listed crimes. Wherefore, a warrant of arrest is requested for Orenthal James Simpson. I declare under penalty of
perjury that the foregoing is true and correct and that this
complaint, Case Number BA097211, consists of 2 counts.
Executed at Los Angeles, County of Los Angeles, on June 17,
1994.

> Philip Vannatter-(LAPD Robbery-Homicide detective)
> Declarant and Complainant.

Simpson Statement to the LAPD

An interrogation conducted by Philip Vannatter (VANNATTER)
and Thomas Lange (LANGE), the Los Angeles Police Department's
chief investigators of the murders of Nicole Simpson and Ron
Goldma n..

VANNATTER: ...my partner, Detective Lange, and we're in an
interview room in Parker Center. The date is June 13, 1994,
and the time is 13:35 hours. And we're here with O.J. Simpson. Is that Orenthal James Simpson?

SIMPSON: Orenthal James Simpson.

VANNATTER: And what is your birthdate, Mr. Simpson?

SIMPSON: July 9, 1947.

VANNATTER: OK. Prior to us talking to you, as we agreed with
your attorney, I'm going to give you your constitutional
rights. And I would like you to listen carefully. If you
don't understand anything, tell me, OK?

SIMPSON: All right

VANNATTER: OK. Mr. Simpson, you have the right to remain
silent. If you give up the right to remain silent, anything
you say can and will be used against you in a court of law.
You have the right to speak to an attorney and to have an
attorney present during the questioning. If you so desire and
cannot afford one, an attorney will be appointed for you
without charge before questioning. Do you understand your
rights?

O.J.: Yes, I do.

VANNATTER: Are there any questions about that?

SIMPSON: (unintelligible)

VANNATTER: OK, you've got to speak up louder than that...

SIMPSON: OK, no.

VANNATTER: OK, do you wish to give up your right to remain silent and talk to us?

SIMPSON: Ah, yes.

VANNATTER: OK, and you give up your right to have an attorney present while we talk?

SIMPSON: Mmm hmm. Yes.

VANNATTER: OK. All right, what we're gonna do is, we want to. . . . We're investigating, obviously, the death of your ex-wife and another man.

LANGE: Someone told us that.

VANNATTER: Yeah, and we're going to need to talk to you about that. Are you divorced from her now?

SIMPSON: Yes.

VANNATTER: How long have you been divorced?

SIMPSON: Officially? Probably close to two years, but we've been apart for a little over two years.

VANNATTER: Have you?

SIMPSON: Yeah.

VANNATTER: What was your relationship with her? What was the...

SIMPSON: Well, we tried to get back together, and it just didn't work. It wasn't working, and so we were going our separate ways.

VANNATTER: Recently you tried to get back together?

SIMPSON: We tried to get back together for about a year, you know, where we started dating each other and seeing each other. She came back and wanted us to get back together, and

VANNATTER: Within the last year, you're talking about?

SIMPSON: She came back about a year and four months ago about us trying to get back together, and we gave it a shot. We gave it a shot the better part of a year. And I think we both knew it wasn't working, and probably three weeks ago or so, we said it just wasn't working, and we went our separate ways.

VANNATTER: OK, the two children are yours?

SIMPSON: Yes.

LANGE: She have custody?

SIMPSON: We have joint custody.

LANGE: Through the courts?

SIMPSON: We went through the courts and everything. Everything is done. We have no problems with the kids, we do everything together, you know, with the kids.

VANNATTER: How was your separation? What that a...?

SIMPSON: The first separation?

VANNATTER: Yeah, was there problems with that?

SIMPSON: For me, it was big problems. I loved her, I didn't want us to separate.

VANNATTER: Uh huh. I understand she had made a couple of crime . . . crime reports or something?

SIMPSON: Ah, we have a big fight about six years ago on New Year's, you know, she made a report. I didn't make a report. And then we had an altercation about a year ago maybe. It wasn't a physical argument. I kicked her door or something.

VANNATTER: And she made a police report on those two occasions?

SIMPSON: Mmm hmm. And I stayed right there until the police came, talked to them.

LANGE: Were you arrested at one time for something?

SIMPSON: No. I mean, five years ago we had a big fight, six years ago. I don't know. I know I ended up doing community service.

VANNATTER: So you weren't arrested?

SIMPSON: No, I was never really arrested.

LANGE: They never booked you or...

SIMPSON: No.

VANNATTER: Can I ask you, when's the last time you've slept?

SIMPSON: I got a couple of hours sleep last night. I mean, you know, I slept a little on the plane, not much, and when I got to the hotel I was asleep a few hours when the phone call came.

LANGE: Did Nicole have a housemaid that lived there?

SIMPSON: I believe so, yes.

LANGE: Do you know her name at all?

SIMPSON: Evia, Elvia, something like that.

VANNATTER: We didn't see her there. Did she have the day off perhaps?

SIMPSON: I don't know. I don't know what schedule she's on.

LANGE: Phil, what do you think? We can maybe just recount last night...

VANNATTER: Yeah. When was the last time you saw Nicole?

SIMPSON: We were leaving a dance recital. She took off and I was talking to her parents.

VANNATTER: Where was the dance recital?

SIMPSON: Paul Revere High School.

VANNATTER: And was that for one of your children?

SIMPSON: Yeah, for my daughter Sydney.

VANNATTER: And what time was that yesterday?

SIMPSON: It ended about 6:30, quarter to seven, something like that, you know, in the ballpark, right in that area. And they took off.

VANNATTER: They?

SIMPSON: Her and her family — her mother and father, sisters, my kids, you know.

VANNATTER: And then you went your own separate way?

SIMPSON: Yeah, actually she left, and then they came back and her mother got in a car with her, and the kids all piled into her sister's car, and they...

VANNATTER: Was Nicole driving?

SIMPSON: Yeah.

VANNATTER: What kind of car was she driving?

SIMPSON: Her black car, a Cherokee, a Jeep Cherokee.

VANNATTER: What were you driving?

SIMPSON: My Rolls-Royce, my Bentley.

VANNATTER: Do you own that Ford Bronco that sits outside?

SIMPSON: Hertz owns it, and Hertz lets me use it.

VANNATTER: So that's your vehicle, the one that was parked there on the street?

SIMPSON: Mmm hmm.

VANNATTER: And it's actually owned by Hertz?

SIMPSON: Hertz, yeah.

VANNATTER: Who's the primary driver on that? You?

SIMPSON: I drive it, the housekeeper drives it, you know, it's kind of a...

VANNATTER: All-purpose type vehicle?

SIMPSON: All-purpose, yeah. It's the only one that my insurance will allow me to let anyone else drive.

VANNATTER: OK

LANGE: When you drive it, where do you park it at home? Where it is now, it was in the street or something?

SIMPSON: I always park it on the street.

LANGE: You never take it in the...

SIMPSON: Oh, rarely. I mean, I'll bring it in — and switch the stuff, you know, and stuff like that. I did that yesterday, you know.

LANGE: When did you last drive it?

SIMPSON: Yesterday

VANNATTER: What time yesterday?

SIMPSON: In the morning, in the afternoon.

VANNATTER: OK, you left her, you're saying, about 6:30 or 7, or she left the recital?

SIMPSON: Yeah.

VANNATTER: And you spoke with her parents?

SIMPSON: Yeah, we were just sitting there talking.

VANNATTER: OK, what time did you leave the recital?

SIMPSON: Right about that time. We were all leaving. We were all leaving then. Her mother said something about me joining them for dinner, and I said no thanks.

VANNATTER: Where did you go from there, O.J. ?

SIMPSON: Ah, home, home for a while, got my car for a while, tried to find my girlfriend for a while, came back to the house.

VANNATTER: Who was home when you got home?

SIMPSON: Kato.

VANNATTER: Kato? Anybody else? Was your daughter there, Arnelle?

SIMPSON: No.

VANNATTER: Isn't that her name, Arnelle?

SIMPSON: Arnelle, yeah.

VANNATTER: So what time do you think you got back home, actually physically got home?

SIMPSON: Seven-something.

VANNATTER: Seven-something? And then you left, and...

SIMPSON: Yeah, I'm trying to think, did I leave? You know, I'm always ...I had to run and get my daughter some flowers. I was actually doing the recital, so I rushed and got her some flowers, and I came home, and then I called Paula as I was going to her house, and Paula wasn't home.

VANNATTER: Paula is your girlfriend?

SIMPSON: Girlfriend, yeah.

VANNATTER: Paula who?

SIMPSON: Barbieri.

VANNATTER: Could you spell that for me?

SIMPSON: B-A-R-B-I-E-R-I.

VANNATTER: Do you know an address on her?

SIMPSON: No, she lives on Wilshire, but I think she's out of town.

VANNATTER: You got a phone number?

SIMPSON: Yeah (number deleted).

VANNATTER: So you didn't see her last night?

SIMPSON: No, we'd been to a big affair the night before, and then I came back home. I was basically at home. I mean, any time I was... whatever time it took me to get to the recital and back, to get to the flower shop and back, I mean, that's the time I was out of the house.

VANNATTER: Were you scheduled to play golf this morning, some place?

SIMPSON: In Chicago.

VANNATTER: What kind of tournament was it?

SIMPSON: Ah, it was Hertz, with special clients.

VANNATTER: Oh, OK. What time did you leave last night, leave the house?

SIMPSON: To go to the airport?

VANNATTER: Mmm hmm.

SIMPSON: About . . . the limo was supposed to be there at 10:45. Normally, they get there a little earlier. I was rushing around — somewhere between there and 11.

VANNATTER: So approximately 10:45 to 11.

SIMPSON: Eleven o'clock, yea, somewhere in that area.

VANNATTER: And you went by limo?

SIMPSON: Yeah.

VANNATTER: Who's the limo service?

SIMPSON: Ah, you have to ask my office.

LANGE: Did you converse with the driver at all? Did you talk to him?

SIMPSON: No, he was a new driver. Normally, I have a regular driver I drive with and converse. No, just about rushing to the airport, about how I live my life on airplanes, and hotels, that type of thing.

LANGE: What time did the plane leave?

SIMPSON: Ah, 11:45 the flight took off.

VANNATTER: What airline was it?

SIMPSON: American.

VANNATTER: American? And it was 11:45 to Chicago?

SIMPSON: Chicago.

LANGE: So yesterday you did drive the white Bronco?

SIMPSON: Mmm hmm.

LANGE: And where did you park it when you brought it home?

SIMPSON: Ah, the first time probably by the mailbox. I'm trying to think, or did I bring it in the driveway? Normally, I will park it by the mailbox, sometimes...

LANGE: On Ashford, or Ashland?

SIMPSON: On Ashford, yeah.

LANGE: Where did you park yesterday for the last time, do you remember?

SIMPSON: Right where it is.

LANGE: Where it is now?

SIMPSON: Yeah.

LANGE: Where, on...?

SIMPSON: Right on the street there.

LANGE: On Ashford?

SIMPSON: No, on Rockingham.

LANGE: You parked it there?

SIMPSON: Yes.

LANGE: About what time was that?

SIMPSON: Eight-something, seven . . . eight, nine o'clock, I don't know, right in that area.
LANGE: Did you take it to the recital?
SIMPSON: No.
LANGE: What time was the recital?
SIMPSON: Over at about 6:30. Like I said, I came home, I got my car, I was going to see my girlfriend. I was calling her and she wasn't around.
LANGE: So you drove the...you came home in the Rolls, and then you got in the Bronco...
SIMPSON: In the Bronco, 'cause my phone was in the Bronco. And because it's a Bronco. It's a Bronco, it's what I drive, you know. I'd rather drive it than any other car. And, you know, as I was going over there, I called her a couple of times and she wasn't there, and I left a message, and then I checked my messages, and there were no new messages. She wasn't there, and she may have to leave town. Then I came back and ended up sitting with Kato.
LANGE: OK, what time was this again that you parked the Bronco?
SIMPSON: Eight-something, maybe. He hadn't done a Jacuzzi, we had... went and got a burger, and I'd come home and kind of leisurely got read to go. I mean, we'd done a few things...
LANGE: You weren't in a hurry when you came back with the Bronco.
SIMPSON: No
LANGE: The reason I asked you, the cars were parked kind of at a funny angle, stuck out in the street.
SIMPSON: Well, it's parked because...I don't know if it's a funny angle or what. It's parked because when I was hustling at the end of the day to get all my stuff, and I was getting my phone and everything off it, when I just pulled it out of the gate there, it's like it's a tight turn.
LANGE: So you had it inside the compound, then?
SIMPSON: Yeah.
LANGE: Oh, OK.
SIMPSON: I brought it inside the compound to get my stuff out of it, and then I put it out, and I'd run back inside the gate before the gate closes.
VANNATTER: O.J., what's you office phone number?
SIMPSON: (number deleted)
VANNATTER: And is that area code 310?
SIMPSON: Yes.
VANNATTER: How did you get the injury on your hand?
SIMPSON: I don't know. The first time, when I was in Chicago and all, but at the house I was just running around.
VANNATTER: How did you do it in Chicago?
SIMPSON: I broke a glass. One of you guys had just called me, and I was in the bathroom, and I just kind of went bonkers for a little bit.
LANGE: Is that how you cut it?
SIMPSON: Mmm, it was cut before, but I think I just opened it again, I'm not sure.
LANGE: Do you recall bleeding at all in your truck, in the Bronco?

SIMPSON: I recall bleeding at my house and then I went to the Bronco. The last thing I did before I left, when I was rushing, was went and got my phone out of the Bronco.
LANGE: Mmm hmm. Where's the phone now?
SIMPSON: In my bag.
LANGE: You have it...?
SIMPSON: In that black bag.
LANGE: You brought a bag with you here?
SIMPSON: Yeah, it's...
LANGE: So do you recall bleeding at all?
SIMPSON: Yeah, I mean, I knew I was bleeding, but it was no big deal. I bleed all the time. I play golf and stuff, so there's always something, nicks and stuff here and there.
LANGE: So did you do anything? When did you put the Band-Aid on it?
SIMPSON: Actually, I asked the girl this morning for it.
LANGE: And she got it?
SIMPSON: Yeah, 'cause last night with Kato, when I was leaving, he was saying something to me, and I was rushing to get my phone, and I put a little thing on it, and it stopped.
VANNATTER: Do you have the keys to that Bronco?
SIMPSON: Yeah.
VANNATTER: OK. We've impounded the Bronco. I don't know if you know that or not.
SIMPSON: No.
VANNATTER: ...take a look at it. Other than you, who's the last person to drive it.
SIMPSON: Probably Gigi. When I'm out of town, I don't know who drives the car, maybe my daughter, maybe Kato.
VANNATTER: The keys are available?
SIMPSON: I leave the keys there, you know, when Gigi's there because sometimes she needs it, or Gigi was off and wasn't coming back until today, and I was coming back tonight.
VANNATTER: So you don't mind if Gigi uses it, or...
SIMPSON: This is the only one I can let her use. When she doesn't have her car, 'cause sometimes her husband takes her car, I let her use the car.
LANGE: When was the last time you were at Nicole's house?
SIMPSON: I don't go in, I won't go in her house. I haven't been in her house in a week, maybe five days. I go to her house a lot. I mean, I'm always dropping the kids off, picking the kids up, fooling around with the dog, you know.
VANNATTER: How does that usually work? Do you drop them at the porch, or do you go in with them?
SIMPSON: No, I don't go in the house.
VANNATTER: Is there a kind of gate out front?
SIMPSON: Yeah.
VANNATTER: But you never go inside the house?
SIMPSON: Up until about five days, six days ago, I haven't been in the house. Once I started seeing Paula again, I kind of avoid Nicole.
VANNATTER: Is Nicole seeing anybody else that you...
SIMPSON: I have no idea. I really have absolutely no idea. I don't ask her. I don't know. Her and her girlfriends, they go out, you know, they've got some things going on right now with her girlfriends, so I'm assuming something's happening

because one of the girlfriends is having a big problem with
her husband because she's always saying she's with Nicole
until three or four in the morning. She's not. You know,
Nicole tells me she leaves her at 1:30 or 2 or 2:30, and the
girl doesn't get home until 5, and she only lives a few
blocks away.

VANNATTER: Something's going on, huh?

LANGE: Do you know where they went, the family, for dinner
last night?

SIMPSON: No. Well, no, I didn't ask.

LANGE: I just thought maybe there's a regular place that
they go.

SIMPSON: No. If I was with them, we'd go to Toscano. I mean,
not Toscano, Poponi's.

VANNATTER: You haven't had any problems with her lately, have
you, O.J. — ?

SIMPSON: I always have problems with her, you know? Our
relationship has been a problem relationship. Probably lately
for me, and I say this only because I said it to Ron yesterday at the — Ron Fischman, whose wife is Cora — at the dance
recital, when he came up to me and went, "Oooh, boy, what's
going on?" and everybody was beefing with everybody. And I
said, "Well, I'm just glad I'm out of the mix." You know,
because I was like dealing with him and his problems with his
wife and Nicole and evidently some new problems that a guy
named Christian was having with his girl, and he was staying
at Nicole's house, and something was going on, but I don't
think it's pertinent to this.

VANNATTER: Did Nicole have words with you last night?

SIMPSON: Pardon me?

VANNATTER: Did Nicole have words with you last night?

SIMPSON: No, not at all.

VANNATTER: Did you talk to her last night?

SIMPSON: To ask to speak to my daughter, to congratulate my
daughter, and everything.

VANNATTER: But you didn't have a conversation with her?

SIMPSON: No, no.

VANNATTER: What were you wearing last night, O.J. — ?

SIMPSON: What did I wear on the golf course yesterday? Some
of these kind of pants, some of these kind of pants — I mean
I changed different for whatever it was. I just had on
some...

VANNATTER: Just these black pants.

SIMPSON: Just these...They're called Bugle Boy.

VANNATTER: These aren't the pants?

SIMPSON: No.

VANNATTER: Where are the pants that you wore?

SIMPSON: They're hanging in my closet.

VANNATTER: These are washable, right? You just throw them in
the laundry?

SIMPSON: Yeah, I got 100 pair. They give them to me free,
Bugle Boys, so I've got a bunch of them.

VANNATTER: Do you recall coming home and hanging them up,
or...?

SIMPSON: I always hang up my clothes. I mean, it's rare that
I don't hang up my clothes unless I'm laying them in my

bathroom for her to do something with them, but those are the only things I don't hang up. But when you play golf, you don't necessarily dirty pants.

LANGE: What kind of shoes were you wearing?

SIMPSON: Tennis shoes.

LANGE: Tennis shoes? Do you know what kind?

SIMPSON: Probably Reebok, that's all I wear.

LANGE: Are they at home, too?

SIMPSON: Yeah

LANGE: Was this supposed to be a short trip to Chicago, so you didn't take a whole lot?

SIMPSON: Yeah, I was coming back today.

LANGE: Just overnight?

SIMPSON: Yeah.

VANNATTER: That's a hectic schedule, drive back here to play golf and come back.

SIMPSON: Yeah, but I do it all the time.

VANNATTER: Do you?

SIMPSON: Yeah. That's what I was complaining with the driver about, you know, about my whole life is on and off airplanes.

VANNATTER: O.J. — , we've got sort of a problem.

SIMPSON: Mmm hmm.

VANNATTER: We've got some blood on and in your car, we've got some blood at your house, and sort of a problem.

SIMPSON: Well, take my blood test.

LANGE: Well, we'd like to do that. We've got, of course, the cut on your finger that you aren't real clear on. Do you recall having that cut on your finger the last time you were at Nicole's house?

SIMPSON: A week ago?

LANGE: Yeah.

SIMPSON: No. It was last night.

LANGE: OK, so last night you cut it.

VANNATTER: Somewhere after the recital?

SIMPSON: Somewhere when I was rushing to get out of my house.

VANNATTER: OK, after the recital.

SIMPSON: Yeah.

VANNATTER: What do you think happened? Do you have any idea?

SIMPSON: I have no idea, man. You guys haven't told me anything. I have no idea. When you said to my daughter, who said something to me today, that somebody else might have been involved, I have absolutely no idea what happened. I don't know how, why or what. But you guys haven't told me anything. Every time I ask you guys, you say you're going to tell me in a bit.

VANNATTER: Well, we don't know a lot of answers to these questions yet ourselves, O.J. — , OK?

SIMPSON: I've got a bunch of guns, guns all over the place. You can take them, they're all there. I mean, you can see them. I keep them in my car for an incident that happened a month ago that my in-laws, my wife and everybody knows about that.

VANNATTER: What was that?

SIMPSON: Going down to...and cops down there know about it because I've told two marshals about it. At a mall, I was going down for a christening, and I had just left — and it was like 3:30 in the morning, and I'm in a lane, and also the car in front of me is going real slow, and I'm slowing down 'cause I figure he sees a cop, 'cause we were all going pretty fast. And I'm going to change lanes, but there's a car next to me, and I can't change lanes. Then that goes for a while, and I'm going to slow down and go around him but the car butts up to me, and I'm like caught between three cars. They were Oriental guys, and they were not letting me go anywhere. And finally I went on the shoulder, and I sped up, and then I held my phone up so they could see the light part of it, you know, 'cause I have tinted windows, and they kind of scattered, and I chased one of them for a while to make him think I was chasing him before I took off.

LANGE: Were you in the Bronco?

SIMPSON: No.

LANGE: What were you driving?

SIMPSON: My Bentley. It has tinted windows and all, so I figured they thought they had a nice little touch...

LANGE: Did you think they were trying to rip you off?

SIMPSON: Definitely, they were. And then the next thing, you know, Nicole and I went home. At four in the morning I got there to Laguna, and when we woke up, I told her about it, and told her parents about it, told everybody about it, you know? And when I saw two marshals at a mall, I walked up and told them about it.

VANNATTER: What did they do, make a report on it?

SIMPSON: They didn't know nothing. I mean, they'll remember me and remember I told them.

VANNATTER: Did Nicole mention that she'd been getting any threats lately to you? Anything she was concerned about or the kids' safety?

SIMPSON: To her?

VANNATTER: Yes.

SIMPSON: From?

VANNATTER: From anybody.

SIMPSON: No, not at all.

VANNATTER: Was she very security conscious? Did she keep that house locked up?

SIMPSON: Very.

VANNATTER: The intercom didn't work apparently, right?

SIMPSON: I thought it worked.

VANNATTER: Oh, OK. Does the electronic buzzer work?

SIMPSON: The electronic buzzer works to let people in.

VANNATTER: Do you ever park in the rear when you go over there?

SIMPSON: Most of the time.

VANNATTER: You do park in the rear.

SIMPSON: Most times when I'm taking the kids there, I come right into the driveway, blow the horn, and she, or a lot of times the housekeeper, either the housekeeper opens or they'll keep a garage door open up on the top of the thing, you know, but that's when I'm dropping the kids off, and I'm not going in. — times I go to the front because the kids have to hit the buzzer and stuff.

VANNATTER: Did you say before that up until about three weeks ago you guys were going out again and trying to...

SIMPSON: No, we'd been going out for about a year, and then the last six months we've had...it ain't been working, so we tried various things to see if we can make it work. We started trying to date, and that wasn't working, and so, you know, we just said the hell with it, you know.

VANNATTER: And that was about three weeks ago?

SIMPSON: Yeah, about three weeks ago.

VANNATTER: So you were seeing her up to that point?

SIMPSON: It's, it's...seeing her, yeah, I mean, yeah. It was a done deal. It just wasn't happening. I mean, I was gone. I was in San Juan doing a film, and I don't think we had sex since I've been back from San Juan, and that was like two months ago. So it's been like...for the kids we tried to do things together, you know, we didn't really date each other. Then we decided let's try to date each other. We went out one night, and it just didn't work.

VANNATTER: When you say it didn't work, what do you mean?

SIMPSON: Ah, the night we went out it was fun. Then the next night we went out it was actually when I was down in Laguna, and she didn't want to go out. And I said, "Well, let's go out 'cause I came all the way down here to go out," and we kind of had a beef. And it just didn't work after that, you know? We were only trying to date to see if we could bring some romance back into our relationship. We just said, let's treat each other like boyfriend and girlfriend instead of, you know, like 17-year-old married people. I mean, 17 years together, whatever that is.

VANNATTER: How long were you together?

SIMPSON: Seventeen years.

VANNATTER: Seventeen years. Did you ever hit her, O.J.?

SIMPSON: Ah, one night we had a fight. We had a fight, and she hit me. And they never took my statement, they never wanted to hear my side, and they never wanted to hear the housekeeper's side. Nicole was drunk. She did her thing, she started tearing up my house, you know? I didn't punch her or anything, but I...

VANNATTER: ...slapped her a couple of times.

SIMPSON: No, no, I wrestled her, is what I did. I didn't slap her at all. I mean, Nicole's a strong girl. She's a...one of the most conditioned women. Since that period of time, she's hit me a few times, but I've never touched her after that, and I'm telling you, it's five-six years ago.

VANNATTER: What is her birth day?

SIMPSON: May 19th.

VANNATTER: Did you get together with her on her birthday?

SIMPSON: Yeah, her and I and the kids, I believe.

VANNATTER: Did you give her a gift?

SIMPSON: I gave her a gift.

VANNATTER: What did you give her?

SIMPSON: I gave her either a bracelet or the earrings.

VANNATTER: Did she keep them or...

SIMPSON: Oh, no, when we split she gave me both the earrings and the bracelet back. I bought her a very nice bracelet — I don't know if it was Mother's Day or her birthday — and I bought her the earrings for the other thing, and when we split — and it's a credit to her — she felt that it wasn't right that she had it, and I said good because I want them back.

VANNATTER: Was that the very day of her birthday, May 19, or was it a few days later?

SIMPSON: What do you mean?

VANNATTER: You gave it to her on the 19th of May, her birthday, right, this bracelet?

SIMPSON: I may have given her the earrings. No, the bracelet, May 19th. When was Mother's Day?

VANNATTER: Mother's Day was around that...

SIMPSON: No, it was probably her birthday, yes.

VANNATTER: And did she return it the same day?

SIMPSON: Oh, no, she...I'm in a funny place here on this, all right? She returned it — both of them — three weeks ago or so, because when I say I'm in a funny place on this it was because I gave it to my girlfriend and told her it was for her, and that was three weeks ago. I told her I bought it for her. You know? What am I going to do with it?

LANGE: Did Mr. Weitzman, your attorney, talk to you anything about this polygraph we brought up before? What are your thoughts on that?

SIMPSON: Should I talk about my thoughts on that? I'm sure eventually I'll do it, but it's like I've got some weird thoughts now. I've had weird thoughts...you know when you've been with a person for 17 years, you think everything. I've got to understand what this thing is. If it's true blue, I don't mind doing it.

LANGE: Well, you're not compelled at all to take this thing, number one, and number two — I don't know if Mr. Weitzman explained it to you — this goes to the exclusion of someone as much as the inclusion so we can eliminate people. And just to get things straight.

SIMPSON: But does it work for elimination?

LANGE: Oh, yes. We use it for elimination more than anything.

SIMPSON: Well, I'll talk to him about it.

LANGE: Understand, the reason we're talking to you is because you're the ex-husband.

SIMPSON: I know, I'm the number one target, and now you tell me I've got blood all over the place.

LANGE: Well, there's blood at your house in the driveway, and we've got a search warrant, and we're going to go get the blood. We found some in your house. Is that your blood that's there?

SIMPSON: If it's dripped, it's what I dripped running around trying to leave.

LANGE: Last night?

SIMPSON: Yeah, and I wasn't aware that it was...I was aware that I... You know, I was trying to get out of the house. I didn't even pay any attention to it, I saw it when I was in the kitchen, and I grabbed a napkin or something, and that was it. I didn't think about it after that.

VANNATTER: That was last night after you got home from the recital, when you were rushing?

SIMPSON: That was last night when I was...I don't know what I was... I was in the car getting my junk out of the car. I was in the house throwing hangers and stuff in my suitcase. I was doing my little crazy what I do...I mean, I do it every-

where. Anybody who has ever picked me up says that O.J. —
he's a whirlwind, he's running, he's grabbing things, and
that's what I was doing.
VANNATTER: Well, I'm going to step out and I'm going to get a
photographer to come down and photograph your hand there. And
then here pretty soon we're going to take you downstairs and
get some blood from you. OK? I'll be right back.
LANGE: So it was about five days ago you last saw Nicole?
Was it at the house?
SIMPSON: OK, the last time I saw Nicole, physically saw
Nicole...I saw her obviously last night. The time before, I'm
trying to think...I went to Washington, D.C., so I didn't see
her, so I'm trying to think...I haven't seen her since I went
to Washington — what's the date today?
LANGE: Today's Monday, the 13 of June.
SIMPSON: OK, I went to Washington on maybe Wednesday. Thurs-
day I think I was in...Thursday I was in Connecticut, then
Long Island Thursday afternoon and all of Friday. I got home
Friday night, Friday afternoon. I played, you know... Paula
picked me up at the airport. I played golf Saturday, and when
I came home I think my son was there. So I did something with
my son. I don't think I saw Nicole at all then. And then I
went to a big affair with Paula Saturday night, and I got up
and played golf Sunday which pissed Paula off, and I saw
Nicole at...It was about a week before, I saw her at the...
LANGE: OK, the last time you saw Nicole, was that at her
house?
SIMPSON: I don't remember. I wasn't in her house, so it
couldn't have been at her house, so it was, you know, I don't
physically remember the last time I saw her. I may have seen
her even jogging one day.
LANGE: Let me get this straight. You've never physically
been inside the house?
SIMPSON: Not in the last week.
LANGE: Ever. I mean, how long has she lived there? About six
months?
SIMPSON: Oh, Christ, I've slept at the house many, many,
many times, you know? I've done everything at the house, you
know? I'm just saying,...You're talking in the last week or
so.
LANGE: Well, whatever. Six months she's lived there?
SIMPSON: I don't know. Roughly. I was at her house maybe two
weeks ago, 10 days ago. One night her and I had a long talk,
you know, about how can we make it better for the kids, and I
told her we'd do things better. And, OK, I can almost say
when that was. That was when I...I don't know, it was about
10 days ago. And then we...The next day I had her have her
dog do a flea bath or something with me. Oh, I'll tell you, I
did see her one day. One day I went...I don't know if this
was the early part of last week, I went 'cause my son had to
go and get something, and he ran in, and she came to the
gate, and the dog ran out, and her friend Faye and I went
looking for the dog. That may have been a week ago, I don't
know.
LANGE: (To Vannatter) Got a photographer coming?
VANNATTER: No, we're going to take him up there.
LANGE: We're ready to terminate this at 14:07.

Investigator's Report

Department of Coroner
> 94-05135
> Goldman, Ronald L.
> FD 6-13-94
> Homicide
> LAPD Rob/Homi
> See 94-05136

INFORMATION SOURCE:
> Det(s) Lange and Vannatter
> At scene investigation
> Louis Brown, father of decedent

LOCATION:
> A private residence, 875 S. Bundy Dr., Los Angeles

INVESTIGATION:
> 94-05135 A 25-year-old male is the victim of an apparent homicide.
> 94-05136 A 35-year-old female is the victim of an apparent homicide.
> The decedents appear to be the victims of sharp force injuries.

STATEMENTS:
> According to Det. Lange, at about 0030 hrs. 6-13-94 a resident observed the dog belonging to the decedent 94-05136 wandering about the neighborhood. The resident reportedly walked the dog back to the above address and observed the decedents unresponsive. Emergency services were called to the scene and death was pronounced by Eng. 19* at 0045 hr.
> The decedent 94-05136 was last known to be alive at about 2300 hrs. speaking to her mother on the telephone. Her mother had left her eyeglasses at a restaurant that evening and the decedent reportedly advised her mother that she should ask if an employee could bring them to her residence.

SCENE DESCRIPTION/BODY EXAMINATION:
> I arrived at the scene at 0905 hr. 6-13-94. The scene is the gated entrance to the decedent's (94-05136) residence. The decedent 94-05135 was observed at the north side of the entrance. He was seated in the dirt (garden area) slumped to his right side. His back was against a small tree stump and iron fence. He was dressed in blue jeans and a light colored cotton-type sweater. His clothes and face were stained with blood. Numerous sharp force injuries were observed at his neck, back, head and hands. Another wound was present at his left thigh area. Lividity was present and fixed, rigor mortis was fully established.
> Lying near the decedent's (94-05135) right foot was a business-size white envelope containing a pair of eyeglasses.
> The decedent 94-05136 was lying at the foot of the stairs at the gate. She was in a fetal position on her left side, wearing a black dress, no shoes. Her legs were posi-

tioned under the stationery portion of the gate and her arms
were bent at the elbow and close to her body. Coagulated and
dried blood stained the walkway leading to the decedent. Paw
prints were present at the side walk, consistent with a dog
present/leaving the location. The gated area is several feet
from the front entrance of the residence. Blood stains were
present on the decedent's legs, arms, and face. Examination
revealed a large sharp force injury at the decedent's neck,
with smaller injuries just to the left side of the neck.
Lividity was fixed and consistent with her position and rigor
mortis was fully established.

EVIDENCE:
94-05135: Hair standards were taken and nail standards
could not be retrieved (nails too short).
94-05136: Hair and nail standards taken as well as
physical evidence by criminologist L. Mahanay (at the Forensic Science Center).

IDENTIFICATION/NOTIFICATION:
94-05135: Identification was established at the scene
by California Drivers License: A1347431. Notification was
established to father, Fred Goldman, by this investigator.
94-05136: Identification was established at the scene
by a passport. Notification was established to father, Louis
Brown, by Det. Lange.

AUTOPSY NOTIFICATION:
PLEASE CONTACT DET(S) LANGE AND VANNATTER AT LEAST TWO HOURS
PRIOR TO EXAMINATION.

Signed,
C. Ratcliffe 203300, 6-13-94

Autopsy Report:
Nicole Brown Simpson

AUTOPSY REPORT
94-05136
I performed an autopsy on the body of BROWN-SIMPSON, NICOLE
at the DEPARTMENT OF CORONER Los Angeles, California on June
14, 1994 @0730 HOURS
From the anatomic findings and pertinent history, I ascribe
the death to: MULTIPLE SHARP FORCE INJURIES Due To Or As a
Consequence of:

Anatomical Summary:
I. Incised wound of neck:
A. Transection of left and right common carotid arteries.

B. Incisions, left and right internal jugular veins
C. Transection of thyrohyoid membrane, epiglottis, and hy-
popharynx.
D. Incision into cervical spine, C3.
II. Multiple stab wound of neck and scalp (total of seven).
III. Multiple injuries of hands, including incised wound, ring
finger of right hand (defense wound).
IV. Scalp bruise, right parietal.

NOTES AND PROCEDURES:
1. The body is described in the Standard Anatomical Position.
Reference is to this position only.
2. Where necessary, injuries are numbered for reference. This
is arbitrary and does not correspond to any order in which
they may have been incurred. All the injuries are antemortem,
unless otherwise specified.
3. The term "anatomic" is used as a specification to indicate
correspondence with the description as set forth in the
textbooks of Gross Anatomy. It denotes freedom from significant, visible or morbid alteration.

EXTERNAL EXAMINATION:
The body is that of a well-developed, well-nourished Caucasian
female stated to be 35 years old. The body weighs 129 pounds
and measures 65 inches from crown to sole. The hair on the
scalp is brown. The irises are brown with the pupils fixed and
dilated. The sclerae and conjunctive are unremarkable, without
evidence of petechial hemorrhages on either. Both upper and
lower teeth are natural, without evidence of injury to the
cheeks, lips or gums.
There are no tattoos, deformities or amputations. Two linear
surgical scars are found beneath each breast, transversely
oriented and measuring 2 inches in length.
Rigor mortis is fixed at the time of autopsy examination
(please see form 1).
The body appears to the examiner as stated above. Identification is by toe-tag and the autopsy is not material to identification. The body is not embalmed.
The head is normocephalic and there is external evidence of
antemortem injury to be described below. Otherwise, the
external auditory canals, eyes, nose and mouth are not remarkable. The neck shows sharp force injury to be described below,
and the larynx is visible through the gaping wound.
No recent traumatic injuries are noted on the chest or abdomen; tan lines are seen on the lower abdomen (bathing suit).
The genitalia are that of adult female with no gross evidence
of injuries. Examination of the posterior surface at the trunk
shows some excoriations compatible with postmortem injuries on
the upper back, right side, on the medial aspect of the right
scapula and on the lateral aspect of the right scapula (compatible with ant to insect bites). An abrasion above the left
scapula measures 3/4 x 1/2 inch and is red-brown in color and
appears antemortem. Otherwise, the lower back and remainder of
the posterior aspect of the body shows no evidence or recent
injuries.
Refer to available photographs and diagrams and the specific
documentation of the autopsy protocol.

CLOTHING:
The decedent was wearing a short black dress, blood stained.
Also, she was wearing a pair of black panties. To the unaided
eye examination there was no evidence of cut or tear.
EVIDENCE OF INJURY:
DESCRIPTION OF INCISED WOUND OF NECK:
The incised wound of the neck is gaping and exposes the
larynx and cervical vertebral column. It measures 5 1/2 x 2
1/2 inches in length and is found at the level of the superior border of the larynx.
After approximation of the edges, it is seen to be diagonally
oriented on the right side and transversely oriented from the
midline to the left side. On the right side it is upwardly
angulated toward the right earlobe and extends for 4 inches
from the midline. On the left side it is transversely oriented and extends 2 1/2 inches to the anterior border of the
left sternocleidomastoid muscle. The edges of the wound are
smooth, with subcutaneous and intramuscular hemorrhage,
fresh, dark red purple, is evident.
On the right side the upwardly angulated wound passes through
the skin, the subcutaneous tissue, the platysma, passing
under the ramus of the right mandible and upward as it passes
through the strap muscles on the right, towards the digastric
muscle on the right, and through the thyrohyoid membrane and
ligament. Further dissection discloses that it passes posteriorly and transects the distal one-third of the epiglottis,
the hypo-pharynx, and passes into the body of the 3rd cervical vertebra where it transversely oriented 3/4 inch incised
wound is seen in the bone, extending it for a depth of 1/4
inch into the bone. The spinal canal and cord are not entered.
On the right side superiorly the wound passes towards the
insertion of the sternocleidomastoid muscle, and then becomes
more superficial and tapers as it terminates in the skin
below the right earlobe.
On the left side the wound is transversely oriented and
extends for 2 1/2 inches where the wound path intersects the
stab wounds on the left side of the neck to be described
below.
Dissection discloses that the right common carotid artery is
transected with hemorrhage in the surrounding carotid sheath
and there is a 1/4 incised wound or nick in the right internal jugular vein with surrounding soft tissue hemorrhage.
On the left side the left common carotid artery is transected
with hemorrhage in the surrounding carotid sheath and the
left internal jugular vein is subtotally transected with only
a thin strand of tissue remaining posteriorly with surrounding soft tissue hemorrhage. The injuries on the left side of
the neck intersect and the pathways of the stab wounds on the
left side to be described below.
There is fresh hemorrhage and bruising noted along the entire
incised wound path.
Depth of penetration is not given because the neck can be
either flexed or extended, and the length of the wound is
greater than the depth.
Opinion: This is a fatal incised wound or sharp force injury,

associated with transection of the left and right carotid
arteries and incisions of the left and right internal jugular
veins with exsanguinating hemorrhage.
DESCRIPTION OF MULTIPLE STAB WOUNDS:
There are four stab wounds on the left side of the neck over
the left sternocledomastoid muscle; they extend to 3 inches
below the external auditory canal.
1. This stab wound overlaps that of the incised wound of the
neck described above. The wound measures 5/8 inch in length,
is vertically oriented, and has a squared-off end inferiorly
approximately 1/32 inch and a pointed end superiorly. The
minimal depth of the penetration, from left to right, is
1 1/2 to 2 inches where it intersects the incised wound.
Penetration is through the skin, subcutaneous tissue and
muscle, and injury to the internal jugular vein or common
carotid artery cannot be excluded.
2. Stab wound of left side of neck: This is a 1/8 inch superficial slit-like incision into the skin and dermis; no
squared-off or dull end is evident.
This is a superficial slit-like wound of the skin, non-fatal.
3. Stab wound on left side of neck: This is a diagonally
oriented stab wound measuring 1/2 inch in length; there is a
pointed end on the posterior aspect and a squared-off end
anterior less than 1/32 inch in length. The edges are smooth,
and dissection disposes a depth of penetration for 1 1/2 to 2
inches where the stab wound intersects that of the incised
wound of the neck; the stab wounds are approximately 1 inch
from the left lateral termination of the incised wound. Fresh
hemorrhage is noted along the wound path which goes through
the skin, subcutaneous tissue and muscle.
Opinion: This stab wound cannot be distinguished from injuries caused by the incised wound of the neck and may have
injured the left common carotid artery and/or the left internal jugular vein.
4. Stab wound of the left side of neck: This is a diagonally
oriented stab wound measuring 7/8 inch in length; on the
posterior aspect there is a pointed end and on the anterior
aspect a squared -off or dull end approximately 1/32 inch in
width; otherwise the edges are smooth. Subsequent dissection
discloses the wound path through the skin, subcutaneous
tissue and muscle where it intersects the incised wound of
the neck. Depth of penetration is 1 - 1/2 inches.
Opinion: This stab wound may have injured the left common
carotid artery and/or the left internal jugular vein as
described above.
5. Stab wound of scalp, left parietal: This diagonally oriented stab wound is located on the left parietal scalp, which
is shaved postmortem for visualization. It measures 1/2 inch
in length and no definite squared-off or dull end is evident,
both ends appearing to be rounded. Depth of penetration is
through the scalp, to the galea, approximately 3/8-1/2 inch.
There is deep scalp hemorrhage and a subgaleal bruise, measuring 1 1/2 x 1 1/2 inches; there is no cutting wound or
injury to the skull and there is no penetration into the
cranium.
Opinion: This is a superficial stab wound or cutting wound of

the scalp, non-fatal.

6. Stab wound or cutting wound of scalp: This is transversely oriented and is found in the right posterior parietal-occipital region. The transversely oriented wound measures 1 1/2 inches in length and has a pointed end to the left and a fork or split into the right. Depth of penetration is 3/8-1 1/2 inches with fresh deep scalp bruising.

Opinion: This is a non-fatal, stabbing or cutting wound of the scalp.

7. Stab wound or cutting wound of the scalp, right parietal-occipital: This is vertically oriented, measures 3/16 inch in length and involves the skin only. No squared-off or dull end is evident, both ends or aspects being pointed or tapered. There is a small amount of deep scalp hemorrhage or bruising, no subgaleal hemorrhage.

Opinion: This is a non-fatal superficial stabbing or cutting wound of the scalp.

8. Blunt force injury to head: On the right side of the scalp, 4 inches above the right external auditory canal there is a scalp bruise; this is revealed after postmortem shaving of the scalp. It measures 1 x 1 inches and is red-violet or purple in color. The skin is smooth, non-abraded or lacer-ated. Subsequent autopsy discloses fresh deep scalp hemor-rhage and fresh dark red-purple subgaleal hemorrhage or bruising measuring 2 x 1 1/4 inches. Inferiorly the bruise extends to the superficial right temporal muscle. There is no associated skull fracture.

INJURIES TO HANDS:

Right hand: There is a 5/8 incised wound of the volar surface of the right index finger at the distal knuckle. This 5/8 inch incised wound is tangentially oriented or cut through the skin and dermis with the avulsed skin inferiorly indicat-ing that the direction is from distal to proximal.

Further examination discloses that there is a split or forked end on the ulnar aspect and pointed end on the radial aspect. There is a small amount of dermal hemorrhage.

On the dorsal surface of the right hand, at the base of the ring finger, there is a 1/16 inch punctate abrasion.

Left hand: On the dorsal surface of the left hand, there is a punctate abrasion, red-brown in color at the base of the ring finger.

There is a 1/2 inch superficial incised skin cut, 1/2 inch in length, diagonally oriented, on the top of the left hand, midportion.

INTERNAL EXAMINATION:

The body is opened with the usual Y-shaped thoracoabdominal incision revealing the abdominal wall adipose tissue to measure 1/4 - 3/8 inch in thickness. The anterior abdominal wall has its normal muscular components and there is no evidence of abdominal wall injury. Exposure of the body cavities shows the contained organs in their usual anatomic locations with their usual anatomic relationships. No free fluid or blood is found within the pleural, pericardial, or the peritoneal cavities. The serosal surfaces are smooth, thin, and glistening and there are no intra-abdominal adhe-sions.

INTERNAL EVIDENCE OF INJURIES:
There are no internal traumatic injuries involving the thorax
or thoracic viscera, abdomen or abdominal viscera.
SYSTEMIC AND ORGAN REVIEW:
Autopsy findings, or the lack of them, are considered apart
from those already stated. The following observations pertain
to findings other than the injuries and changes that are
described above.
MUSCULOSKELETAL SYSTEM—SUBCUTANEOUS TISSUE—SKIN:
Examination of the breasts reveals bilateral silastic implants that are intact. Otherwise, no other significant
changes are noted in the breasts. The remainder of the musculoskeletal system and subcutaneous tissue are anatomic.
HEAD—CENTRAL NERVOUS SYSTEM:
The external injuries to the scalp have been described. A
small abrasion, red-brown in color, measuring 3/8 x 1/4 inch
and appearing to be antemortem is found lateral-posterior to
the right eyebrow and this is a non-patterned superficial
abrasion.
The hemorrhage beneath the scalp, due to the sharp force
injuries have been described. There is no hemorrhage deep
into the temporal muscles.
There are no tears of the dura mater and no recent epidural,
subdural, or subarachnoid hemorrhage.
The dura is stripped to reveal no fractures of the bones of
the calvarium or base of the skull.
The pituitary gland is normally situated in the sella turcica
and is not enlarged.
The cranial nerves are enumerated and they are intact, sym-
metrical and anatomic in size, location and course.
The component vessels of the circle of Willis are identified.
They are anatomic in size, course, configuration and distribution. The blood vessels are intact, free of aneurysms or
other anomaly, and non-occluded and show no significant
atherosclerosis.
Examination of the non-formalin fixed, fresh brain shows: The
cerebral hemispheres, cerebellum, brainstem, pons and medulla
to show their normal anatomical structures. The cerebellar,
the pontine and medullary surfaces present no lesions. Multiple sections reveal an anatomic appearing cortex, white
matter, ventricular system and basal ganglia. There is no
evidence of hemorrhage, cyst or neoplasm involving the brain
substance.
The spinal chord, in the vicinity of the cervical incised
wound is dissected; there is no evidence or intraspinal
hemorrhage and no evidence of sharp force injury to the
spinal chord.
ORGANS OF SPECIAL SENSES:
Not dissected.
RESPIRATORY SYSTEM—THROAT STRUCTURES:
The oral cavity, viewed from below, is anatomic. The teeth
are examined and there is no evidence of injury and there is
no evidence of injury to the cheeks, lips, gums, or tongue.
No blood is present.
Injuries to the upper airway including the incised wound of
the hypopharynx and epiglottis have been described. Other-

wise, the mucosa of the larynx, piriform sinuses, trachea and major bronchi are anatomic. No mucosal lesions are evident and no blood is present.

The hyoid bone and thyroid cartilages are intact, inasmuch as the incised wound passes through the thyrohyoid membrane and ligament and both greater cornuas of the thyroid cartilage are intact. Hemorrhage is present in the tissue adjacent to the neck organs due to the incised would as described above. There is no hemorrhage into the substance of the thyroid gland which anatomic in size and location. The parathyroid glands are not identified.

Lungs: Right lung weighs 330 grams; left lung 300 grams. The external appearance and that of the sectioned surface of the lungs show minimal congestion and otherwise no injuries or lesions. No foreign material, infarction, or neoplasm is encountered. The pulmonary arteries are free of thromboemboli.

CARDIOVASCULAR SYSTEM:

The heart weighs 280 grams, and is anatomic in size and configuration. The chambers, valves and myocardium are anatomic, and a minimal amount of liquid blood is found within the cardiac chambers. No focal endocardial, valvular, or myocardial lesions are seen. There are no congenital anomalies.

Multiple transverse sections of the left and right coronary arteries reveal them to be thin-walled and patent throughout with no significant atherosclerosis. The aorta and major branches are anatomic and show only minimal lipid streaking of the intima. The portal and caval veins and the major branches are anatomic.

Note: The injuries of the common carotid arteries and internal jugular veins have been described above.

GASTROINTESTINAL SYSTEM:

The mucosa and wall of the esophagus are intact and gray-pink and no lesions or injuries are evident.

The gastric mucosa is intact and pink. No mucosal lesions are evident and there are no residuals of medication or blood. Examination of the gastric contents reveals approximately 500 ml. of chewed semisolid food in the stomach. Recognizable food particles are identified as follows: pieces of pasta appearing to be rigatoni, fragments of apparent spinach leaves; and the remainder, chewed, partially digested non-recognizable food material.

The mucosa of the duodenum, jejunum, ileum, colon and rectum are intact. The lumen is patent. No mucosal lesions are evident, and no blood is present. The fecal content is usual in appearance.

HEPATOBILIARY SYSTEM—PANCREAS:

The liver weighs 1370 grams. The capsular surface is intact. The subcapsular and the cut surface of the liver are uniformly brown-red in color, and free of nodularity and are usual in appearance. The biliary duct system, including the gallbladder, are free of anomaly and no lesions are evident. The mucosa is intact and bile stained. The lumen are patent and no calculi are present.

The pancreas is anatomic both externally and on cut surface.

HEMOLYMPHATIC SYSTEM—ADRENAL GLAND:

The spleen weighs 90 grams and has an intact capsule. Cut surface shows the usual dark red-purple parenchyma which is

firm and no lesions are evident.
The blood, the bone marrow and the usually-named aggregates
of lymph nodes do not appear to be significantly altered.
The thymus gland is no identifiable.
The adrenal glands are their usual size and location and cut
surface presents no lesions.
URINARY SYSTEM:
Each kidney weighs 100 grams. The kidneys are anatomic in
size, location and configuration. The capsules are stripped
to show a pale brown surface. On section the cut surface
shows no abnormalities of the cortex and medulla.
The calyces, pelves, ureters and urinary bladder are unaltered in appearance. The mucosa is gray-pink, no calculi are
present and no blood is present.
The urinary bladder contains a few ml. of clear urine.
GENITAL SYSTEM (female):
The uterus, tubes, and adnexa are anatomic. Cut surface of
the uterus shows no lesions and a thin light brown en-
dometrium. The vagina has its normal mucosal surface and no
lesions or injuries are evident.
HISTOLOGY:
Representative portions of the various organs, including the
larynx and hyoid, are preserved in 10% formaldehyde and
placed in a single storage container.
TOXICOLOGY:
A sample of cardiac chamber blood and urine are submitted for
toxicologic analysis.
SEROLOGY:
A sample of intracardiac blood is submitted in an EDTA tube,
RADIOLOGY:
None.
PHOTOGRAPHY:
In addition to the routine identification photographs, perti-
nent photographs are taken of the external injury.
WITNESSES:
Detective Vannatter and Lange, Los Angeles Police Department,
Robbery-Homicide, were present during the autopsy.
DIAGRAMS USED:
Forms 16, 20, 20D, 20F, 20G, 20H, 22, 23, 24 and 29 were
utilized during the performance of the autopsy.
OPINION:
Death is attributed to multiple sharp force injuries, includ-
ing a deep incised wound of the neck and multiple stab wounds
of the neck.
The sharp force injuries led to transection of the left and
right common carotid arteries, and incisions of the left and
right internal jugular vein causing fatal exsanguinating
hemorrhage. The sharp force injury to the scalp were superficial, non-fatal.
Injuries present on the hands, including the incised wound of
the right hand are compatible so-called defense wounds.
Routine toxicologic studies were ordered.

/s/ Irwin L. Golden M.D. IRWIN L. GOLDEN
DEPUTY MEDICAL EXAMINER
June 16, 1994 Date

Autopsy Report: Ronald Lyle Goldman

AUTOPSY REPORT 94-05135
I performed an autopsy on the body of GOLDMAN, RONALD at the
DEPARTMENT OF CORONER Los Angeles, California on June 14,
1994 @1030 HOURS
From the anatomic findings and pertinent history, I ascribe
the death to: MULTIPLE SHARP FORCE INJURIES Due To Or As a
Consequence of:

Anatomical Summary:
1. Sharp force wound of neck, left side, with transection of
left internal jugular vein.
2. Multiple stab wounds of chest, abdomen, and left thigh:
Penetrating stab wounds of chest and abdomen with right
hemothorax and hemoperitoneum.
3. Multiple incised wounds of scalp, face, neck, chest and
left hand (defense wound).
4. Multiple abrasions upper extremities and hands (defense
wounds).

NOTES AND PROCEDURES:
1. The body is described in the Standard Anatomical Position.
Reference is to this position only.
2. Where necessary, injuries are numbered for reference. This
is arbitrary and does not correspond to any order in which
they may have been incurred. All the injuries are antemortem,
unless otherwise specified.
3. The term "anatomic" is used as a specification to indicate
correspondence with the description as set forth in the
textbooks of Gross Anatomy. It denotes freedom from significant, visible or morbid alteration.

EXTERNAL EXAMINATION:
The body is that of a well-developed, well-nourished Caucasian male stated to be 25 years old. The body weighs 171
pounds, measuring 69 inches from crown to sole. The hair on
the scalp is brown and straight. The irides appear hazel with
the pupils fixed and dilated. The sclerae and conjunctive are
unremarkable, with no evidence of petechial hemorrhages on
either. Both upper and lower teeth are natural, and there are
no injuries of the gums, cheeks, or lips.
There is a picture-type tattoo on the lateral aspect of the
left upper arm. There are no deformities, old surgical scars
or amputations.
Rigor mortis is fixed (see Form 1 of autopsy report).
The body appears to the Examiner as stated above. Identification is by toe tag and the autopsy is not material to identification. The body is not embalmed.
The head is normocephalic, and there is extensive evidence of
external traumatic injury, to be described below. Otherwise,
the eyes, nose and mouth are not remarkable. The neck shows
sharp force injuries to be described below. The front of the
chest and abdomen likewise show injuries to be described

below. The genitalia are that of an adult male, with the
penis circumcised, and no evidence of injury.
Examination of the posterior surface of the trunk reveals no
antemortem traumatic injuries.
Refer to available photographs and diagrams and to the specific documentation of the autopsy protocol.
CLOTHING:
The clothes were examined both before and after removal from
the body. The decedent was wearing a long-sleeved type of
shirt/sweater; it was extensively bloodstained.
On the front, lower right side, there was a 1 1/2 inch long
slit-like tear. Also on the lower right sleeve there was a 1
inch slit-like tear. On the back there was a 1/2 inch slit-
like tear on the right lower side.
Decedent was wearing a pair of Levi jeans bloodstained. On
the outside of the left hip region there was a 1-1/2 inch
long slit-like tear. The decedent also was wearing 2 canvas
type boots and 2 sweat socks.
EVIDENCE OF THERAPEUTIC INTERVENTION: None.
EVIDENCE OF INJURY:
SHARP FORCE INJURIES OF NECK:
1. Sharp force injury of neck, left side, transecting left
internal jugular vein. This sharp force injury is complex,
and appears to be a combination of a stabbing and cutting
wound. It begins on the left side of the neck, at the level
of the midlarynx, over the left sternocleidomastoid muscle;
it is gaping, measuring 3 inches in length with smooth edges.
It tapers superiorly to 1 inch in length cut skin. Dissection
discloses that the wound path is through the skin, the subcutaneous tissue, and the sternocleidomastoid muscle with
hemorrhage along the wound path and transection of the left
internal jugular vein, with dark red-purple hemorrhage in the
adjacent subcutaneous tissue and fascia. The direction of the
pathway is upward and slightly front to back for a distance
of approximately 4 inches where it exits, post-auricular, in
a 2 inch in length gaping stab/incised wound which has undu-
lating or wavy borders, but not serrated. Intersecting the
wound at right angle superior inferior is a 2 inch in length
interrupted superficial, linear incised wound involving only
the skin. Also, intervening between the 2 gaping stab-incised
wounds is a horizontally oriented 3-1/2 inch in length interrupted superficial, linear incised wound of the skin only.
In addition, there is a 1/2 inch long, linear-triangular in
size wound of the inferior portion of the left earlobe.
The direction of the sharp force injury is upward (rostral),
and slightly front to back with no significant angulation or
deviation. The total length of the wound path is approximately 4 inches. However, there is a 3/4 inch in length,
linear, cutting or incised wound of the top or superior
aspect of the pinna of the left ear; a straight metallic
probe placed through the major sharp force injury shows that
the injury of the superior part of the ear can be aligned
with the straight metallic rod, suggesting that the 3 injuries are related; in this instance the total length of the
wound path is approximately 6 inches. Also, in the left
postauricular region, transversely oriented, extending from

the auricular attachment laterally to the scalp is a 1-1/8 inch in length linear superficial incised skin wound.
Opinion: This sharp force injury of the neck is fatal, associated with transection of the left internal jugular vein.
2. Sharp force wound of the right side of neck. This is a complex injury, appearing to be a combination stabbing and cutting wound. The initial wound is present on the right side of the neck, over the sternocleidomastoid muscle, 3 inches directly below the right external auditory canal. It is diagonally oriented, and after approximation of the edges measures 5/8 inch in length; there is a pointed or tapered end inferiorly and a split or forked end superiorly approximately 1/16 inch in maximal width. Subsequent autopsy shows that the wound path is through the skin and subcutaneous tissue, without penetration of injury of a major artery or vein; the direction is front to back and upward for a total wound path length of 2 inches and the wound exits on the right side of the back of the neck, posterior to the right sternocleidomastoid muscle where a 2 inch long gaping incised/stab wound is evident on the skin; both ends are tapered; superiorly there is a 1 inch long superficial incised wounds extension on the skin to the back of the head; inferiorly there is a 2 inch long incised superficial skin extension, extending inferiorly towards the back of the neck. There is fresh hemorrhage and bruising along the wound path; the direction, as stated, is upward and slightly front to back.
Opinion: This is a nonfatal sharp force injury, with no injury or major artery or vein.
3. At the level of the superior border of the larynx there is a transversely oriented, superficial incised wound of the neck, extending from 3 inches to the left of the anterior midline; it is 3 inches in length and involves the skin only; a small amount of cutaneous hemorrhage is evident.
Opinion: This is a nonfatal superficial incised wound.
4. Immediately inferior and adjacent to incised wound #3 is a transversely oriented, superficial incised wound involving the skin and subcutaneous tissue; there is a small amount of dermal hemorrhage.
Opinion: This is a nonfatal superficial incised wound.
SHARP FORCE INJURIES OF FACE:
1. There is a stab wound, involving the right earlobe; it is vertically oriented, and after approximation of the edges measures 1 inch in length with forked or split ends superiorly and inferiorly approximately 1/16 inch in total width both superior and inferior. Subsequent dissection discloses that the wound path is from right to left, in the horizontal plane for approximately 1-1/4 inches; there is fresh hemorrhage along the wound path; the wound path terminates in the left temporal bone and does not penetrate the cranial cavity.
Opinion: This is a nonfatal stab wound.
2. There is a group of 5 superficial incised or cutting wounds on the right side of the face, involving the right cheek and the right side of the jaw. They are varied in orientation both diagonal and horizontal; the smallest is 1/4

inch in length; the largest 5/8 inch in length. They are
superficial, involving the skin only, associated with a
small amount of cutaneous hemorrhage.
3. On the back of the neck, right side, posterior to the ear
and posterior border of the right sternocleidomastoid muscle
there is vertically oriented superficial incised skin wound,
measuring 3/4 inch in length.
4. There are numerous superficial incised wounds or cuts,
varied in orientation, involving the skin of the right
cheek, intersection and mingled with the various superficial
incised wounds described above. The longest is a 3 inch long
diagonally oriented superficial incised wound extending from
the right side of the forehead to the cheek; various other
superficial wound vary from 1/2 to 1 inch.
5. On the right side of the cheek, adjacent to the ramus of
the mandible, right, there is a 1-1/2 x 3/4 inch superficial
nonpatterned red-brown abrasion with irregular border,
extending superiorly towards the angle of the jaw where
there are poorly defined and circumscribed abrasions adjacent to the superficial cuts or abrasions described above.
It should be noted that the 5th superficial incised wound of
the right side of the mandible which measures 5/8 inch in
length is tapered on the posterior aspect and forked on the
anterior aspect where it has a width of 1/32 inch.
6. On the left ear, there is a superficial incised wound
measuring 1/4 inch, adjacent to the posterior border of the
pinna. Just below this on the inferior pinna, extending to
the earlobe, there is an interrupted superficial linear
abrasion measuring 1 inch in length.

SHARP FORCE INJURIES OF SCALP:
1. The scalp is shaved postmortem for visualization. On the
right posterior parietal region of the scalp there is a
sharp force wound, diagonally oriented, and after approximation of the edges it measures 5/8 inch in length with a
perpendicularly oriented skin cut at the midpoint.
Depth of penetration is approximately 1/4 to 3/8 inch into
the scalp, with associated deep scalp hemorrhage and a
subgaleal hemorrhage beneath the wound measuring 2 x 2
inches in transverse diameter. There is no underlying fracture of the skull or penetration of the cranium.
Opinion: This is a sharp force wound that may represent
either a cutting wound of a superficial stab wound; nonfatal.
2. On the posterior parietal region, midline, to the left of
the wound described above there is a 1/4 inch superficial
incised wound or skin cut measuring 1/4 inch in length; both
ends are pointed or tapered; extension is 1/4 inch into the
scalp with a small amount of deep scalp hemorrhage but no
subgaleal hemorrhage.
3. On the left posterior parietal region there is an injury
that is an abrasion, 1/4 x 1/8 inch in maximal diameter and
an ovoid in configuration; it is red-brown with a small
amount of superficial skin bruising.
Opinion: This is a skin abrasion-bruise, noncharacteristic.

DESCRIPTION OF MULTIPLE STAB WOUNDS:
On the right side of the chest adjacent to the stab wound

there are multiple, irregular, brown abrasions consistent with ant bites.

1. Stab wound of right side of chest.

The stab wound is located on the right side of the chest, 22 inches below the top of the head and 5 inches from the back of the body; it is vertically oriented and after approximation of the edges it measures 5/8 inch in length. Inferiorly there is a squared off or dull end approximately 1/32 in length; superiorly the wound is tapered.

Subsequent autopsy shows that the pathway is through the skin, the subcutaneous tissue, and through the right 7th rib at the approximately midaxillary line where the rib is totally incised. Thereafter, it enters the right pleural cavity which at the time of autopsy contains approximately 100-200 ml of predominantly liquid blood. The path is through the lateral base of the border of the right lower lobe as the path is through the pleura and the immediately subjacent pulmonary parenchyma which is hemorrhagic; the pleural wounds are approximately 1/2-3/4 inch in length; thereafter the pathway is from right to left and back to front and through the pleural cavity where the wound path terminates on the anterior rib cage where a 3/4 cutting wound is found on the posterior aspect of the right 4th rib anteriorly at the approximate midclavicular line; there is overlying bruising in the adjacent intercostal musculature. Estimated length of the total wound path is 4 inches and as stated the direction is right to left and back to front with no other angulation measurable.

Opinion: This is a fatal wound associated with perforation of the right lung and a hemothorax.

2. Stab wound of right side of chest.

This wound is located on the right side of the chest, 21 inches below the top of the head and 2 inches from the back of the body. After approximation of the edges it measures 1-1/2 inches in length and is diagonally oriented; the posterior aspect is dull or flat, measuring 1/32 inch and the anterior aspect is pointed or tapered.

Subsequent autopsy shows that the wound is through the skin, the subcutaneous tissue, and the intercostal musculature and it penetrates into the pleural cavity through the 8th right intercostal space without striking rib. Thereafter the pathway is similar to stab wound #1 as it passes obliquely through the pleura and subjacent hemorrhagic parenchyma at the base of the right lower lobe; 1/2 inch and 3/4 inch pleural cuts are evident both posteriorly and anteriorly. No other terminating point is evident.

There is fresh hemorrhage and bruising noted along the wound path as well as the hemothorax described above.

The direction is right to left with no other angulation or deviation determined because of absence of fixed reference points. Estimated minimum total depth of penetration is 2-3 inches.

Opinion: This is a fatal stab wound associated with perforation of the lung and hemothorax.

3. Stab wound of right flank.

This is a diagonally oriented wound, on the right flank, 29

inches below the top of the head and 3-1/2 inches to the back
of the body. It measures 3/8 inch in length and involves the
skin and subcutaneous tissue without penetrating the chest
wall or abdominal wall. No square or dull edges are evident.
Both ends are rounded or tapered.
Opinion: This is a superficial cutting wound, representing
either a superficial stab wound or an incised wound.
4. Stab wound of left thigh.
This is a transversely oriented stab wound on the lateral left
thigh, 33 inches above the left heel and 4 inches from the
back of the thigh. After approximation of the edges it measures 2-1/8 inches in length and posteriorly there is a dull
or flat end 1/32 inch and anteriorly a pointed or tapered end.
Subsequent autopsy shows that the wound path is through the
skin, the subcutaneous tissue, and the muscle without striking
bone. There is fresh hemorrhage along the wound path. The
depth of penetration is 3 to 3-1/2 inches from left to right
without angulation or deviation.
Opinion: This is a stab wound of the soft tissue and muscle of
the left thigh, nonfatal.
5. Stab wound of left side of abdomen.
This is a transversely oriented stab wound on the left side of
the abdomen, located 45 inches above the left heel. After
approximation of the edges it measures 3/4 inch in length with
the anterior end pointed or tapered and the posterior end
forked or split.
Subsequent autopsy shows that the wound passes through the
skin, the subcutaneous tissue, and through the retroperitoneal
tissue which is hemorrhagic; the pathway is through the left
ilio-psoas muscle associated with fresh hemorrhage and bruising. The path is from left to right and slightly back to
front; the wound path terminates in the abdominal aorta
approximately 1 1/4 inches proximal to the bifurcation. Two
perforating 1/2 inch wounds are seen in the wall of the aorta
with surrounding para-aortic hemorrhage. In addition to the
retroperitoneal hemorrhage, including hemorrhage into the
mesocolon, approximately 100 ml of liquid blood is found free
within the peritoneal cavity.
In addition to the fresh bruising and hemorrhage along the
wound path the entire length of the wound path is approximately 5-1/2 inches.
The direction is left to right, and a slightly back to front
direction with no other angulation or deviation evident.
Opinion: This is a fatal stab wound associated with perforation of the abdominal aorta with retroperitoneal and intra-
abdominal hemorrhage.
6. Stab wound of the right upper chest, lateral border of
right clavicle.
This vertically oriented superficial stab wound or incised
wound is located on the lateral border of the right clavicle,
is vertically oriented, and measures 1/2 inch in length;
involves the skin and subcutaneous tissue; inferiorly the
wound is split or forked and superiorly it is tapered or
pointed. It should be noted that all of the split or forked
ends of the previously mentioned stab wounds overall measure
approximately 1/16 to 1/8 inch in overall width. There is a

small amount of fresh cutaneous hemorrhage.
No direction can be evident except for front to back, inasmuch as it is superficial.

Opinion: This is a nonfatal superficial stab wound or cutting wound.

SHARP FORCE INJURIES OF HANDS:
1. On the palmar surface of the right hand, at the base of the index finger, there is a cutting or incised wound, 3/4 inch in length and 1/2 inch deep involving the skin and subcutaneous tissue with hemorrhage in the margins. Both ends are rounded or tapered.
Opinion: This is compatible with a defense wound.
2. On the palmar surface of the right hand, just proximal to the web of the thumb, there is a triangular or Y-shaped cutting wound measuring 1/2 inch in length maximally and 1/4 inch deep with hemorrhage at the margins.
Opinion: This is compatible with a defense wound.
3. On the palmar surface of the left hand at the web of the thumb, there is a 3/4 inch in size or cutting wound involving the skin, and subcutaneous tissue; it is approximately 1/4 inch deep with hemorrhage at the margins. Both ends are tapered or pointed with smooth edges similar to the 2 wounds described above.
Opinion: This is compatible with a defense wound.

OTHER INJURIES TO HANDS AND UPPER EXTREMITIES:
1. On the lateral aspect of the right distal forearm, adjacent to the wrist, there is a 3/4 x 1/2 inch abrasion on the ulnar surface, red-brown in color, nonpatterned.
2. On the lateral or outer aspect of the left forearm there are multiple abrasions both linear and one that is approximately triangular measuring 3/4 x 1/2 inch; they are all brown to red-brown in color and antemortem; the longest linear abrasion is 3/4 inch in length.
3. On the dorsal surface of the right hand there are fresh bruises (red-purple in color) and fresh red-brown abrasions. On the proximal knuckle of the right middle finger a 1 x 3/4 inch bruise with no overlying abrasion. On the middle knuckle of the index finger a 1/2 x 1/2 inch bruise surrounding a 1/8 nondescript abrasion; just distal on the middle phalanx of the middle finger a 1/8 nondescript abrasion. On the proximal knuckle of the right index finer there is a 1/2 x 1/2 inch fresh bruise surrounding a linear diagonally oriented 1/2 inch red-brown abrasion.
There is a 1/2 x 1/2 inch fresh bruise on the middle of the right ring finger surrounding 2 punctate abrasions approximately 1/8 inch in maximal diameter; on the middle knuckle of the right 5th finger there is a 1/16 inch punctate nondescript abrasion.
4. On the dorsal side of the left hand there are multiple red-brown abrasions irregular in configuration and border, involving the 3 knuckles of the left index finger; maximal dimension 1/4 x 3/8 inch, all red-brown in color.
There is an irregularly configured abrasion on the proximal knuckle of the left middle finger consisting of an apparent 3 linear 1/2 inch abrasions converging at the center having a

somewhat configuration of the letter W. These are all superficial skin abrasions. On the dorsal side of the left hand
adjacent to the web of the thumb there is a linear, 3/4 inch
long skin abrasion terminating in a 1/8 inch nondescript
punctate abrasion near the base of the thumb.
There is a fresh bruise, 1-1/4 x 1-1/2 inch on the dorsal
surface of the left hand adjacent to the wrist surrounding a
punctate abrasion.
5.. There are 2 fresh bruises on the ulnar surface of the
left wrist, nonabraded, measuring respectively 3/8 x 3/8 inch
and 1/2 x 1/2 inch, with the bruising involving the skin and
dermis.

INTERNAL EXAMINATION:
The body is opened with the usual Y-shaped thoracoabdominal
incision revealing the abdominal adipose tissue to measure
1/2 to 3/4 inch in thickness. The anterior abdominal wall has
its normal muscular components and no blunt force injuries
are evident. Exposure of the body cavities shows the contained organs in their usual anatomic locations with their
usual anatomic relationships. The serosal surfaces are
smooth, thin, and glistening and the free blood within the
peritoneal cavity due to the stab wound as previously described; this also includes the left retroperitoneal hemorrhage, hemorrhage into the left ilio-psoas muscle, and the
mesocolon.

INTERNAL EVIDENCE OF INJURY:
Aside from the stab wounds of the chest and abdomen, there
are no other internal traumatic injuries involving the thoracic or abdominal viscera.

SYSTEMIC AND ORGAN REVIEW:
Autopsy findings, or lack of them, considered apart from
those already stated. The following observations pertain to
findings other than the injuries and changes that are described above.

MUSCULOSKELETAL SYSTEM—SUBCUTANEOUS TISSUE-SKIN:
Anatomic except as otherwise stated or implied.

HEAD—CENTRAL NERVOUS SYSTEM:
The brain weighs 1,100 grams. The external indications of
injury as well as the deep scalp and subgaleal hemorrhage
have been described above. There is no hemorrhage into the
temporal muscle or the orbits.
There are no tears of the dura mater and no recent epidural,
subdural, or subarachnoid hemorrhage. The dura is stripped
revealing no fractures of the bones of the calvarium or base
of the skull.
The pituitary gland is normally situated in the sella turcica
and is not enlarged.
The cranial nerves are enumerated and they are intact, sym-
metrical and anatomic in size, location and course.
The component vessels of the circle of Willis are identified
and they are anatomic in size, course and configuration. The
blood vessels are intact, free of aneurysm or other anomaly,
are non-occluded, and show no significant atherosclerosis.
Multiple coronal sections of the non-formalin-fixed, fresh
brain shows: The cerebral hemispheres, cerebellum, brain
stem, pons and medulla to show their normal anatomical struc-

tures. The cerebellar, the pontine and the medullary surfaces present no lesions. The cerebral cortex, the white matter, the ventricular system and basal ganglia are anatomic. There is no evidence of hemorrhage, cysts or neoplasm involving the brain substance.

The spinal chord is not dissected.

ORGANS OF SPECIAL SENSES: Not dissected.

RESPIRATORY SYSTEM—THROAT STRUCTURES:

The oral cavity, viewed from below, is anatomic and no lesions are seen. The mucosa is intact and there are no injuries to the lips, teeth or gums.

There is no obstruction of the airway. The injury to the left internal jugular vein has been previously described. The mucosa of the epiglottis, glottis, piriform sinuses, trachea and major bronchi are anatomic. No injuries are seen and there are no mucosal lesions.

The hyoid bone, the thyroid, and the cricoid cartilages are intact. No hemorrhage is present in the tissues adjacent to the throat organs nor is there hemorrhage into the substance of the anatomic appearing thyroid gland. The parathyroid glands are not identified.

Lungs: The lungs weight: Right, 420 grams; left 320 grams. The external appearance and that of the sectioned surface of the left lung shows a pink external surface without evidence of injuries. There is minimal congestion, otherwise not remarkable. No foreign substance, infarction or neoplasm is encountered.

The right lung shows basilar atelectasis due to the hemothorax caused by the stab wound to the right lower lobe described above. Otherwise the external appearance of the sectioned surface shows no focal lesion; there is no evidence of foreign material, infarction or neoplasm.

CARDIOVASCULAR SYSTEM:

The heart weighs 290 grams, and has a normal size and configuration. The chambers, valves, and the myocardium are anatomic. There are no focal endocardial, valvular or myocardial lesion and no congenital anomalies.

Multiple transverse sections of the left and right coronary arteries reveal them to be thin-walled and patent throughout with no significant atherosclerosis. The aorta and its branches are anatomic; the perforating stab wound injury of the distal abdominal aorta has been previously described.

The portal and caval veins and the major branches are anatomic.

GASTROINTESTINAL SYSTEM:

The mucosa and wall of the esophagus are intact and gray-pink, without lesions or injuries.

The gastric mucosa is intact and pink without injury. There are no focal lesions, no residual medications, and no swallowed blood is present. Approximately 200 ml of partially digested semisolid food is found in the stomach with the presence of fragments of green leafy vegetable material compatible with spinach.

The mucosa of the duodenum, jejunum, ileum, colon and rectum are intact. The lumen is patent. There are no mucosal lesions or injuries and no blood is present. The fecal content is usual in appearance.

The vermiform appendix is present.

HEPATOBILIARY SYSTEM—PANCREAS:

The liver weighs 1,360 grams and is normal size and configuration. The subcapsular and the cut surfaces of the liver are uniformly brown-red in color, free of nodularity, and usual in appearance. The biliary duct system, including the gallbladder, is free of anomaly and no lesions are seen. The mucosa is intact and bile stained. The lumina are patent and no calculi are present.

The pancreas is anatomic both externally and on cut surface.

HEMOLYMPHATIC SYSTEM—ADRENAL GLAND

The spleen weighs 210 grams and has an intact capsule. Cut surface shows a normal coloration with a firm red-purple parenchyma and no focal lesions.

The blood, the bone marrow and the usually-named aggregates of lymph nodes do not appear to be significantly altered.

The thymus gland is not identified.

The adrenal glands are usual in size and location and the cut surface presents no lesions or injuries. However, there is a small amount of left periadrenal hemorrhage due to the retroperitoneal hemorrhage caused by the stab wound.

URINARY SYSTEM:

The kidneys weigh: Left, 150 grams; right, 140 grams. The kidneys are anatomic in size, shape and location. The capsules are stripped to show a smooth, pale brown surface. On section the cortex and medulla are anatomic without lesions. The calyces, the pelves, the ureters and urinary-bladder are unaltered in appearance. The mucosa is gray-pink. No calculi are present, and no blood is present.

The urinary bladder contains no measurable urine.

MALE GENITAL SYSTEM:

The testicles, the penis, the prostate gland are anatomic to dissection.

HISTOLOGY:

Representatives portions of the various organs, including the larynx, are preserved in 10% formaldehyde and placed in a single storage container.

TOXICOLOGY:

A sample of right pleural blood as well as bile are submitted for toxicologic analysis. Stomach contents are saved.

SEROLOGY:

A sample of right pleural blood is submitted in the EDTA tube.

RADIOLOGY: None.

PHOTOGRAPHY:

In addition to the routine identification photographs; pertinent photographs are taken of the external injuries.

WITNESSES:

Detectives Van Natter and Lange, LAPD, Robbery Homicide Division, were present during the autopsy.

DIAGRAMS USED:

Form 42, 16, 20F, 20H, 21 and 24 were utilized during the performance of the autopsy.

OPINION:

The decedent sustained multiple sharp force injuries, includ-

ing multiple stab wounds involving the chest and abdomen; multiple incised-stab wounds of the neck; and multiple incised or cutting wounds. Fatal wounds were identified involving the neck where there was transection of the left internal jugular vein and stab wounds of the chest and abdomen causing intrathoracic and intraabdominal hemorrhage.
Of note the cutting wounds of the left and right hands, compatible with defensive wounds. In addition there were a number of blunt force injuries to the upper extremities and hands, likewise compatible with defensive wounds. The remainder of the autopsy revealed a normal, healthy adult male with no congenital anomalies. Routine toxicologic studies were ordered.

/s/ IRWIN L. GOLDEN, M.D. DEPUTY MEDICAL EXAMINER
June 17, 1994 DATE

The Bill of Rights

The Constitution of the United States of America is the fundamental law of the U.S. federal system. It defines the principal organs of government and their jurisdictions, as well as the basic rights of citizens. The basic text was drafted by the Constitutional Convention in 1787 and declared in effect by the Congress on March 4, 1789. On September 25, 1789, Congress proposed 12 amendments constituting a Bill of Rights; 10 were ratified by the States and adopted on December 15, 1791. The 26th Amendment was the last to be ratified, on July 5, 1791.

We present here the familiar preamble, skipping over the basic text of seven articles, to the Bill of Rights, the first ten amendments. Amendments IV through VII came up repeatedly in the Simpson matter.

Preamble

We the People of the United States, in Order to form a more perfect Union, establish Justice, insure domestic Tranquility, provide for the common defence, promote the general Welfare, and secure the Blessings of Liberty to ourselves and our Posterity, do ordain and establish this Constitution for the United States of America.

Bill of Rights

The following is a transcription of the first 10 amendments to the United States Constitution. Called the Bill of Rights, these amendments were ratified on December 15, 1791.

Amendment I: Congress shall make no law respecting an establishment of religion, or prohibiting the free exercise thereof;

or abridging the freedom of speech, or of the press; or the right of the people peaceably to assemble, and to petition the Government for a redress of grievances.

Amendment II: A well regulated Militia, being necessary to the security of a free State, the right of the people to keep and bear Arms, shall not be infringed.

Amendment III: No Soldier shall, in time of peace be quartered in any house, without the consent of the Owner, nor in time of war, but in a manner to be prescribed by law.

Amendment IV: The right of the people to be secure in their persons, houses, papers, and effects, against unreasonable searches and seizures, shall not be violated, and no Warrants shall issue, but upon probable cause, supported by Oath or affirmation, and particularly describing the place to be searched, and the persons or things to be seized.

Amendment V: No person shall be held to answer for a capital, or otherwise infamous crime, unless on a presentment or indictment of a Grand Jury, except in cases arising in the land or naval forces, or in the Militia, when in actual service in time of War or public danger; nor shall any person be subject for the same offence to be twice put in jeopardy of life or limb; nor shall be compelled in any criminal case to be a witness against himself, nor be deprived of life, liberty, or property, without due process of law; nor shall private property be taken for public use, without just compensation.

Amendment VI: In all criminal prosecutions, the accused shall enjoy the right to a speedy and public trial, by an impartial jury of the State and district wherein the crime shall have been committed, which district shall have been previously ascertained by law, and to be informed of the nature and cause of the accusation; to be confronted with the witnesses against him; to have compulsory process for obtaining Witnesses in his favor, and to have the assistance of counsel for his defence.

Amendment VII: In Suits at common law, where the value in controversy shall exceed twenty dollars, the right of trial by jury shall be preserved, and no fact tried by a jury, shall be otherwise reexamined in any Court of the United States, than according to the rules of the common law.

Amendment VIII: Excessive bail shall not be required, nor excessive fines imposed, nor cruel and unusual punishments inflicted.

Amendment IX: The enumeration in the Constitution, of certain rights, shall not be construed to deny or disparage others retained by the people.

Amendment X: The powers not delegated to the United States by the Constitution, nor prohibited by it to the States, are reserved to the States respectively, or to the people.

Notes

Chapter 1. THE PROSECUTION

1. *Los Angeles Times* staff, *In Pursuit of Justice, The People vs. Orenthal James Simpson* (Los Angeles: The *Los Angeles Times* Syndicate, 1995), pp. 29-31. Copyright 1995, *Los Angeles Times*. Reprinted by permission.

2. Christopher Darden with Jess Walter, *In Contempt* (New York: HarperCollins/Regan Books, 1996), p. 336.

3. *O.J. Simpson, The Interview* (H&K, LLC, 1996), videocassette.

4. *Larry King Live*, 2 January 1996.

5. Karl Gude, Eileen Glanton, William Schroeder, "The Trail of Blood" (Associated Press, 1994). Reprinted by permission.

6. Darden, *In Contempt*, p. 280.

7. Donald Freed, interview with Robert Heidstra, Los Angeles, 25 March 1996.

Chapter 2. THE DEFENSE

1. Alan M. Dershowitz, *Reasonable Doubts: The O.J. Simpson Case and the Criminal Justice System* (New York: Simon & Schuster, 1996), p. 32.

2. Ian Bowater, interview with Dr. Kary Mullis, Los Angeles, 19 January 1996.

3. *Larry King Live*, 2 January 1996.

4   Donald Freed, interview with Pablo Fenjves, Los Angeles, 10 March 1996.

5. Rob Hernandez, "O.J. Simpson's Estate," Copyright 1995, *Los Angeles Times*. Reprinted by permission.

6. Faye D. Resnick with Mike Walker, *Nicole Brown Simpson: The Private Diary of a Life Interrupted* (California: Dove Books, 1994), p. 82.

7. Ibid., p. 224.

Chapter 3. THE SECOND MAN

1. Clifford Linedecker, *OJ A to Z: The Complete Handbook to the Trial of the Century* (New York: St. Martin's Press, 1995), p.244.

2. *O.J. Simpson, The Interview*.

3. Darden, *In Contempt*, p. 337.

CHAPTER 4. ALL-AMERICAN DRUGS

1. Jeffrey Toobin, "Drop-Dead Georgeous," *New Yorker,* 18 September 1995.
2. Resnick, *Nicole Brown Simpson,* p. 216.
3. Sheila Weller, *Raging Heart: The Intimate Story of the Tragic Marriage of O.J. and Nicole Brown Simpson* (New York: Pocket Books/Simon & Schuster, 1994) p. 274.
4. Ian Bowater, interview with Dr. Jennifer Ameli, Los Angeles, 4 March 1996.
5. Marjorie Lambert and Battino Batts Jr., "Man's Past No Help in Solving Slayings," *Fort Lauderdale Sun-Sentinel,* 29 June 1994, Palm Beach Edition.
6. Ibid.
7. Alex Constantine, *The Florida/Hollywood Mob Connection* (Los Angeles, 1995), pp. 5-6. Reprinted by permission of the author.
8. Ian Bowater, interview with Christian Reichardt, Los Angeles, 17 February 1996.
9. Weller, *Raging Heart,* p. 241.
10. Ibid., p. 265.
11. Ibid., p. 279.
12. Resnick, *Nicole Brown Simpson,* p. 91.
13. Ibid., p. 208.
14. *O.J. Simpson, The Interview.*
15. Donald Freed, interview with unnamed informant, Los Angeles, 22 May 1996.

Chapter 5. KILLER OR KILLERS UNKNOWN

1. Weller, *Raging Heart.* p. 172.
2. "O.J. Wants to Frame Me for Nicole's Murder," *Examiner,* 13 February 1996.
3. Resnick, *Nicole Brown Simpson,* p. 216.
4. Ibid., p. 226.
5. Cora Fischman, civil trial deposition, 2 April 1996.
6. Marcus Allen, civil trial deposition, 31 May 1996.
7. Weller, *Raging Heart.* p. 370.
8. Bowater, interview with Christian Reichardt.
9. Ian Bowater, interview with unidentified chief medical examiner, Los Angeles, 15 January 1996.
10. Bowater, interview with Christian Reichardt.

Chapter 6. THE FUHRMAN TIMELINE

1. Darden, *In Contempt,* p. 284.
2. Fox Butterfield, "A Portrait of the Elusive Police Detective in

the O.J. Whirlpool," *The New York Times*, 2 March 1996.

3. Letter from Kathleen Bell, 1994 WL 77410 at 1 (Cal.Super. Trans. 19 July 1994).

4. Darden, *In Contempt*, p. 284.

5. Butterfield, "A Portrait of the Elusive Police Detective in the O.J. Whirlpool."

6. Ibid.

7. Stephen Singular, *Legacy of Deception* (Beverly Hills: Dove Books, 1995), p. 130. Reprinted by permission of the author.

8. Darden, *In Contempt*, p. 282.

9. Singular, *Legacy of Deception*, pp. 22-24.

10. Linedecker, *OJ A to Z*, p. 193.

11. Donald Freed, interview with unnamed sources close to the Defense, February 1996.

12. Singular, *Legacy of Deception*, pp. 154-55.

13. Despite being named in this report, Fuhrman was promoted to the rank of detective. Another officer named in the report was a Sergeant Koons of the K-9 division. Koons and his K-9 were also at the Bundy crime scene in the early hours of June 13.

14. Darden, *In Contempt*, p. 176.

15. Ibid.

16 Ibid., p. 178.

Chapter 7. THE OPEN TIMELINE

1. *O.J. Simpson, The Interview.*

2. Stephanie Simon, "Simpson Detective Deviated from Usual Practice, Expert Testifies," *Los Angeles Times*, 7 June 1996.

3. Donald Freed, interview with unnamed source, Los Angeles, 3 July 1996.

4. John F. Kennedy, "Showdown: the shocking truth behind JFK's Secret Summit with Tabloid Honcho Iaim Calder!" *George*, August 1996.

5. Mercury Morris, interview, *Globe* (Quebec: *Globe* International Inc.), 12 January 1996.

6. *Globe*, January 1996.

7. Francis Winnover, "Nicole's Grave Is Empty," *World Weekly News*, 23 January 1996.

8. Henry Louis Gates, Jr., "Thirteen Ways of Looking at a Black Man," *New Yorker*, 23 October 1995.

9. Ibid.

10. O.J. Simpson, civil trial deposition, 19 February 1996.

11. Donald Freed and Ian Bowater, interview with unnamed researcher, 7 February 1996.

12. Darden, *In Contempt*, p.192.

13. Bill Boyarsky, "Simpson Case Catches Up to D.A.'s Race," *Los Angeles Times*, 25 February 1996.

14 *O.J. Simpson, The Interview.*

15. Linda Deutsch, "Simpson Reflects on Days in Jail, Rebuilding His Life," Associated Press, 1 July 1996.

Index *

* *Numbers in italics indicate information in charts, maps, timelines, or other diagrams.*

About the Authors

Donald Freed is a historian, dramatist, and novelist, whose work Harold Pinter has described as "a unique and fearless marriage of politics and art." He is the author of *Secret Honor, Circe & Bravo, Executive Action, The Killing of RFK, The Secret Life of Ronald Reagan, Agony in New Haven,* and *The Spymaster.* A Visiting Distinguished Professor of Humanities at Loyola Marymount University, he also teaches at the University of Southern California. His many honors include Rockefeller awards, Louis B. Mayer awards, the Berlin Critics Award, and a National Endowment for the Arts award for distinguished writing. He lives in Los Angeles.

Raymond P. Briggs, Ph.D., is an awardwinning visual and cognitive scientist and research fellow of the National Academy of Sciences. Currently Director of Research at the Southern California College of Optometry, he has developed visual standards for law enforcement for the State of California and appeared as an expert witness for the U.S. military, the U.S. Department of Justice, and other clients. A specialist in using computers to reconstruct and simulate real-life events, he is currently developing the virtual reality version of *Killing Time.* He lives in Fullerton, California.

212